SOUTH ASIA
The Spectre of Terrorism

SOUTH ASIA
The Spectre of Terrorism

Editors

P.R. KUMARASWAMY

IAN COPLAND

LONDON AND NEW YORK

First published 2009
by Routledge

2 Park Square, Milton Park, Abingdon, Oxfordshire OX14 4RN
711 Third Avenue, New York, NY 10017

Routledge is an imprint of the Taylor & Francis Group, an informa business

First issued in paperback 2018

Transferred to Digital Printing 2009

Copyright © 2009 P.R. Kumaraswamy and Ian Copland

Originally published as a special issue of *South Asia: Journal of South Asian Studies* (vol. XXX(1), April 2007). Reprinted with permission of Taylor & Francis Ltd (http://www.informaworld.com).

Typeset by
Star Compugraphics Private Limited
5–CSC, First Floor, Near City Apartments
Vasundhara Enclave
Delhi 110 096

All rights reserved. No part of this book may be reprinted or reproduced or utilised in any form or by any electronic, mechanical, or other means, now known or hereafter invented, including photocopying and recording, or in any information storage or retrieval system, without permission in writing from the publishers.

Notice:
Product or corporate names may be trademarks or registered trademarks, and are used only for identification and explanation without intent to infringe.

British Library Cataloguing-in-Publication Data
A catalogue record of this book is available from the British Library

ISBN: 978-0-415-48321-6 (hbk)
ISBN: 978-1-138-37682-3 (pbk)

Contents

INTRODUCTION *by* P.R. Kumaraswamy		7
1.	Terrorism in South Asia: The Changing Trends P.R. KUMARASWAMY	11
2.	Unholy Alliance: Religion and Political Violence in South Asia ROBERT G. WIRSING	29
3.	Understanding the 1993 Mumbai Bombings: *Madrassas* and the Hierarchy of Terror MARIKA VICZIANY	47
4.	Force and Compromise: India's Counter-Insurgency Grand Strategy RAJESH RAJAGOPALAN	79
5.	Ethno-Nationalism and the Politics of Terror in India's Northeast WASBIR HUSSAIN	97
6.	Identity Politics and Minorities in Pakistan RASUL BAKHSH RAIS	115
7.	The Evolution of Sectarian Conflicts in Pakistan and the Ever-Changing Face of Islamic Violence FRÉDÉRIC GRARE	131
8.	Islamic Militancy in Bangladesh: The Threat from Within SREERADHA DATTA	149
9.	Political Terrorism of the Liberation Tigers of Tamil Eelam (LTTE) in Sri Lanka GAMINI SAMARANAYAKE	175
NOTES ON CONTRIBUTORS		188
INDEX		189

Introduction

P.R. Kumaraswamy

Especially since the partition of the subcontinent along communal lines, political violence has become endemic to South Asia. Although there was a sharp decline in mass violence after 1947 which continued through the 1950s, since the 1960s the region has become—to a far greater extent than during British times—a hotbed of religiously-, ethnically- and ideologically-driven violence that has left no part of it immune. Today, more and more groups, from the majority and minority communities alike, are resorting to violence either in their quest for power or to redress perceived grievances. As a result, assassinations, insurgencies, large-scale communal riots and other forms of extremist violence have become an integral part of the South Asian political landscape. Terrorism is one such manifestation of this violence. None of the major states in the region is immune from this scourge.

The September 11 attacks in the United States in 2001 merely dramatised the impact of terrorism and endangered the safety and security of ordinary people. That so many people were killed while going about their daily routines underscores the devastating message of terrorism: innocent bystanders are not safe. Post-9/11, life in the US has not been the same.

Although South Asia has escaped cataclysmic catastrophes like 9/11, the cumulative effect of the various forms of political violence has been far more severe in material damage and still costlier in human lives. The prolonged terrorism in the Punjab, militancy in Kashmir, ethnic conflict in Sri Lanka, turmoil in India's north-eastern states, sectarian violence in the streets of Pakistan and Maoist insurgency in Nepal have each individually accounted for more deaths than the September 11 attacks on the US. For instance, at least 2,974 people in the US were killed instantly, and another 24 were missing and presumed dead. According to the data compiled by the New Delhi-based *South Asia Terrorism Portal* (SATP), between 1994 and 2005, over 10,000 civilians were killed in militancy in Kashmir. During the same period, over 7,000 non-combatants were killed in the turbulence in the north-east. The Maoist insurgency in Nepal claimed over 13,000 lives between 2000 and early 2008. Likewise, over 3,600 Pakistani civilians were killed in terrorism-related violence between 2003 and May 2008.

South Asian leaders were for long indifferent to or complacent about the growing menace of terrorism. Blatant targeting of civilians in different parts of the world, including within the region, were once treated as a genuine expression of national aspirations. Groups engaging in terrorist violence were sometimes given political patronage, economic assistance and even military training and supplies by some short-sighted governments. Terrorism in neighbouring countries too was exploited to promote national interests. Acts of internal political violence were denounced as 'terrorism', while similar acts in neighbouring countries were either hailed or excused as manifestations of *jihad*, 'freedom struggle', or popular resistance.

This duality, however, could not be sustained. The rapid growth of terrorism in Punjab, Kashmir, Nepal, Sri Lanka and Pakistan eventually forced South Asian countries to see the long-term consequences of the evil. Even if most of them have so far failed to evolve a viable politico-military counter strategy, the fallout from the September 11 attacks is gradually forcing them to recognise terrorism in its true colours. Today there is a greater awareness in South Asia of the threat of terrorism. Nevertheless, any meaningful action to fight terrorism in the region will have to begin with this basic premise: even genuine political grievances are no excuse for terrorism.

So where do things stand? The civil war in Sri Lanka is well into its third decade. Sikh militancy in Punjab and the Mohajir violence in Sindh each lasted for over a decade. The tribal insurgency in the north-eastern states of India continues to fester. The Maoist insurgency in Nepal lasted for over a decade until the monarch was forced in 2008 to relinquish his absolute powers as the price for the Maoists to join the political process. In India, Hindu–Muslim communal violence peaked in the 1980s with around 1,100 incidents and 1,200 deaths each year during the latter part of the decade, a level not seen since the dark days of partition. It has since lessened, but not significantly.

Contrary to popular notions of external factors, much of this political violence, especially terrorism, has been an indigenous development. Official neglect of and indifference towards genuine political grievances have resulted in marginalised groups and communities resorting to arms. The truism in South Asia is that only violence leads to the redressal of injustice. Short-sighted policies towards social problems often transform them into a major menace to the society.

The ethnic violence in Sri Lanka can be traced to the prolonged marginalisation of the Tamil minorities in the island republic and their deprival of the fruits of development. The refusal to recognise the multi-cultural nature of the country and accommodate the non-Sinhalese minority was the root cause of terrorism in Sri Lanka. The same is the case with Pakistan's immigrant Mohajirs who have never been fully accepted by the local Sindhis and Punjabis—even though the Pakistani state was conceived as a homeland for the Muslims of British India. The situation in north-east India fits into the same category. The peoples of the region feel utterly neglected by the central authority in New Delhi. Likewise, a strong sense of social injustice has been identified as the main reason for Maoist violence in Andhra Pradesh and Bihar. Conservative Nepal needed a Maoist insurgency to put an end to a corrupt monarchical regime.

The common factor here is a sense that the state is indifferent. Failures of governance in India and of the electoral system in Pakistan and Sri Lanka have driven many groups to resort to extremism as a means of conveying their cause to a larger public.

There is a strong and irrefutable link between religion and political violence in South Asia. Indeed much of terrorist activity in the region during the past few decades can be directly linked to religion-centric violence. Much of the literature on the religious dimension of political violence in South Asia has focused on the Kashmir problem, but Kashmir is only part of a wider phenomenon. When a minority feels threatened by the chauvinism of the majority, violence often becomes attractive. The flashpoint comes when the minority group reaches its limit of tolerance. The Muslim grievance over the demolition of the controversial Babri Masjid in December 1992 by Hindu militants directly contributed to the spate of terrorist attacks that rocked Mumbai in 1993. It would be impossible to deny a direct link between the two. A host of terror attacks in India since then have been invariably linked to the failure of the Indian state to protect its Muslim citizens. The same is true for the Mohajirs of Pakistan, the Tamils of Sri Lanka and the Sikhs in Punjab.

Yet it is not only representatives of minority groups who resort to violence. The rise of the Right in India has contributed to the growing tension between the Hindu majority and minority groups like the Muslims and Christians. When a majority feels 'threatened' by a minority then violence becomes likely. The relatively new phenomenon of anti-Christian violence in India and Pakistan can be traced to this sense of insecurity among the majority.

However, if a targeted minority community is perceived as threatening the purity of the dominant faith—as is the case with the Ahmadiyyas in Pakistan—the consequences are far worse. Under public pressure and political blackmail by the *ulema*, the governments of Pakistan—of late Bangladesh—have contributed to the marginalisation of minority communities like the Ahmadiyyas, even as they remain passive spectators of the anti-minority violence.

Nor does every deprived group resort to violence. If they are extremely socially disadvantaged, or few in number, minorities tend to become resigned to their fate. The reluctance of the Hindus in Bangladesh or Christians in Pakistan to resort to terrorism probably has more to do with their weakness than to any ecumenical disposition.

With these considerations as a backdrop, the volume offers a serious and scholarly assessment of various aspects of terrorism that are affecting the region. Eight scholars of international repute take a closer look at the problem.

The inaugural chapter by Robert G. Wirsing examines the 'unholy alliance' between religion and political violence in South Asia. Then follows a micro-study by Marika Vicziany of the well-coordinated Mumbai bomb blasts of 12 March 1993, which takes us into the shadowy world of Mumbai's criminal syndicates and exposes the bureaucratic corruption that allowed this organised attack to take place. This is followed by two analyses of the violence in the north-east by Wasbir Hussein and Rajesh Rajagopalan. Hussein looks at the roots of the ethnic violence in the region and how it was allowed to flourish as a result of short-sighted policies. Rajagopalan analyses India's strategy of counter-insurgency and its effectiveness in the region. The next two chapters deal with the situation in Pakistan. In the essay by Rasul Bakhsh Rais, we see how the marginalisation of the minorities has been institutionalised in Pakistan. Analysing the phenomenon of Shia-Sunni violence, Frédéric Grare points out that the sectarian violence within Pakistan is not a 'monocausal phenomenon [but] has deep social, political and geographical roots'.

Religious extremist violence in Bangladesh forms the core of the chapter by Sreeradha Datta who argues that Islamic militancy 'has largely been home grown and has emanated from, and thrives on, domestic issues and agendas'; while Gamini Samaranayake examines the recourse to terrorism by the LTTE and its role in perpetuating the ethnic violence in Sri Lanka. Building on these various assessments, the final chapter looks at the changing debate in South Asia, and among South Asianists, towards the phenomenon of terrorism.

This volume would not have materialised without the willing cooperation and participation of the contributors. I am grateful to all of them. Special mention is reserved for Vivien Seyler at Monash University and Omita Goyal at Routledge for making this volume possible. I am also grateful to my friend Shyam Babu for his prolonged help and partnership.

Terrorism in South Asia: The Changing Trends

P.R. Kumaraswamy[1]

Since the end of the colonial period collective violence has been an unsavoury but integral part of South Asian politics, dashing the hopes of the region's freedom fighters, who had expected the withdrawal of colonialism to usher in a more peaceful era. The communal bloodbath between Hindus and Muslims in the aftermath of the partition of the subcontinent in 1947 was followed by innumerable intercommunal and sectarian riots, political murders, armed insurgencies, militant struggles and other forms of organised violence.

None of the countries in South Asia is free from the scourge of ethnic confilct and carnage—including India, whose leaders have internationally championed the peaceful resolution of disputes and purport to be guided by the country's Buddhist and Gandhian traditions. Indian governments since 1947 have frequently used force to quash sub-national political aspirations in different parts of the country, especially in the north-eastern region and in the states of Punjab and Jammu and Kashmir.

Similarly, since the early 1950s sectarian violence has tormented Pakistan, a country conceived as a homeland for the Muslims of British India. Irreconcilable ethnic differences between predominantly Punjabi West Pakistan and Bengali East Pakistan, though both are overwhelmingly Muslim, led to massacres in 1971 by the Pakistani military, and eventually caused the break-up of the country. And when East Pakistan emerged as Bangladesh the cycle of violence continued. More recently the disease has spread to Sri Lanka and the Kingdom of Nepal. Thanks to the influx of militant groups from India's Northeast as well as from Nepal, even the remote Himalayan Kingdom of Bhutan is no longer free from organised violence.

Because of the modern revisionist tendency to rewrite the past to suit present needs, there has been a tendency among scholars to treat all forms of political violence as terrorism.[2] But while political violence has been common in South Asia, arguably a

---

[1] The author is grateful to D. Shyam Babu for his valuable and critical comments.
[2] See for example Kanti Bajpai, *Roots of Terrorism* (New Delhi: Penguin Books, 2002).

large portion of the violence that dominates its political landscape does not fall into that category. What, then, can be said to constitute terrorism within the South Asian context?

Definitional Problems

The major problem facing a serious discussion on terrorism comes from the proliferation of nomenclatures for political violence. Such violence comes in different forms and categories: assassination; separatism; militancy; armed struggle; rebellion; insurgency; 'communal riots'; sectarian violence; etc. All of them have to varying degrees a political component—the essential ingredient that differentiates terrorism from other forms of violence.

However, in each category, there are exceptions and ambiguities. Political murder or assassination has become a recurrent phenomenon in South Asia. Real or perceived grievance of an ethnic group or religious community results in individuals or groups taking up arms on behalf of the 'injured' party. Such violence is often directed at political personalities held to be responsible for their misery. These include the assassinations of Mahatma Gandhi in 1948, Indira Gandhi in 1984 and Rajiv Gandhi in 1991, and scores of Sinhalese and Tamil personalities including Sri Lanka's Defence Minster Ranjan Wijeratne in March 1991, President Ranasinghe Premadasa in May 1993, Opposition Leader Gamini Dissanayake in October 1994 and moderate Tamil leader Neelan Thiruchelvam in July 1999.[3]

Some scholars draw a line between assassinations carried out by individuals and by organised groups. But in the South Asian case the distinction is blurred. The killings of former Indian Army chief A.S. Vidya in August 1985, Punjab Chief Minister Beant Singh in July 1995, and Akali leader Harchand Singh Longowal in September 1985 were all directly related to Sikh militancy. On the other hand, Pakistan's first Prime Minister Liaquat Ali Khan fell to a tribal assassin's bullets in October 1951, and military officers pulled the trigger on Bangladeshi leaders Mujibur Rahman in August 1975 and Zia ur-Rahman in May 1981.

Other forms of political violence, however, do not fall so squarely within the gamut of terrorism. Communal riots, a frequent occurrence in India, have been driven by economic as well as political considerations. The anti-Tamil violence in Sri Lanka and the anti-Ahmadiyya violence in Pakistan as well as Bangladesh have strong party-political overtones, being primarily targeted against unarmed civilian populations in pursuance of a specific political agenda; so too the

---

[3] Robert Rotberg, *Creating Peace in Sri Lanka: Civil War and Reconciliation* (Washington DC: Brookings Institution Press, 1999).

anti-foreigner violence in Assam in the 1990s and the anti-Pundit violence in Kashmir. However, if one defines terrorism as premeditated political violence directed against civilian populations with an intention of conveying a message to a larger society, then some of the above campaigns could be classed as terrorism.

Moreover, even explicitly insurgent movements have often turned their guns against non-combatants suspected of providing support to the state or its arms. For example in June 1991, K. Doraiswamy, a senior executive of the Indian Oil Corporation, was abducted by Kashmiri militants who demanded the release of four of their jailed colleagues in return for his release. The militants killed Doraiswamy following the government's refusal to accept their demand. When groups do not make any distinction between combatants and non-combatants, their anti-state violence falls into the category of terrorism.

However the real problem lies elsewhere. The term 'terrorism' came into popular vocabulary quite recently and invoking that label in the context of the activities of any group now amounts to declaring that group beyond the pale. Governments in South Asia regularly ban organisations on the grounds that they are 'extremist' or 'terrorist' outfits. But at the same time, they also de-notify such organisations and lift the bans on them in order to start a political dialogue. Again, South Asia has been reluctant to treat even extreme violence as terrorism—partly because of the region's traditional support for liberation movements, and partly because it recognises that some kinds of ethno-nationalist terrorism may not be amenable to a military solution. In the words of one writer, 'If freedom fighters meet standards of representativeness, rationality, and responsibility, then their resort to violence may be justified'.[4]

The Terrorist versus Freedom Fighter Dilemma[5]

Any discussion on terrorism in South Asia has to consider the development that shaped, sharpened and eventually shifted the thinking in the region, namely, that terrorism is no longer a distant phenomenon. At one level, the countries of the South Asian region, like the rest of the developing world, are committed to supporting the cause of national liberation. This support for the nationalist aspirations of other people in Asia, Africa and Latin America was in tune with their own anti-colonial and anti-imperialist traditions and their commitment to the principle of freedom. Finding a common cause with various nationalisms, South Asian

---

[4] Bajpai, *Roots of Terrorism*, p.15.
[5] For more on the different definitions of terrorism, see Boaz Ganor, 'Defining Terrorism: Is One Man's Terrorist Another Man's Freedom Fighter?' [http://www.ict.org.il/articles/define.html].

countries have generally extended an unqualified support to movements which have, at times, indulged in activities that arguably fall into the category of terrorism.

South Asian support for the Palestinian movement since the 1960s is a classic example. In their desire to endorse the legitimacy and righteousness of the Palestinian cause and support for Arab nationhood generally, the region's governments rarely came out against the terrorist activities such as hijacking and the premeditated killing of civilians committed from time to time by elements of the Palestine Liberation Organisation. The same was true of anti-regime violence in colonial Angola and in South Africa during the apartheid era. Although the South Asian countries did not go to the extent of justifying these excesses, they took the view that they were aberrations that did not invalidate the larger cause.

Even India, which claimed a tradition of non-violence, never linked its support for overseas national liberation movements to their abandoning violence. Ironically, by focusing solely on the political demands of these movements, India and other South Asian countries bestowed a kind of legitimacy upon their operational tactics—which sometimes included terrorism.

Indeed, taking a lenient view of terrorism has paid political dividends for South Asian governments. A general indifference to terrorism in far-off places has a sound political logic. The cause of national liberation abroad has enjoyed consistent domestic popularity across the region. As well, ruling parties have found giving support to liberation movements a useful way to brandish their 'progressive' credentials. Finally, both India and Pakistan have freely employed the 'Palestine card' in an effort to out-bid the other internationally. Support for the Palestinian cause also enabled Pakistan to mitigate domestic criticism over the pro-American foreign policy pursued by its leaders since 1947.

The stand taken by the Colombo summit of the Non-Aligned Movement (NAM) in 1976 exemplified the regional position. In July 1976 an Air France plane en route to Paris was hijacked by a group of Palestinian guerrillas who commandeered it to Entebbe in Uganda. Subsequently a successful rescue operation was carried out by Israel, which many Western countries came to see as a milestone in counter-terrorism. But the NAM countries, meeting in Sri Lanka a few months later, threw in their lot not only with the Palestinians but also with the Ugandan leader Idi Amin. The communiqué of the summit expressed its disappointment over the failure of the UN Security Council to condemn 'Israeli military aggression against Uganda', and condemned Israel for its violation of Uganda's territorial integrity and 'for thwarting humanitarian efforts by the

President of Uganda to have all [the] hostages released'. But it remained silent on the hijacking *per se*.[6]

Moreover, this stance was made easier because the terrorism pursued by national liberation movements was generally directed against the West rather than against the communist East or the developing South. Immune to its consequences, the countries of the South could go along with the Soviet Union and its allies in blaming the West for causing the deprivation that drove people to terrorism.

With the passing of time, however, the benign position adopted by South Asia *vis-à-vis* national liberation movements became increasingly untenable.

Boomerang Effect
South Asia had a collective legacy of suffering from separatist agitation and ethnic conflict. Yet even as it fought this politically-motivated violence *within* the region, it had simultaneously supported similar activities *outside*. This contradiction was explained/justified by the spurious claim that the internal agitations were 'separatist', while similar movements in other parts of the world were 'national liberation struggles'. The usage of different nomenclatures enabled South Asian regimes to adopt different yardsticks.

But eventually the chickens came home to roost. Driven by considerations of *realpolitik*, some South Asia governments began to embrace the cause of, and at times enlist the support of, groups fighting for political rights in neighbouring countries. Soon, numerous *jihadi* groups in Kashmir, Tamil militants in Sri Lanka, Sikh extremists in Punjab, and Bengali nationalists in the erstwhile East Pakistan were receiving ideological as well as logistical support from neighbouring states.

Each country adopted the familiar 'freedom fighter' logic to explain and justify this support. Because they shared and endorsed the ultimate political objective of these groups, namely greater autonomy, these countries turned a blind eye to the extremist activities of some of these groups, including the premeditated killing of unarmed civilians. Once a government took the risky step of making common cause with a group fighting the state of its neighbour, it usually had no inhibitions about implicitly endorsing all the means adopted by the insurgent group.

Thus virtually all South Asian countries are victims of terrorism supported by their neighbours—in particular, India, Pakistan, Bangladesh and Nepal. The support the

---
[6] Government of India, *Documents of the Gathering of the Non-Aligned Countries, 1961–79* (New Delhi: Ministry of External Affairs, 1981), p.203. Even though Pakistan was not a member of the Non-Aligned Movement at that time, its position was not different.

region has extended to terrorism ranges from 'moral support' to active military help, including arms supply and training. In other words, at one time or another all these states have indulged in what is now commonly referred to as 'state-sponsored terrorism'. But there are no real winners in this tit-for-tat game. The end result of South Asian states justifying and supporting militant activities in the neighbourhood has been to weaken their own power.

Pakistan periodically accused India and its intelligence agencies of fomenting the ongoing sectarian violence in the country.[7] This charge remains largely unproven. On the other hand, Indian involvement in the internal violence in Sri Lanka, Bangladesh and to a lesser extent Nepal, is quite well-known. The prolonged ethnic conflict in Sri Lanka was partly fuelled in the early years by active Indian involvement. And even if New Delhi did not endorse the idea of a separate state for the Sri Lankan Tamils, it desired and supported the idea of a greater autonomy for the Tamils within a federal Sri Lanka. New Delhi's sympathy for the plight of the Tamils in Sri Lanka was further reinforced by domestic political calculations and pressures from the All-India Anna Dravida Munnetra Kazhagam (AIADMK), then a major regional ally of the ruling Congress Party.

While fighting for a separate Tamil homeland in northern Sri Lanka, the Liberation Tigers of Tamil Eelam (LTTE) and other Tamil militant groups were also indulging in large-scale violence against the local civilian population. Despite this, India was instrumental in strengthening the nascent LTTE that was spearheading the separatist movement. It is widely accepted that the Tamil Tigers fighting the Sri Lankan army received training from the Indian army[8] and it is alleged that the Tigers were provided with substantial financial support by the government of Tamil Nadu.[9] According to J.N. Dixit, India's high commissioner in Colombo at the height of the conflict, 'Tamil Nadu Chief Minister M.G. Ramachandran provided sufficient finances to the LTTE to purchase arms and supplies even after the IPKF (Indian Peace Keeping

---

[7] See for example 'RAW camps in Balochistan', *The Dawn* (Karachi) (31 August 2004).
[8] The in-camera testimony of witnesses before the Jain Commission that examined the assassination of Rajiv Gandhi provided more substantial evidence about the extent of Indian involvement in providing military training to Tamil groups. During the tenure of Indira Gandhi, the intelligence agency Research and Analysis Wing (RAW) selected and trained Sri Lankan Tamils in the use of modern arms in camps organised in Tamil Nadu, Karnataka, Uttar Pradesh, New Delhi and elsewhere. The idea was that the Sri Lankan Tamils would be sent back to northern Sri Lanka to engage Sri Lankan troops in guerrilla warfare. Even the relevant state governments were kept in the dark about this top-secret operation. See Coomi Kapoor, 'Uppermost in our Minds was to Save the Gandhis' Name', *The Indian Express* (12 December 1997) [http://www.expressindia.com/ie/daily/19971212/34650923.html].
[9] See T.S. Subramanian, 'Full of Holes', in *Frontline*, Vol.14, no.24 (29 Nov.–12 Dec. 1997) [http://www.frontlineonnet.com/fl1424/14240260.htm]. See also Rohan Gunaratna, 'International and Regional Implications of the Sri Lankan Tamil Insurgency', Institute for Counter-Terrorism (2 Dec. 1998) [http://www.ict.org.il/articles/articledet.cfm?articleid=57].

Force) was launched against this militant group'.[10] Later, however, the Indian government thought better of the strategy. The failure of the militants to surrender their arms following the signing of the Indo–Sri Lankan accord of July 1987 led to India withdrawing its patronage of the Tigers. Then the entry of the Indian Army into Sri Lanka resulted in the IPKF taking on the Tamil militants in battle. However, it was only after the assassination of Rajiv Gandhi by members of the Tamil Tigers in May 1991 that India finally banned the LTTE from operating on its territory. Indeed there are still voices in Tamil Nadu that call for the revocation of the ban imposed upon the LTTE.[11] For instance Vaiko, a lawmaker from Tamil Nadu, was tried (without success) under the draconian anti-terrorist laws for making pro-LTTE statements.[12]

Likewise, from the early 1980s India provided shelter and logistical support to the ethnic Chakmas who were fighting the Bangladeshi government. For long, New Delhi tried to convince Dhaka that its policy of settling Bengali outsiders in the Chakmas' traditional homeland of the Chittagong Hill Tracts (CHT) was destroying their lifestyle and creating social unrest among the tribal population, resulting in a large number of Chakmas fleeing to India as refugees. But Dhaka turned a deaf ear. The post-Mujibur regimes did not view India favourably. When some of the refugees decided to take up arms under the banner of the Parbattya Chattagram Jana Sanghati Samiti (United Peoples' Party of Chittagong Hill Tracts or PCJSS) in defence of their rights, India found a suitable opening.[13] It allowed the Chakma rebels to operate from its north-eastern states, and provided logistical support to them in the form of rations, financial help and even small quantities of arms.[14] When India later 'abandoned' its support, mainstream Chakmas led by Santanu Larma concluded the Chittagong Hill Tracts accord with the Sheikh Hasina government in December 1997.[15]

Politically India adopted a similar position vis-a'-vis Nepal. At different times, both the Congress as well as the opposition parties provided patronage to Nepalese groups and individuals fighting the monarchy. Indeed some of the latter were even given refuge in the homes of leading Indian politicians. But not all these activists were fervent

---

[10] J.N. Dixit, *Assignment Colombo* (New Delhi: Konark, 1998), p.232. See also *Growth of Sri Lankan Tamil Militancy in Tamil Nadu, Chapter 1 Phase-II (1987–88), Jain Commission Interim Report* [www.tamilnation.org].

[11] 'Lift the Ban on LTTE: Tirumavalavan', *The Hindu* (9 June 2004).

[12] These statements were made at a public rally on 29 June 2002, and resulted in his arrest by the Tamil Nadu government.

[13] Subir Bhoumik, *Insurgent Crossfire: North-East India* (New Delhi: Lancer, 1996), p.272.

[14] *Ibid.* See also Sanjoy Hazarka, *Rites of Passage: Border Crossings, Imagined Homelands, India's East and Bangladesh* (New Delhi: Penguin, 2000), p.89.

[15] *Chittagong Hill Tracts Treaty, 1997* [http://www.satp.org/satporgtp/countries/bangladesh/document/actandordinances/CHT1990.htm].

democrats. In February 2006 Maoists from Nepal organised a large rally in New Delhi. It was attended by representatives of the Left parties whose support is crucial for the Manmohan Singh government.[16] However Indian support for the Nepalese rebels remained largely non-governmental—political parties rather than government agencies.

When Indian involvement was official, as in the cases of the LTTE and the Chakmas, security and foreign policy considerations influenced New Delhi's behaviour. It found the militant groups useful tools for exerting political pressure upon neighbouring governments. By adopting a tolerant and lenient view towards these militants, New Delhi sought to further its national interests.

Likewise, the support of Pakistan and Bangladesh for regional terrorism in South Asia was equally driven by self-interest. While Pakistan cannot be held responsible for the origin of the problem, it benefited immensely from the Sikh militancy that haunted India in the 1980s. Unlike the Kashmir situation, the struggle for an independent Sikh homeland or Khalistan did not have any ideological roots in Pakistan. On the contrary, Sikhism had emerged as a reaction to the weak response of Hinduism to the growth of Islam in northern India. Rather, the ethno-religious violence in India offered an opportunity to the Pakistan government led by General Zia ul-Haq to tie down the neighbouring state and thereby minimise security threats emanating from the east. The Soviet presence in Afghanistan also played a role in his calculations as he was trying to neutralise India's potential to collaborate with Moscow and sandwich Pakistan between the two. Under such circumstances, tacit support for Sikh militancy was a logical strategy for Pakistan.

The role of Pakistan in the Kashmir militancy is, by contrast, underpinned by strong ideological fervour and popular emotional sentiment. Islamabad has never accepted Indian control over the Kashmir Valley, but in the summer of 1990 it began to play a major role in the direction of the Kashmir revolt. Since then, coincidentally or not, militant groups fighting for separation from India have become more ruthless in targeting the civilian population, in particular those Kashmiris whom they suspect of collaborating with the Indian Army. Suicide attacks, killings, kidnappings and other forms of violence against civilian targets have become commonplace. The mass exodus during 1990 of the Kashmiri Pundit community was one direct result of terrorism. According to Indian estimates, between 1989 and January 2000 nearly 23,000 people died as a result of the insurgency—of this number a staggering 43.9 percent were civilians.[17]

---

[16] 'Protest Against Bid to Stifle Democracy', *The Hindu* (13 Feb. 2006).

[17] 10 percent were security personnel and the remaining 46.1 percent were militants. See 'Jammu and Kashmir: Backgrounder' [www.ict.org.il/articles/backgrounder_j_k.htm].

Pakistan has provided political, ideological, financial, military and logistical support to the Kashmiri separatists. Besides allowing its territory to be used for anti-Indian violence, it has established, organised and run training camps for militants in the Pakistan-administered territory of Azad Kashmir (Free Kashmir).[18]

For long Pakistan denied its culpability in the militancy that was raging in Kashmir and maintained that its support was purely political and ideological. Gradually it reverted to the logic of the liberation struggle. Kashmiri militants, Pakistani leaders maintained, were 'freedom fighters' or *jihadis*, not terrorists.[19] In August 1984 Kashmiri militants commandeered a domestic Indian flight and hijacked it to Pakistan. Though all the passengers were eventually released unharmed, according to some passengers, Pakistani security officials provided weapons to the hijackers.[20] Occasionally Kashmiri militants carried out terrorist attacks in other parts of India as well.

Of late the distinction between Kashmiri militants and Islamic terrorists has become somewhat blurred. It is not easy to connect violent attacks like that on the Akshardham Temple in Gujarat, or the foiled attack on the Rashtriya Swayamsevak Sangh (RSS) headquarters in Nagpur in Maharashtra, with militancy in Kashmir, because not all the militants/terrorists captured or killed by police were from Kashmir. Similarly, with several countries having endorsed the Indian government's charge that Pakistan abets terrorism in India, the 'Pakistan-link' is taken as given. Therefore, people in general tend to believe Pakistan's hand is behind every act of terrorism that takes place in the country. For example, the attack on the Indian Parliament in December 2001 brought India and Pakistan to the brink of war, as New Delhi believed that the attackers, all killed in the incident, were Pakistani nationals. Though the police failed to establish an external conspiracy in court, public perception of Pakistan's involvement remains intact.

In the early 1990s along with Iran, Iraq and Syria, Pakistan was almost branded by Washington as a state sponsoring international terrorism. It was only its geo-strategic importance *vis-à-vis* Afghanistan (first as a base for combating the Soviets and then as a springboard for smiting the Taliban/al Qaeda) that prevented the US from publicly castigating Islamabad.

---

[18] See for example K. Santhanam, Sreedhar, Sudhir Saxena, and Manish, *Jihadis in Jammu and Kashmir: A Portrait Gallery* (New Delhi: Sage Publications, 2003).
[19] "'Jihad' in Kashmir is not Terrorism: Musharraf', *The Hindu* (5 Feb. 2000).
[20] K. Subrahmanyam, then the director of the Institute for Defence Studies and Analyses (IDSA) who was also a passenger, provided a first-person account of the hijack drama. These articles appeared in the *Indian Express* between 28 and 31 August 1984.

That said, it should be noted that terrorism and other forms of political violence in Kashmir dropped considerably after Pakistani President Pervez Musharraf, in response to the post-9/11 global environment and intense American pressure, abandoned the *jihadi* forces and opted for a political dialogue to resolve the Kashmir problem. In turn, post-9/11, the US came to accept India's complaints that Kashmiri militants were receiving support from Pakistan.

Recently Musharraf has gone further and declared some Kashmiri militant groups to be terrorists.[21] The Indo–Pakistani talks that followed that shift dramatically eased tensions between the two large South Asian neighbours. If this thaw continues it might even result in an eventual Indo–Pakistani *détente*.[22]

Bangladesh was also a willing accomplice to terrorism in South Asia. The *bonhomie* of Indo–Bangladeshi relations came to an end following the brutal assassination of Mujibur Rahman in August 1975. A host of political and economic issues have contributed to periodic tension between the two. However there is also a terrorism angle. A number of militants who have been fighting in India's north-eastern states have taken refuge in Bangladesh.

Since the late 1990s, and especially since Khaleda Zia returned to power in October 2001, New Delhi has accused Dhaka of harbouring and sponsoring various militant groups. It is said that numerous militants' camps are located inside Bangladesh close to its borders with India. According to one estimate as many as 172 such camps were reportedly in existence in 2005.[23]

Periodically India has presented Dhaka with a list of these militants' camps and demanded their closure. But they continue to thrive. The United Liberation Front of Asom (ULFA), the most prominent and perhaps the largest militant group in the Northeast, has developed large business interests in Bangladesh and now owns seven up-market hotels in Dhaka and Chittagong.[24] Meanwhile several prominent

---

[21] For a detailed discussion see Peter R. Lavoy, 'Pakistan's Kashmir Policy after the Bush Visit to South Asia', in *Strategic Insights*, Vol.4, no.4 (April 2006) [http://www.ccc.nps.navy.mil/si/2006/Apr/lavoyApr06.asp].

[22] D. Shyam Babu, 'Detente in South Asia: Euphoria needs Caution', *Power and Interest News Report* (2 May 2005) [http://www.pinr.com/report.php?ac=view_report&report_id=292&language_id=1].

[23] Press Release, Border Security Force, 'India–Bangladesh Border Coordination Conference Concludes: Joint Record of Discussions Signed' (New Delhi: Ministry of Home Affairs, 30 Sept. 2005) [http://bsf.nic.in/press/pr49.htm].

[24] They were identified as the Surma International, Hotel Mahammadia and Hotel Padma International in Dhaka, Hotel Keya International and Hotel Yamuna in Sylhet, and Hotel Basundhara and Hotel Raj King in Chittagong. *Indian Express* (4 June 2005). The Border Security Force also alleged that it had identified three bank accounts operated by the ULFA in Bangladesh and that the militant outfit was running a number of nursing homes in Bangladesh. This charge, however, was quickly denied by Bangladesh. See *The Daily Star* (5 June 2005) and *The Hindu* (6 June 2005).

militants including the ULFA's Anup Chetia and Sanjib Debbarma of the National Liberation Front of Tripura sought and received political asylum in Bangladesh. Yet the Bangladesh government continues to deny any involvement in the militancy going on in India's north-eastern states.

To a point, one can understand why the Bangladesh government has vacillated. Rugged terrain, porous ill-defended borders and frequently-changing water lines along the Indo–Bangladeshi border enable the north-eastern militants to easily cross over into Bangladesh. A deteriorating internal law and order situation and the rise of domestic militancy have further impeded the ability of the Bangladesh government to act decisively. Yet reflecting the traditional view, some Bangladesh leaders, including Khaleda Zia, have insisted on describing the ULFA cadres as 'freedom fighters'.[25]

Driven by their national-interest calculations, Bangladesh, India and Pakistan have all lent a helping hand to terrorist groups in their neighbouring states. While India demanded that Pakistan cease support for cross-border terrorism in Kashmir, it pressed ahead with support for LTTE terrorist violence in Sri Lanka. Similarly, both Bangladesh and Pakistan found it convenient to support militant groups active in India.

Domestic Terrorism

Domestically, too, South Asian countries adopted policies that contributed to the growth of terrorism in the region. If national-interest calculations forced governments to be supportive of some terrorist groups in neighbouring states, narrow political calculations often resulted in parties and leaders adopting a benevolent attitude towards terrorism and its perpetrators within their states.

Again, India constituted the classic case. Let us begin with the Punjab crisis. As is well known, the onset and growth of Sikh militancy in the 1980s was primarily the result of a power struggle between the Congress Party and the locally-powerful Akali Dal:

> During that period, prominent figures of the Congress Party—including [Prime Minister] Indira Gandhi—quietly channelled funds and assistance to extremist Sikh religious leaders.. .. Their intention was to fragment the Sikh community in order to split the Sikhs' sectarian political

---

[25] Jaideep Saikia, *Contours: Essays on Security and Strategy*, Ch.2, '*Swadhin Asom or Brihot Bangladesh*' (Urbana-Champaign: Arms Control, Disarmament and International Security (ACDIS), University of Illinois, 2001) [http://www.acdis.uiuc.edu/Research/ OPs/Saikia/contents/chap_two.html].

party, the Akali Dal. If that party could be divided, the likely beneficiary in Punjab politics would have been the Congress Party which drew support from a minority of Hindus. Prominent among the Sikh militants receiving this assistance was.. .Sant Jarnail Singh Bhindranwale.[26]

But these men were for the most part avowed enemies of the Indian state. However, Indira Gandhi and her home minister (later president) Giani Zail Singh covertly lent their support to those very Sikh extremists who would later spearhead a violent movement for the creation of Khalistan, a separate Sikh homeland. While this extremist movement would have developed anyway, one cannot ignore the role the Congress Party and its central leadership played in the process.

Likewise Indian leaders have often failed to take a resolute stand in the face of terrorist challenges. On 20 December 1978 two little-known Congress workers, Bholanath Pandey and Devendra Pandey, hijacked a domestic airliner and demanded the release of opposition leader Indira Gandhi who had been arrested by the Janata Party government. The hijacking ended peacefully and in 1980 both men were elected to the Uttar Pradesh legislature on a Congress Party ticket. Again, in the summer of 1990, several convicted terrorists were released from prison following the kidnapping of a daughter of Indian Home Minister Mufti Mohammed Sayyid by Kashmiri militants. Some of them went on to become key figures in the Kashmiri militancy.[27] Ironically the same government—headed by V.P. Singh—refused to make similar concessions when some foreigners and senior civil servants were kidnapped in Kashmir—a principled stand that resulted in their gruesome murder by the militants.[28] The Bharatiya Janata Party (BJP) had presented itself at the hustings as a party resolutely committed to fighting terrorism in all its forms. But in the wake of the hijacking of Indian Airlines IC 814 to Kandahar in December 1999, the BJP-led government buckled under public pressure and released three Kashmiri militants in a bid to secure the release of the passengers.[29]

Last but not least, political calculations have frequently influenced governmental decisions regarding the proscription of groups regarded as terrorist. As mentioned earlier, India banned the LTTE only after the assassination of Rajiv Gandhi. In July 2004 the Congress government of Andhra Pradesh revoked an eleven-year-old

---

[26] James Manor, 'Collective Conflict in India', in *Conflict Studies*, No.212 (June 1988), p.14.
[27] Bhavna Vij, 'Rewind to '89: Govt. Crawled when Militants asked it to Bend', *Indian Express* (15 Oct. 2001).
[28] Since 1989, for example, as many as 21 foreigners have been kidnapped by the militants. They were from Britain, France, Germany, Holland, Israel, Japan, Norway, Sweden and the US. *The Tribune* (Chandigarh) (23 July 1998).
[29] However Foreign Minister Jaswant Singh's journey to Kandahar with the three militants provoked strong criticism and disapproval inside the country.

official ban on the Naxalite People's War Group (PWG) in the hope of starting a 'peace process'. This olive branch was extended to the Naxalites despite evidence that they were continuing to murder landlords in Andhra Pradesh and other states[30]. Similarly, the inclusion and exclusion of various north-eastern groups in the terrorist watch-list maintained by the Indian Home Ministry has been motivated, to a large extent, by political considerations.

Still, this apparent duality in policy is essential if there is to be a peaceful resolution of disputes. While South Asian states can afford to adopt an uncompromising position *vis-à-vis* terrorist groups located outside their territories, such a policy is counter-productive in respect of local groups. Willy-nilly these groups have to be recognised, brought into the negotiation process and accommodated politically. It is a matter of political calculation. The desire of the Sri Lankan government to seek a political settlement with the LTTE and India's willingness in recent times to seek a negotiated settlement with the 'moderate' segments of various north-eastern militant groups both emanate from this equation.

Bangladesh faces a similar dilemma. The support of the religious parties, especially the Jamaat-e-Islami, was critical to Khaleda Zia's success in the Jatiya Sangsad elections of October 2001. Brought into the ruling coalition and given places in the cabinet, the Jamaat-e-Islami now wields considerable influence, which has constrained Khaleda from adopting a strong stand against religious extremism. While the opposition Awami League argues that there are as many as 33 militant groups active in the country,[31] the government chose to ban only three.[32] The Bangladesh media, which has repeatedly highlighted a nexus between militant groups and the Bangladesh Nationalist Party (BNP)-led ruling coalition, is similarly ignored.[33]

The Role of Religion
Since the days of Partition when the subcontinent was divided along communal lines, religion has become a primary factor contributing to the growth of terrorism and numerous other forms of political and sectarian violence in South Asia. For a long time riots were not seen as terrorism, but merely as inter-communal violence.

---

[30] Moreover, in October 2003 the then Andra Chief Minister Chandra Babu Naidu narrowly escaped a Naxalite attack in the temple town of Tirupati.
[31] Awami League, 'Growing Fanaticism & Extremism in Bangladesh: Shades of the Taliban' [http://www.albd.org/aldoc/growing/growing.fanaticism.pdf].
[32] While the Jamaatul-Mujahideen Bangladesh (JMB) and Jagrata Muslim Janata Bangladesh (JMJB) were banned in Feb. 2005, the Harakat-ul-Jihad-al-Islami (HUJI) was proscribed only on 17 October 2005.
[33] Following a series of bomb blasts, *The Daily Star* carried a series of articles on the militancy–politician nexus between 22 and 24 August 2005.

The tension between two communities in a particular locality takes a violent turn and transforms itself into a riot. The provocation can be external or some local development. Much of post-1947 Indian polity has been dominated by Hindu–Muslim communal violence in which the minority Muslims are usually the prime targets and victims. However although there is not always an organised structure behind this violence, some of the communal riots clearly fall into the category of terrorism.

The destruction of the controversial Babri Mosque at Ayodhya in December 1992 symbolised the communal frenzy which gripped the region in the late twentieth century. The state was unable to prevent a frenzied mob of a few thousand from destroying the mosque. Despite prolonged political agitation over the issue of the mosque's future and the public declaration by Hindu militants that they intended to build a temple in its place, neither the central nor state governments took adequate preventive measures.[34] The result was the destruction of the mosque and a wave of communal violence across the country culminating in Bombay, where on 12 March 1993 eleven bombs were detonated by religious militants in various parts of the city.

The religion–terrorism nexus often shows itself in places of worship being utilised for terrorist activities. The Sikh insurgency in Punjab reached its climax in June 1984 when Akali militants led by Bhindranwale took refuge in the sacred Golden Temple in Amritsar. Capitalising on the holy status of the venue, the militants used it to stockpile large quantities of small arms, ammunition and heavy weapons. This eventually led to a confrontation between the militants holed up there and the Indian Army. The action—codenamed Operation Blue Star—is one of the bloodiest events in India's recent history.[35]

Ten years later, in October 1994, a group of Kashmiri militants took refuge in the Hazratbal Shrine in Srinagar. According to Kashmiri traditions, the mosque is believed to house a strand of the Prophet Mohammad's beard. The army laid a siege that lasted a month, after which the militants surrendered. In the process, however, more than 50 civilians demonstrating in support of the holed-up militants were killed by the Indian security forces. When in March 1996 another group of militants took refuge in the same shrine, the stand-off was resolved peacefully, with the militants being allowed 'to slip' from the shrine with their weapons.

The religion–terrorism nexus is also killing people in Pakistan. For the past decade, Shia–Sunni violence has rocked the country. Much of this sectarian violence is

---

[34] Prominent BJP leaders including L.K. Advani, who later became the deputy prime minister, are still facing criminal trial for their alleged involvement in the destruction of the mosque.
[35] For an account of Operation Blue Star, see Mark Tully and Satish Jacob, *Amritsar: Mrs. Gandhi's Last Battle* (London: Macmillan, 1986).

unleashed in markets, places of worship and other meeting places, often following Friday noon prayers. While there are no explicit political motives, the violence has taken a heavy toll.

Pakistani involvement in Kashmir and Afghanistan was rooted in, rationalised and sustained through the Islamic prism. Both its military and civilian rulers perceived support for the Kashmiri cause as an article of faith and an essential duty of Pakistan. Support for the *jihadi* movement in Kashmir was not confined to the establishment but was widespread. Through volunteers and financial contributions, ordinary Pakistanis not only sustained the militancy in Kashmir but also compelled the government to adopt a sympathetic view of the militants. Any perception of a 'dilution' of support for Kashmir's secession from India and its unification with Pakistan was politically counter-productive. When he deposed the elected government and took over the reins of power in October 1999, General Musharraf justified his action by saying that under Prime Minister Nawaz Sharif Pakistan had 'abandoned' the Kashmiris.[36]

And Bangladesh, too, now regularly experiences communal riots, especially against the minority Hindus and Ahmadiyyas. In the past anti-Hindu violence in Bangladesh was sporadic and linked to communal tensions in India. In recent years, especially since the BNP victory in 2001, it has become sui *generis*.[37] The violence against the religious minorities is seen by its perpetrators as a means of suppressing and even erasing their religious identity. Certainly, in the case of the Hindus, it has had the effect of forcing many to flee.[38]

The heterodox Ahmadiyyas have been another target of communal violence in South Asia. In the early 1950s, West Pakistan saw a prolonged agitation directed against the Ahmadiyyas. While the onset of military rule in 1958 saved them from immediate oblivion, the Ahmadiyyas fared badly under the following civilian regime. Yielding to public pressure, in 1974 Prime Minister Zulfikar Ali Bhutto declared them to be non-Muslims and forbade them from representing themselves as Muslims.[39] And now, Bangladesh appears to be going down the same path. Ahmadiyyas and their places of worship are becoming the target of organised violence by various

---

[36] 'Text of Speech by Gen. Pervez Musharraf' [http://www.chowk.com/show_article.cgi?aid=00000669&channel=civic%20center].
[37] Sreeradha Datta, 'Post Election Hindu–Muslim Violence in Bangladesh', in *Strategic Analysis*, Vol.26, no.2 (April–June 2002), pp.316–21.
[38] Meghna Guhathakurta, 'Assault on Minorities in Bangladesh: An Analysis' [http://www.meghbarta.net/ 2002/january/ minor.html#minor1].
[39] For a detailed discussion, see Yohanan Friedmann, *Prophecy Continues: Aspects of Ahmadi Religious Thought and its Medieval Background* (Berkeley: University of California Press, 1989).

Islamic groups and organisations.[40] The government of Khaleda Zia has come under intense pressure, especially from its coalition partners, to 'clarify' the status of the Ahmadiyyas within Islam. Not willing to alienate its support-base among conservative voters, in January 2004 the government imposed a ban on Ahmadiyya publications. According to an official report by the US State Department, only Washington's intervention prevented Bangladesh from declaring the Ahmadiyyas non-Muslims and introducing legislation that 'would have created blasphemy laws based on the Pakistani model'.[41]

The violence in Sri Lanka, though mainly ethnic in nature, also has a religious dimension. Arguably, pressure from the Buddhist clergy contributed significantly to the inflexibility of various Sri Lankan governments towards the political demands of the minority Tamil population—a point that has not received adequate attention and scrutiny.[42] And the desire of the (mainly Buddhist) Sinhalese-dominated Sri Lankan governments to pursue the military option against the Tamil militants in the 1980s probably owed something to the same source. Certainly the clergy played a leading role in galvanising the Sinhalese public against the Indo–Sri Lankan agreement of 1987 that visualised a federal solution to the ethnic problem. Moreover, there is a suggestion that some Sinhalese terrorist groups such as the Janatha Vimukthi Peramuna (People's Liberation Front or JVP) also enjoyed the support of the Buddhist religious establishment. If so, the latter must bear a heavy responsibility for helping to prolong the civil war. In its turn, however, the LTTE, while nominally secular, has not hesitated in targeting Buddhist institutions. For instance in January 1998 the LTTE carried out a bomb attack on the Dalada Malagawa in Kandy in which 13 worshippers, including a number of children, were killed. Known as Temple of the Tooth, it is the holiest Buddhist shrine in the country.

There are similar examples in Pakistan. Much of the Shia–Sunni sectarian violence involves places of worship. Either weapons are stored in mosques or they become the venue for killing members of rival groups. Wahhabi-influenced Sunni Islam does not recognise Shias as proper Muslims and hence Sunnis do not recognise Shia mosques. In turn, attacks on Shia mosques have sparked revenge assaults from Shia Muslims against Sunni institutions. Indeed, post-Friday noon prayer is the most frequent

---

[40] Human Rights Watch, *Breach of Faith: Persecution of the Ahmadiyya Community in Bangladesh* (New York: Human Rights Watch, June 2005) [http://hrw.org/reports/ 2005/bangladesh0605/bangladesh0605.pdf, accessed 26 February 2006].

[41] Bureau of Democracy, Human Rights, and Labor, Department of State, 'International Religious Freedom 2004' [http://www.state.gov/g/drl/rls/ irf/ 2004/, accessed 18 May 2004].

[42] Jeyaraja Tambiah, *Buddhism Betrayed? Religion, Politics and Violence in Sri Lanka* (Chicago: University of Chicago Press, 1992).

occasion for communal violence in Pakistan. But at times allegations of blasphemy have led to attacks against places of worship of other communities too. In October 2001, for example, 16 worshippers were killed in a church in Bahawalpur town near Multan.

Likewise in Bangladesh, mosques have become places not only of religious contestation but also bases for terror networks. After the August 2005 nationwide bomb blasts, large quantities of arms and ammunition were seized from mosques and *madrassas* operated by various Islamic groups and organisations.

Conclusion

As 'terrorism' became a popular label, especially in the wake of 9/11, South Asian governments began to represent much of the domestic political violence in the region as terrorist-inclined or -inspired. These days all kinds of politically-motivated violence—insurgency, militancy, armed struggle, religiously-motivated *jihad*, low-intensity conflict, political killings and assassinations, Left-wing violence and even communal riots—are routinely classified as terrorism. This tactic enables governments to put such groups outside the 'legal' framework and proscribe their existence and operations.

At the same time, South Asian governments know that there is no simple military solution to the so-called terrorist menace. While an uncompromising posture is tenable towards outside groups, it is an impractical way to deal with 'internal' groups espousing terrorism as a means of securing political rights. Most South Asian insurgencies, on the other hand, have proven amenable to solution through a mixture of force and negotiation. So, governments in the region are increasingly adopting a reconciliatory posture *vis-à-vis* terrorism. This is sensible. Alienated groups need to be recognised, brought into the negotiation process, and a political accommodation sought with them. This is true equally of the Tamil Tigers, the Sikh militants, the Chakmas and the Maoist rebels in Nepal. Sooner or later, governments must reach out to 'moderate' elements among these groups and find a basis for a political settlement.

Clearly, the terrorist attacks on the World Trade Centre in New York and on the Pentagon in Washington DC on 11 September 2001 have changed the way Western states think about terrorism in the wider world. Until 9/11 the United States, in general, gave precedence to maintaining human rights in developing countries over fighting terrorism. Thus India's human rights' 'record' in Kashmir was a major problem in its otherwise-good bilateral relations with the US. Post-9/11, the US started taking a zero-tolerance attitude towards terrorism—especially towards *jihadi* terrorism. This resulted in Pakistan having to openly dissociate itself from the Kashmiri terrorists, paving the way for an Indo–Pakistani peace process which has so far been more robust than anything comparable in the past. Moreover the categorical stand of the US against global terrorism has undoubtedly constrained many countries, including some in South Asia, from brazenly supporting terrorism in other countries as liberation struggles or in some other guise.

Of course a principled global stand on the issue is welcome, insofar as it delegitimises terrorism under any pretext. However one still needs to look into the ground-level causes of the conflicts that sustain the violence. While global consensus can be effective in dissuading support for cross-border terrorism, home-grown terrorist movements may still fester, even without outside support. The renewed violence in Sri Lanka and the near-collapse of the state in Nepal are reminders of how far the region has to go before the fight against terrorism is won. Still, there is no alternative to the state upholding due process and promoting civic engagement with the social problems and grievances that underlie the region's many ethno-religious disputes.

Unholy Alliance: Religion and Political Violence in South Asia

Robert G. Wirsing

In an informal discussion I had not long ago on the Kashmir conflict, the assertion was made to me: 'There is *no jihad* in Kashmir'.[1] The comment, atypical though it certainly was, would still not have seemed especially startling but for the fact that the speaker was a very senior official in India's counter-insurgency apparatus in the violence-infested Muslim-majority state of Jammu and Kashmir. Expressed straightforwardly and without any apparent irony, the speaker's implied denial that Kashmir was the site of a religion-inspired holy war or that the Muslim militants fighting Indian forces there were to any significant degree motivated by Islamic zealotry ran directly counter to much that has been claimed about the Kashmiri Muslim insurgency since its onset in the state in 1989, whether by India's political leadership or other observers.[2] It is with the wider conceptual and policy ramifications of this remark—not only in connection with violence in Kashmir but, more broadly, with religion-connected collective political violence arising anywhere in South Asia—that this article is concerned.

In South Asia, religion-connected collective political violence has taken a variety of forms, ranging from communal to sectarian, separatist, terrorist, or even interstate violence. At one time or another, and in one context or another, all of the region's major religious groupings (or, rather, portions of them)—be they Christians, Muslims, Hindus, Sikhs, Buddhists, or some sectarian offshoot of any of these—have perpetrated and/or been the victims of collective political violence. The nature, intensity, and frequency of the violence have, of course, varied considerably

---

[1] The views expressed in this article are those of the author and do not necessarily reflect the official policy or position of the Asia-Pacific Centre for Security Studies, the US Pacific Command, the US Department of Defence or the US Government.
[2] For but one of many examples of the claim that Islamic extremism is a major driver of the insurgency, see K. Santhanam, Sreedhar, Sudhir Saxena, and Manish, *Jihadis in Jammu and Kashmir: A Portrait Gallery* (New Delhi: Sage Publications, 2003).

from country to country, from place to place, and over time. Given the region's extraordinary ethno-religious heterogeneity and the equally extraordinary variation found in the local environments and social circumstances of its ethno-religious groups, professional analysts of the region's ethno-religious conflicts have had plenty to argue about. They have debated nothing more heatedly, however, than the character of the linkage between political violence and religion—in particular, the extent to which and the manner in which the latter has driven the former.[3]

Adding enormously to the pre-existing and inevitable complexities of this debate over the violence/religion interface has been the huge information dissemblance between the sometimes impenetrable explanations of it given by professional analysts and academic experts and the glib, all-too-readily accessible public discourse on the subject offered up by the media and by a host of far from impartial governmental and nongovernmental agencies. As often as not, these self-appointed purveyors of public information have obeyed the impulse to conceal or misrepresent the truth. This ever-present impulse has grown substantially since the onset of the global war on terrorism, which has vastly increased the stakes in the rivalry for control of public opinion. Nowhere have the effects of this been put more plainly on display than in discussions of religion and violence in South Asia.

When the subject of collective political violence comes up nowadays in public discussion of South Asia, it very often is accompanied by references to religious identity drawn from a repertoire of deprecatory adjectives, including 'fanatic', 'radical', 'fundamentalist', 'extremist', 'medievalist', 'fascist', and so on—all words calculated to conjure up both a direct and negative association between violence and religious

---

[3] The relationship between political violence and religion in South Asia has been examined frequently and from a variety of perspectives. For a sampling, see: Chris Bayly, 'The Pre-History of Communalism? Religious Conflict in India, 1700–1860', in *Modern Asian Studies*, Vol.19, no.2 (1985), pp.177–203; Praful Bidwai, Harbans Mukhia and Achin Vanaik (eds), *Religion, Religiosity and Communalism* (Delhi: Manohar, 1996); Paul Brass, *The Production of Hindu-Muslim Violence in Contemporary India* (Seattle: University of Washington Press, 2003); Paul Brass, *Theft of an Idol* (Princeton: Princeton University Press, 1997); Veena Das (ed.), *Mirrors of Violence: Communities, Riots, and Survivors in South Asia* (Delhi: Oxford University Press, 1990); Ainslee T. Embree, *Utopias in Conflict: Religion and Nationalism in Modern India* (Berkeley: University of California Press, 1990); Asghar Ali Engineer (ed.), *Communal Riots in Post-Independence India* (Hyderabad: Sangam Books, 1984); Sudhir Kakar, *The Colors of Violence: Cultural Identities, Religion, and Conflict* (Chicago: University of Chicago Press, 1996); David Ludden(ed.), *Contesting the Nation: Religion, Community, and the Politics of Democracy in India* (Philadelphia: University of Pennsylvania Press, 1996); Gyanendra Pandey, *The Construction of Communalism in Colonial North India* (Delhi: Oxford University Press, 1990); Beth Roy, *Some Trouble with Cows: Making Sense of Social Conflict* (Berkeley: University of California Press, 1994); Stanley J. Tambiah, *Leveling Crowds: Ethnonationalist Conflicts and Collective Violence in South Asia* (Berkeley: University of California Press, 1997); Ashutosh Varshney, *Ethnic Conflict and Civic Life: Hindus and Muslims in India* (New Haven: Yale University Press, 2002); Ashutosh Varshney and Steven I. Wilkinson, *Hindu-Muslim Riots 1960–93: New Findings, Possible Remedies* (Delhi: Rajiv Gandhi Institute for Contemporary Studies, 1996); Steven I. Wilkinson (ed.), *Religious Politics and Communal Violence* (Delhi: Oxford University Press, 2005); and Steven I. Wilkinson, *Votes and Violence: Electoral Competition and Ethnic Riots in India* (New York: Cambridge University Press, 2004).

identity. Notice, for example, some widely circulated post-9/11 articles about Bangladesh. One, a September 2002 *Asia Times* online piece, bore the arresting headline: 'Bangladesh: Breeding Ground for Muslim Terror'.[4] Another, an October 2002 *Time Asia* online dispatch under the heading 'Deadly Cargo', observed that 'signs abound that Bangladesh has become a safe haven for Islamic jihadis—including Taliban and al-Qaeda fighters fresh off the boat from Afghanistan'.[5] Or witness the comments of Jim Hoagland, a two-time Pulitzer Prize-winning journalist, in an article that appeared in *The Washington Post* on 24 October 2002—hot on the heels of charges that Pakistan had supplied to North Korea equipment for enriching uranium. Headlined 'Nuclear Enabler: Pakistan Today Is the Most Dangerous Place on Earth', the article declared that

> Pervez Musharraf's Pakistan is a base from which nuclear technology, fundamentalist terrorism and life-destroying heroin are spread around the globe. American and French citizens and Christians of any nationality, including Pakistani, are indiscriminately slaughtered by fanatics as occasion arises. This nuclear-armed country is in part ungoverned, in part ungovernable.[6]

It was not necessary for Hoagland to name the religion that had spawned 'fundamentalist' terrorism and the indiscriminate slaughters of Westerners and Christians by 'fanatics' for his readers to get the (Islamic) point. In fact, in the nearly three years that have passed since 9/11, sentiments of the kind Hoagland had expressed have come close to becoming the media norm, at least in the United States.[7] Pakistan, it was commonly asserted, was

---

[4] Bertil Lintner, 'Bangladesh: Breeding Ground for Muslim Terror', *Asia Times* (online) [www.atimes.com/atimes/South_Asia/DI2 1Df06.html].

[5] Alex Perry, 'Deadly Cargo', *Time Asia* (online) (14 Oct. 2002) [http://www.time.com/time/asia/magazine/article/0,13673,501021021-364423,00.html]. The article told of a midnight rendezvous in December 2001 off the coast of Bangladesh, where over a hundred heavily-armed al-Qaeda fighters, fleeing American bombing in Afghanistan, were allegedly off-loaded and sped to hiding places presumably in the Chittagong Hill Tracts.

[6] Jim Hoagland, 'Nuclear Enabler: Pakistan Today is the Most Dangerous Place on Earth', *Washington Post* (24 Oct. 2002), p.A35.

[7] See, for example, the editorial 'Pakistan, a Troubled Ally', in *The New York Times* (Internet edition) (21 Sept. 2003); Tim McGirk and Massimo Calabresi, 'Is Pakistan a Friend or Foe?', *Time Magazine* (29 Sept. 2003), p.34; and Leon Hadar, 'Outsourcing the Hunt for Bin Laden: Pakistan Should be at the Top of Bush's "Axis of Evil"', *Los Angeles Times* (Internet edition) (1 April. 2004). Hadar, a research fellow in foreign policy studies at Washington's Cato Institute, claimed that

> the job of wiping out the leaders of the group responsible for the worst attack on the homeland has been outsourced to a corrupt and incompetent regime that is ruling a country where anti-American Islamist groups roam the streets—and the corridors of power.
> Indeed, Pakistan's military and security services, which are in charge of hunting Bin Laden and his troops, were once allied with the Taliban, the former Al Qaeda protectors in Afghanistan. And some of its members are sympathetic to a radical Islamist agenda. Until recently, the nation's top nuclear scientist was selling his country's secret military technology to Iran, Libya and North Korea.

Pakistan, Hadar argued, instead of being designated a non-NATO major ally, 'should have topped President Bush's "axis of evil" list'.

itself a chief breeding ground for *jihad*-inspired recruits to a violent religious crusade and the globe's primary epicentre of terrorism. Its thousands of religious academies or *madrassas,* it was alleged, were sites of hate-arousing religious indoctrination and, in some cases, also served as training camps for guerrilla fighters being prepared for cross-border terrorist assaults upon targeted adjacent states.

Yet by no means has the casual bracketing of religion and violence been confined to the popular media. It has cropped up, for instance, in prestigious taskforce documents such as the report, co-sponsored by the Council on Foreign Relations and the Asia Society, that was released in November 2003. The report was explicitly intended to influence Washington policy makers. 'Pakistan', said the report's authors in the Executive Summary,

> presents one of the most complex and difficult challenges facing U.S. diplomacy. Its political instability, entrenched Islamist extremism, economic and social weaknesses, and dangerous hostility with India have cast dark shadows over this nuclear-armed nation. Even though Pakistan offers valuable help in rooting out the remnants of al-Qaeda, it has failed to prevent the use of its territory by Islamist terrorists as a base for armed attacks on Kashmir and Afghanistan.[8]

'The United States', the report conceded, 'has a major stake in a stable Pakistan at peace with itself and its neighbours and should be prepared to provide substantial assistance toward this end'.[9] In line with this observation, the report urged a number of unequivocally affirmative actions, including early congressional approval, in its broad outlines, of the Bush Administration's five-year $US3 billion assistance package for FYs 2005 through 2009 promised during President Pervez Musharraf's June 2003 visit to Washington.

The task force report made abundantly plain, however, that what its authors had in mind would place the US/Pakistan relationship on a substantially different—and, from Islamabad's point of view, far less permissive—footing than the Bush Administration had thus far allowed. *'The extent of U.S. assistance'*, it observed pointedly, *'should be calibrated with Islamabad's own performance and conduct'.*[10] In its discussion of planned U.S. assistance to Pakistan, the report observed that the proposed aid package, though generally commendable, had to

---

[8] Chairmen's Report of an Independent Task Force, *New Priorities in South Asia: U.S. Policy Toward India, Pakistan, and Afghanistan* (Washington D.C., New York: Council on Foreign Relations and the Asia Society, Nov. 2003), pp. 1–2.
[9] *Ibid.*
[10] *Ibid.,* p.2 (emphasis added).

put more weight on economic and less on security aid. 'Instead of the fifty-fifty split proposed by the executive branch', the report advised, the split should be 'two-thirds for economic assistance and one-third for security help. U.S. assistance should be emphasising support for economic, social, and political reforms, not further strengthening of Pakistan's defence establishment'.[11] The baseline assistance program, it went on to suggest, should be halved to $US 1.5 billion, the remaining half to 'be released in line with Pakistan's progress in implementing the domestic reform agenda, cooperating in the war on terrorism, and fulfilling non-proliferation responsibilities'. Most revealing of its authors' mindset—and an unambiguous display of their assumptions about the causal linkage between religion and violence—was the report's recommendation that education, including 'reform of the *madrassas'*, should be the aid program's top priority, and that the US Agency for International Development (USAID) should support an international effort to map a strategy for overhauling Pakistan's schooling institutions.[12]

There can be little doubt that post-9/11 acceleration in the casual bracketing of religion and violence has been most conspicuous in public discussions of Islam and the Islamic world. In the South Asian context, this has translated, of course, into a great deal of bad publicity for Pakistan and, to a lesser extent, also for Bangladesh; but Hindu-majority India has certainly not been bypassed. Led from 1999 until spring 2004 by a coalition government dominated by the Hindu nationalist Bharatiya Janata Party (BJP), India has also been seen as a country where religion drives politics. Specifically, commentators have been quick to attribute excesses coupling collective violence in India to passions stirred up by fanatic stalwarts of the Hindu religion. The information disconnection between the professional and popular explanations of the violence/religion interface is *not* thus confined to any one religion.[13]

The balance of this article focuses on the question: What, if anything, have professional analysts and academic specialists to say on the subject of religion's relationship with

---

[11] *Ibid.*, p.49.
[12] *Ibid.*, pp.49–52.
[13] For an illuminating commentary on the alleged 'religious' roots of Hindu nationalism, see Arun R. Swamy, 'Ideology, Organization and Electoral Strategy of Hindu Nationalism: What's Religion Got to Do With It?', in Satu Limaye, Mohan Malik, and Robert Wirsing (eds), *Religious Radicalism and the Security of South Asia* (Honolulu: Asia-Pacific Centre for Security Studies, 2004), pp.73–100. Swamy comments: 'Whether or not Hindu Nationalism is "fascist", it is most assuredly not "fundamentalist". Hindu Nationalists are concerned with the strength and unity of Hindus as a political community, not with their forms of worship. They have charged religious minorities with divided loyalty and have been responsible for organized mass violence against Muslims. However, they have not, historically, been concerned with imposing any view of Hindu religion on its practitioners or punishing Hindus who violate the precepts of the "true" religion. In short, for Hindu Nationalists, there are traitors, but not apostates'. Swamy, pp.73–4.

collective political violence in South Asia that might help diminish the gross simplifications and outright misrepresentations of it now dominant in public discourse? Examination of this question will focus on two cases: separatist violence in Kashmir; and Hindu–Muslim communal violence in India.

Separatist Violence in Kashmir

Is there *a jihad* in Kashmir? Though variously phrased, this question has been asked over and over by many professional analysts of the South Asian region. It meant, of course: What was Islam's role, in particular what was *militant* Islam's role, in the separatist violence in Kashmir? The reply to this question that begins this article was unusually categorical, to be sure; but in its substance it did not differ greatly from what a number of professional analysts had been saying all along. In an examination of 'the problem of religious identity' in Kashmir that I undertook a few years ago, I found, in fact, that there was nothing resembling a consensus in serious scholarly writing on the motivation for Kashmiri Muslim separatism. Some writers, I found, placed relatively little emphasis, others a whole lot, on the religious variable.[14]

My study of separatism's motivation surveyed the published work of six well-known authors—five of them academic specialists or professional analysts (Sumit Ganguly, Sumantra Bose, Yoginder Sikand, Ayesha Jalal, and Navnita Chadha Behera), one of them a bureaucrat/politician turned writer (Malhotra Jagmohan). All of them conceded some role in the Kashmir dispute to religious identity. Four of them assigned it a major role. Only two of them, however, Jagmohan and Sikand, maintained that Kashmiri separatism was driven largely by radicalised pan-Islamic identity. These two agreed that Pakistan had a commanding role in the orchestration of radicalised Islam's cross-border activity; but only Jagmohan, whom New Delhi had twice named governor of the State of Jammu and Kashmir in the last two decades of the twentieth century, took the position that Kashmiri Muslim separatism itself was a foreign import, with but meagre indigenous roots, cynically disguised in Islamic dress by its Pakistani paymasters.[15] Sikand's position, in contrast, was that Kashmiri separatism, even though increasingly under the sway of Islamic radicalism, was neither a fabrication of Pakistani intelligence services nor without a just indigenous cause.[16]

---

[14] Robert G. Wirsing, *Kashmir in the Shadow of War* (Armonk: M.E. Sharpe, 2002), esp. pp.151–68.
[15] Malhotra Jagmohan, *My Frozen Turbulence in Kashmir* (New Delhi: Allied Publishers, 2nd ed., 1992).
[16] Yoginder Sikand, 'Changing Course of Kashmiri Struggle: From National Liberation to Islamist Jihad?', in *Economic and Political Weekly* (20 Jan. 2001), pp.218–27.

The two others who assigned religious identity a major role as a driver of Kashmiri separatism, Jalal and Behera, differed in important respects both from Jagmohan and Sikand but also from one another. For Jalal, not Muslim but *Hindu* communalism, rising parallel to the steady decline of India's increasingly formalistic commitment to secularism, was the principal culprit. 'Majoritarian communalism, after all,' she wrote, 'has been since the early 1980s New Delhi's favourite ideological weapon against movements of regional dissidence'. Conceding that separatism in Kashmir had multiple roots, and that these included 'the repeated denial of the political as well as the economic and social rights of citizenship', she insisted that it was the combination of these 'with the inversion of secularism to promote a crude form of Hindu communalism that [led Kashmiris] to agitate for complete independence from India'.[17] Behera's position, which acknowledged that India's nationalist discourse, centrist ideology, unitary political institutions, and interventionist strategies bore most of the responsibility for the emergence of Kashmiri Muslim political alienation and separatism, resembles that of Jalal. However, by shifting the focus of analysis to the contending sub-national identities of Jammu and Kashmir state and to the undoubtedly majoritarian (hence, further fragmenting) Sunni Muslim and Kashmiri-speaking impulses of its National Conference government, she achieved greater balance.[18] A few years ago I wrote that Behera's study was

> unique in the attention paid not only to the clash between national and sub-national cultural identities but also to the clash among rival sub-national cultural identities (Hindu, Muslim, Buddhist) *within* Jammu and Kashmir. Behera thus recognizes (like Jalal and Sikand) that religion's entry into the Kashmir dispute can come from *Indian* state-building strategies, driven at least in part by majoritarian Hindu communalism, as readily as it can come from Pakistan's. She also recognizes, and dwells at length upon, the fact that *Muslim* majoritarian communalism welded to the state-building strategy of Jammu and Kashmir's own local Muslim rulers can spawn its own destructive and fragmenting species of religious politics. She reminds us, in other words, that in the multilevel politics of Kashmir, their religious identity may serve Kashmiri Muslims no less as sword than as shield.[19]

---

[17] Ayesha Jalal, *Democracy and Authoritarianism in South Asia: A Comparative and Historical Perspective* (Cambridge: Cambridge University Press, 1995), pp.179–80.
[18] Navnita Chadha Behera, *State, Identity and Violence: Jammu, Kashmir and Ladakh* (Delhi: Manohar, 2000). Behera returns to the main themes of this book and greatly enlarges upon them in a new study, *Demystifying Kashmir* (Washington, DC: Brookings Institution Press, 2006).
[19] Wirsing, *Kashmir in the Shadow of War*, pp.167–8.

Both Behera and Jalal, one might add, offered the useful insight that when it comes to Kashmir, it could as easily be said that there were two, or even three, *jihads* simultaneously in progress in the state, not just the one associated with the Kashmiri Muslim insurgency.

The remaining two authors, Ganguly and Bose, both focused their explanations of Kashmiri separatism primarily on secular forces relating mainly to political and socioeconomic developments within India. Ganguly, borrowing heavily from modernisation theory, argued that two powerful contemporary trends—one of them mass *political mobilisation* arising largely from the spread of education, literacy, and economic development, the other *de-institutionalisation* resulting from the fairly recent erosion of the legal, political, and administrative norms and institutions India had inherited at independence—had combined in Kashmir to produce an environment ripe for alienation and violence. For him, the mobilisation of ethno-religious identities that took place in Kashmir was basically unplanned and adventitious, the far-from-predetermined outcome of *secular* developments—some positive (literacy), some negative (political malpractices)—that happened to come to maturity in the state at about the same time. Religion got involved, in other words, not because it had been premeditatedly transformed into a potent political weapon by a radicalised and supranational Islamic movement but because the state *happened to be multi-religious*—politically divided along communal lines and vulnerable to outside interference by Pakistan, which naturally took advantage of its neighbouring adversary's distress.[20]

Like Ganguly, Bose maintained that Kashmiri Muslim separatism was overwhelmingly the outcome of a secular trend—democratic decline—although he departed significantly from Ganguly's understanding of the decline, seeing it not as the relatively recent and fairly superficial product of political changes ushered in during the period of Indira Gandhi's rule but rather as ideologically and institutionally deep-rooted, originating in the Nehru era at the very foundation of Indian democracy. When it came to the matter of religious identity, however, he and Ganguly were more nearly alike. Bose conceded that Kashmiri separatism drew upon 'a deeply-felt collective Muslim identity';[21] but this identity was not of an aggressive or assertive kind. On the contrary, Bose and Ganguly both hold that Kashmiri culture—*kashmiriyat*—is uniquely tolerant and syncretic. Both maintained that the most politically-charged species of religious communalism in the region was located in Pakistan.

---

[20] Sumit Ganguly, *The Crisis in Kashmir: Portents of War, Hopes of Peace* (New York: Cambridge University Press, 1997).
[21] Sumantra Bose, *The Challenge in Kashmir: Democracy, Self-Determination and a Just Peace* (New Delhi: Sage Publications, 1997), p.85.

Kashmir, for both of them, was at bottom a political, not a cultural, problem. It most certainly was not, for either of these authors, an arena for 'the clash of civilizations'.[22]

There are clearly cavernous differences in the positions staked out by the above authors on the primary issues of this article—the extent to which and the manner in which religion may be considered a driver of collective violence in South Asia. Some of them gave it peripheral, others central, importance. If they had all somehow been held to a common and restrictive definition of 'religion', whether as belief, institution, or group cultural identity, perhaps there would have been less discrepancy among them. My hunch, however, is that the differences among them, which are deep-rooted, would persist.

Regrettably, my own research on Kashmir has not resolved these issues—at least not in a final and definitive manner. It has, however, planted me quite firmly on the side of those for whom relentless scepticism is perhaps the defining characteristic. When my informant asserted that there was no *jihad* in Kashmir, I welcomed it not because the statement seemed incontrovertible. On the contrary, the statement on its face was outrageous—and in more than one sense flatly wrong. There is mountainous evidence that there have been religious fanatics fighting in Kashmir, guided by fanatical doctrine, and with fanatical goals in mind. Apart from being outrageous, however, the statement was—and was intended to be—heretical. And in that sense, it had the hugely salubrious effect of flinging open the door to reconsideration of the popular orthodoxies it was clearly meant to upset.

And these orthodoxies, it goes without saying, do need reconsideration. Interviews about the subject of Kashmir on several continents over nearly two decades, with literally hundreds of people of diverse backgrounds and nationalities, have persuaded me that the concept of *jihad,* whatever it is intended to imply about religious motivation and solidarity, hardly even begins to capture what it is that drives the violence in Kashmir. In the early 1990s, soon after the insurgency broke out there, it was already amply clear to observers that motivations on *all* sides—Indian and Pakistani, Kashmiri Muslim and Kashmiri Hindu, security forces and armed militants—were bewilderingly and frustratingly mixed. I wrote then of the sadism and brutality that had become near constants in the behaviour of both insurgents and counter-insurgents. I wrote also of the widespread corruption—the 'commercialization' of separatism,

---

[22] Bose again emphasises the Kashmir insurgency's *political* (that is, non-religious) inspiration in his newest book, *Kashmir: Roots of Conflict, Paths to Peace* (Cambridge: Harvard University Press, 2003). 'The prime reason for the radicalization of political dissent in IJK, culminating in insurrection in 1989–1990 was the purposeful stifling of opposition *within institutional politics* by the Indian state, operating in collusion with local client elites, since the 1950s' (p.198) (emphasis in original).

in other words—that dominated the calculations of many involved in the insurgency.[23] I have been told on countless occasions, in persuasive terms, that material profits from the insurgency have been vast and have enriched many—on all sides of the conflict, including many of exalted position in the civil, military and insurgent ranks—and that these many are today far from enthusiastic about ending the insurgency. I have been told, again convincingly, that *Hindu* youths from desperately impoverished localities in Jammu and Kashmir have been recruited to fight shoulder to shoulder with Muslims in the Kashmiri *jihad,* that they were well paid so long as they survived the sledgehammer blows of Indian security forces, and that they, or rather their parents, who in effect leased their *non-Muslim* sons' lives to an ostensibly rival religious cause in order to escape grinding poverty, were handsomely and unfailingly indemnified when they finally perished. These and other reports compel us to give serious consideration to the possibility that the term *jihad* mainly misses the point, and that it may *conceal* more than it reveals about what motivates separatism in the state of Jammu and Kashmir. Among other things, one must wonder, for instance, whether the region's *poverty,* more than its *piety,* is not the larger driver of separatist violence—and not just in Kashmir.

Hindu–Muslim Communal Violence in India

The explanation of Hindu–Muslim communal violence in India has stimulated heated controversy. The heat has been nearly as evident in scholarly explanations of it as in the popular media. Given the large size and political importance of the Muslim minority (generally held to range between 12.5 and 15 per cent of India's billion-plus total population), the considerable frequency and ferocity of communal riots, and the grim statistics of riot fatalities, neither the controversy nor the heat is surprising. After all, the implications of one's explanation of communal violence, just as of Kashmiri separatist violence, can be far-reaching. If, for instance, Hindu Indians, who may well take pride in their country's reputation for non-violent, even saintly, behaviour, find that reputation turned on its head, their religion held up as the spawning ground for savage fanatics, and their country's leadership and political institutions charged with reckless and ruthless disregard for the well-being of the defenceless Muslim minority, they have ample reason to resist. How religious minorities fare at the hands of religious majorities is an issue no longer reserved as an exclusive subject of sovereign states; and the penalty for 'getting it wrong' can be substantial.

An important focus in recent scholarly controversy over Hindu–Muslim communal violence has been the explanation of riots. The 'deadly ethnic riot' has been defined

---

[23] See, for instance, Robert Wirsing, *India, Pakistan, and the Kashmir Dispute* (New York: St. Martin's Press, 1994), pp.137, 148, 153, 159.

in a recent and magisterial comparative study of the subject by Duke University's Donald L. Horowitz as 'an intense, sudden, though not necessarily wholly unplanned, lethal attack by civilian members of one ethnic group on civilian members of another ethnic group, the victims chosen because of their group membership. So conceived, ethnic riots are synonymous with what are variously called "communal", "racial", "religious", "linguistic", or "tribal" disturbances'.[24] Riots vary enormously, of course, not only in terms of the cultural identity of the groups involved but also in the number of individuals who participate in them, in the physical damage they inflict, and in what motivates them, whether in terms of immediate precipitant or underlying cause. Religion is a frequent but not essential element in them. By far the most lethal species of religious violence, the riot has been both common and extensively reported on in India. Indian cases, overwhelmingly of Hindu-Muslim communal violence, figure very prominently in Horowitz's book. Like other scholars interested in the riot phenomenon, Horowitz brought to his deliberation of riots a lifetime of serious reflection on the nature of ethnic identity and the roots of ethnic conflict. His interpretation of riots, as that of the other scholars, is thus inevitably infused with the theoretical and philosophical understandings acquired over the course of that reflection. Therein, of course, lie most of the grounds for the controversy.

As Horowitz has pointed out, ethnic or communal riots, wherever they occur, are a 'bizarre fusion of coherence and frenzy', 'an amalgam of apparently rational-purposive behaviour and irrational-brutal behaviour'—a mix, in other words, of passion and calculated interest, of impulsive and instrumental activity.[25] They lend themselves, as Horowitz has insightfully observed, as easily to a primordial or 'hard' understanding of ethnic identity, where ethnic groups are seen as real historical entities with firm boundaries, distinct cultural traditions, and strong emotional bonds, as to an instrumental or 'soft' understanding, where ethnic groups are seen as imagined entities with malleable boundaries, and whose behaviour is decided more often than not by calculation and strategic manipulation. For the 'hard' school, ethnicity is made of stone; for the 'soft' school, it is made of putty.[26] In their discussions of communal riots in India, scholars generally leaned toward one or the other understanding.

Paul Brass's most recent book, provocatively titled *The Production of Hindu–Muslim Violence in Contemporary India,* mounts the most powerful argument made so far from the 'soft' perspective about India's Hindu–Muslim

---

[24] Donald L. Horowitz, *The Deadly Ethnic Riot* (Berkeley: University of California Press, 2001), p.1.
[25] *Ibid.,* pp.12, 13, 44, 522.
[25] *Ibid.,* p.44.

communal riots. Notably consistent with instrumentalist theoretical positions Brass has taken over many years of study of nationalism, religion, and ethnic violence,[27] the book maintains that most riots are far from being random, unplanned, and spontaneous events. On the contrary, they are for the most part deliberate, useful, and purposive political *productions*. Riots, from Brass's point of view, generally unfold in relatively predictable phases—of preparation/rehearsal, activation/enactment, and explanation/interpretation. Where they are endemic, they take the form of 'institutionalized riot systems'—patterned events 'in which known persons and groups occupy specific roles in the rehearsal for and the production of communal riots'. In such systems, key roles are played by what Brass calls 'conversion specialists'— 'those', he says, 'whose task it is to decide when a trivial, everyday incident will be exaggerated and placed into the communal system of talk, the communal discourse, and allowed to escalate into communal violence'.[28] Communal riots in India, he avers, are not accidents or products of momentary societal breakdown. On the contrary, they have always been an integral part of the Indian political process, benefiting Muslim political elites as well as their Hindu counterparts, secularists as well as religious fundamentalists.[29] It was not beyond the *capacity* of India's ruling classes to curb the riots, in other words, but, since independence, there had been little *interest* in doing so.

Another major work from the 'soft' theoretical perspective is that of Ashutosh Varshney. Though in substantial agreement with Brass on the issue of ethnicity's plasticity and manipulability (neither taking a primordial view of ethnic identity), Varshney—breaking away sharply from Brass's none-too-kindly view of the Indian political elite's fundamental culpability for communal violence—maintains that communal violence is far from ubiquitous in India; that 'ethnic peace' is commonplace in many Indian cities, towns, and villages; and that what accounts for the difference between communal peace and violence is the existence in some places of an 'institutionalized peace system'—organised local networks of civic engagement between Hindus and Muslims. 'Where such networks of engagement exist', he writes, 'tensions and conflicts were regulated and managed; where they are missing, communal identities led to endemic and ghastly violence'.[30]

---

[27] Notable expositions of Brass's instrumentalist theoretical approach are *Language, Religion, and Politics in North India* (Cambridge: Cambridge University Press, 1974); *Ethnicity and Nationalism: Theory and Comparison* (Newbury Park, CA: Sage, 1991); *Theft of an Idol;* and 'Elite Interests, Popular Passions, and Social Power in the Language Politics of India', in *Ethnic and Racial Studies*, Vol.27, no.3 (May 2004), pp.353–75.

[28] Brass, *The Production of Hindu–Muslim Violence in Contemporary India*, p.32.

[29] According to Brass, riots are *'creations of specific persons, groups, and parties operating through institutionalized riot networks within a discursive framework of Hindu–Muslim communal opposition and antagonism that in turn produces specific forms of political practice that makes riots integral to the political process'*. Ibid., p.369 (emphasis in original).

UNHOLY ALLIANCE: RELIGION AND POLITICAL VIOLENCE IN SOUTH ASIA 41

Varshney mounted his argument at two levels—one, a survey of all reported Hindu–Muslim riots in India between 1950 and 1995, the other, a paired comparison of six cities—three of them riot-prone, three of them peaceful. As for the first level, he found that communal rioting in rural villages accounted for less than 4 percent of deaths in communal violence. Riots, in other words, were overwhelmingly an urban phenomenon. But even in urban India, they were concentrated in a relatively small handful of cities. Indeed, only eight cities (Ahmedabad, Bombay, Aligarh, Hyderabad, Meerut, Baroda, Calcutta, and Delhi), together representing only 5 per cent of India's entire population, accounted for nearly half of all urban deaths from rioting in the period studied.[31]

A clear implication of Varshney's findings is that it is not the political reckonings of India's political elites or the institutions of political democracy that matter in producing communal violence so much as the structure of civil society. The structure of civil society found in any particular locality in India has been dependent, in turn, on the particular historical development of inter-communal civic networks experienced in that locality. In this, says Varshney, the role of the Congress Party over the many years of the independence movement was crucial, for it laid the foundation of India's contemporary associational civic order. Where that order flourished, the resulting 'institutionalized peace system' acted as a powerful constraint on the behaviour of politicians. Where it did not, communal violence occurred. 'The historical lines of causation', he argued, 'run from mass movement to civic order to violence or peace'.[32]

Illustrative of the 'hard' perspective on India's Hindu-Muslim communal violence is Sudhir Kakar's widely cited study, *The Colors of Violence*. In this book, Kakar took strong issue with Brass's position, arguing that instrumentalist theory, in downplaying the psychological wellsprings of mob violence, gave undue prominence to the elite instigators of religious violence. 'In concentrating on the instigators', he wrote,

> [instrumentalist theory] underplays or downright denies that there are 'instigatees', too, whose participation is essential to transform animosity between religious groups into violence. The picture it holds up of evil politicians and innocent masses is certainly attractive since it permits us a disavowal of our own impulses toward violence and vicious ethnocentrism. We all have different zones of indifference

---

[30] Ashutosh Varshney, *Ethnic Conflict and Civic Life: Hindus and Muslims in India* (New Haven: Yale University Press, 2002), p.9.
[31] *Ibid.*, pp.6–7.
[32] *Ibid.*, p. 18.

beyond which our own ethnocentrism, in some form or the other, will become a salient part of our identity.

A part of the instrumentalist or instigator theory's appeal, he suggested, was that it allowed 'a projection of the unacceptable parts of ourselves onto "bad" politicians'.[33]

Religious identity plays an extremely important role in Kakar's psychoanalytic portrait of the Hindu–Muslim riot. In sharp contrast with Brass's institutionalised riot systems, where riots typically are carefully pre-planned, rehearsed, and staged productions, in which group religious identities are callously manipulated for political ends, Kakar sees the riot as 'a battle, an outbreak of hostilities in a long simmering war',[34] or as 'the bursting of a boil, the eruption of pus, of "bad blood" between Hindus and Muslims which has accumulated over a few days or even weeks in a particular location. In some cities and towns. . .where the boil is a festering sore, the tension never really disappears but remains at an uncomfortable level which is below that of violent eruption'.[35] It is not calculated elite manoeuvring for political advantage but group psychology—marked in periods of rising social tension by mass persecutory fantasies, the dominance of invidious group stereotypes, and the virtual replacement of individual by group identity—that counts most for Kakar. For him, intolerance is a constant in human society. As it grows, so does the predisposition to group violence.

Conclusions

This sampling of scholarly opinion on the character and extent of religion's relationship with collective political violence in South Asia hardly begins to scratch the surface of contemporary scholarship pertinent to this topic. It is perhaps enough, however, to warrant a preliminary set of findings in response to the question raised at the beginning: What, if anything, have professional analysts and academic specialists to say on this subject that might help diminish the gross simplifications and outright misrepresentations of it now dominant in public discourse? This article concludes with three findings:

1. *The question of religion's connectedness with collective political violence in South Asia is undoubtedly one of the most consequential, both domestic and international policy-relevant issues that can be addressed today in regard to that region.*

---

[33] Kakar, *The Colors of Violence: Cultural Identities, Religion, and Conflict*, p. 151.
[34] *Ibid.*, p.70.
[35] *Ibid.*, p.41.

2. *The precise nature of the connection between religion and collective political violence in South Asia is far from having been conclusively established.*
3. *Religion's connection with collective political violence in South Asia is far less than is generally believed.*

The question of religion's connectedness with political violence in South Asia constantly crops up not only in discussions of Kashmiri separatism and Hindu–Muslim communal riots but also in discussions, for instance, of Muslim–Christian violence in Pakistan, of Hindu–Christian violence in India, and of Muslim–Hindu or Muslim–Christian violence in Bangladesh. Sunni–Shia sectarian violence in Pakistan alone has generated enormous international attention and a vast literature.[36] Its implications for the domestic political stability of Pakistan as well as for Sunni-majority Pakistan's strategically vital relationship with neighbouring Shia-majority Iran are undoubtedly vast.

And how one understands the religion–violence connection inevitably has major implications also for fundamental judgments about the efficacy of particular political institutional arrangements. Witness, for instance, Steven Wilkinson's portentous finding that India's often-praised consociational (including ethnic preferential) policies, instead of having acted, as some predicted, to decrease inter-group tensions and violence, had actually had the reverse effect: Those years in which India had been most consociational, in other words, had been precisely the years with the highest per capita levels of ethnic, including Hindu–Muslim, violence.[37]

How the religion–violence connection is understood also impacts heavily, of course, on the way in which nations react to and shape policies about movements of self-determination—as in the Kashmir case. As Jonathan Fox has pointed out, the great majority of severe ethnic conflicts on the planet, since there is no religious difference between the majority and the minority involved in the conflict, 'do not even have the potential to involve issues of religious identity'. He also pointed out, however, that in those ethnic conflicts where differences in religious identity were present, religious factors of one sort or another—complaints of past or present religious discrimination, for instance—did generally crop up. 'In short',

---

[36] For a sampling of this literature, see S.V.R. Nasr, 'Islam, the State and the Rise of Sectarian Militancy in Pakistan', in Christophe Jaffrelot (ed.), *Pakistan: Nationalism Without a Nation?* (New Delhi: Manohar Publishers, 2002), pp.85–114; Yunas Samad, 'The Religious Right and Violence', paper prepared for a conference on Religion, Violence and the State in South Asia, Balliol College, Oxford University, 26 Mar. 2004; and Khaled Ahmed, 'Islamic Extremism in Pakistan', in *South Asian Journal*, Vol.2 (Oct.–Dec. 2003), pp.33–44.
[37] Steven Ian Wilkinson, 'India, Consociational Theory, and Ethnic Violence', in *Asian Survey*, Vol.15, no.5 (Sept.–Oct. 2000), p.770. Wilkinson's theoretical positioning is more fully developed in his book-length study, *Votes and Violence: Electoral Competition and Ethnic Riots in India* (New York: Cambridge University Press, 2004).

Fox concluded, 'while most ethnic conflicts are not primarily about religion, most ethno-religious conflicts involve some religious factors'.[38]

In a section of *The Deadly Ethnic Riot* entitled 'The State of Violence Theory', Donald Horowitz laments the failure of theorists, after many years of strenuous effort, to answer satisfactorily the questions of 'why ethnic riots occur, or why they occur when or where they occur, or why particular groups of people initiate them and others are victimized in them, or any of the other questions that need to be asked about such events'. 'Disappointingly', he says, 'little has come of the prodigious literature on violence. No theory is clearly supported by empirical evidence. Few if any specific findings can be said to be firmly established'.[39] Coming from one who has spent a lifetime focused on violent inter-group conflict, this confession is somewhat surprising. Since it comes in a field of research whose professional practitioners have not been particularly renowned for the modesty of their theoretical claims, it is also highly welcome.

Especially welcome among Horowitz's theoretical ruminations in this book is the admission that ample room has to be left in any future coherent theory of collective violence for both the instrumentalist *and* primordialist schools of thought. Sweeping dismissals of either are not warranted. Varshney builds a strong case for his civil society-based 'institutionalized peace systems'; but Brass's point that it may prove difficult in the end for 'institutionalized peace systems' to withstand the wilfully-crafted 'institutionalized riot systems' apparently favoured by many political leaders cannot be simply wished away. However, neither the 'peace' nor the 'riot' system, both of them highly rationalistic formulations, may prove in the end capable of resisting what looms as a yet more powerful and pervasive explanation of collective violence or its absence—the natural inclination of humans to distrust and fear social or cultural groups unlike themselves. Evidence troubling for liberal notions of the human condition has been mounting for years, in fact, that humans are 'hard-wired' for prejudice and hurtful stereotypes—that inter-group intolerance and violence may have evolutionary roots, in other words, making it not only tempting, but practically 'natural', for different identity groups to both hate and fear—and to engage in violent fights with—the 'Other'.[40]

Thus Horowitz strikes just the right note when he counsels, in the face of the persistent explanatory gaps,

---

[38] Jonathan Fox, 'Correlated Conflicts: The Independent Nature of Ethnic Strife', in *Harvard International Review*, Vol.25, no.4 (Winter 2004), p.59.
[39] Horowitz, *The Deadly Ethnic Riot*, pp.34, 39.
[40] Nancy Wartik, 'Hard-Wired for Prejudice? Experts Examine Human Response to Outsiders', *The New York Times* (Internet edition) (20 Apr. 2004).

> leaving open some issues prematurely assumed away by macro-level theorists of violence. In particular, I leave open at the outset the extent to which violence is organized and, if so, for what purpose; the possibility that the infliction of harm is an end, not necessarily a means to some other end; and the related possibility that the violence is generated by antipathy and that the cruelty so prominently displayed in the violence results from that antipathy, or from poorly controlled impulses, or from both.[41]

Enough has already been said here of the character of the connection to require much additional elaboration either of its complexity or of the large and troublesome gap that exists between scholarly understanding and public rhetoric. Clearly, the commonplace reduction to 'Hindu fanaticism' or 'Islamic militancy' of violent phenomena that serious scrutiny reveals to have vastly more complicated, or at least more uncertain, motivations substantially jeopardises understanding of them. There may be, as suggested earlier in this article, a species of zealously anti-Hindu Muslim 'holy war' being waged in Kashmir; but there is another species of 'holy war' currently in progress that is targeted against Islam itself. As a Muslim writer asserted recently, there has grown up in the West

> an Islam industry—a popular and political culture that encourages the production of books, articles, and movies that deal with Islam and the Middle East. This production is closely tied (through financing and through ideological affinity) with the prevalent trends about Islam in the United States. The Islam industry features the works of Middle East and Islam experts at US universities who have revived the classical Orientalist approach, as well as of a swarm of untrained newcomers whose primary qualifications appear to be their ideological orientations and religious zealotry. September 11th has only increased the rate of production of sensational works that promise to reveal the true evil intentions of Muslims and Islam. Scholarly works receive less attention; and the public seems eager to consume books and articles that contain the persistent dogmas and recycled cliches of classical Orientalism, or of the production of the terrorism industry.[42]

By now the meaning of 'unholy alliance' in the title of this article may have become clear. In one sense (the more obvious), the coupling of these two

---
[41] Horowitz, *The Deadly Ethnic Riot,* p.42. In spite of these formidable theoretical allowances, Horowitz remains, at bottom, an ethnic optimist. In this regard, see the concluding comments in his book, pp.560–5.
[42] As'ad Abu Khalil, '"The Islam Industry" and Scholarship', in *Middle East Journal,* vol.58, no.1 (Winter 2004), pp. 130–1.

phenomena—religion and collective political violence—is 'unholy' simply because religion, as a sacred phenomenon, seems an unsuitable companion to profane acts of collective violence, such as have been witnessed on countless occasions over the course of the separatist movement in Kashmir as well as in countless instances of Hindu–Muslim rioting in India. In another (less obvious but much more important) sense, however, the alliance of religion and collective political violence is 'unholy' because religion is often *not* the driver, or at least not the *primary* driver, of the violence—the *real* drivers of which are more secular than sacred in nature. Of course, religion, whether as belief system or form of group identity, does get implicated in the violence; but so also do the manoeuvrings of electoral strategists, the covert machinations of foreign intelligence agencies, the compulsions of impoverished populations and, perhaps not least, the psychological shortcomings of individual humans.

Understanding the 1993 Mumbai Bombings: *Madrassas* and the Hierarchy of Terror

Marika Vicziany

The *madrassas* (Islamic religious schools and colleges) of early nineteenth century British India were much admired by Europeans. In the words of Colonel William Sleeman:

> He who holds an office worth twenty rupees a month commonly gives his sons an education equal to that of a prime minister.... After his seven years of study, the young Muhammadan binds his turban upon a head almost as well filled with the things that appertain to these branches of knowledge as the young man raw from Oxford.[1]

Today, the *madrassas* have a dark image: not only are they seen as providing poor quality education, they are also characterised as '*jihadi* factories' producing intolerant, young, hot-headed and violent 'Islamists'. Religious extremism, *jihad,* sectarianism and international terrorism have all become congealed into a compound metaphor for '*madrassa*'. The consequences of this stereotyping are serious, both for the countries of South Asia and for international attempts to control transnational terrorism.

There has, however, been a recent questioning of these views. Sageman is perhaps the best known critic of the simplistic idea that international *jihadis* are the product of *madrassas*. Published five years after 9/11, his study of 137 terrorists

---

This article has benefited from the comments by Dr. Aneela Babar (Honorary Research Fellow, Monash Asia Institute), Kannan Srinivasan (PhD candidate, Monash Asia Institute) and Maseeh Rahman (Indian journalist, New Delhi). But the views in it are my own.
[1] William Sleeman quoted in William Dalrymple, *The Last Mughal: The Fall of a Dynasty, Delhi 1857* (London: Bloomsbury, 2006), p.95

showed that a minority of only 17 percent had attended any *madrassa*.² He concluded that 'the data refute the notion that global Salafi terrorism comes from madrassa brainwashing, with the exception of the Indonesian network'.³ Moreover, whereas *madrassa* education is narrowly religious and rarely extends beyond high school level, he found that '[o]ver 60 percent [of *jihadis*] have had at least some college education'.⁴ College education also reflected the relatively high socioeconomic status of the terrorists he studied: about 74 percent came from upper- and middle-class families.⁵

Robert Pape's analysis of 315 suicide attacks and 462 suicide attackers in the thirteen years up to 2003 looks at the question of terrorism in an even wider spectrum not limited to Islamic *jihad*.⁶ He concludes that his data shows that 'there is little connection between suicide terrorism and Islamic fundamentalism, *or any one of the world's religions*'. 7 Tamil terrorists in Sri Lanka, for example, who accounted for 24 percent of the 315 suicide attacks—the largest single group involved in this kind of terrorism—are fighting for a homeland rather than a religion.⁸ The majority of suicide bombers—57 percent—were secular.⁹ And Pape's data on the educational and economic background of the Arab cohort in his study confirms Sageman's earlier work: college-educated suicide attackers were the largest group amongst both religious and secular terrorists[10] and only a small minority were poor or unemployed.[11]

Between them Sageman and Pape collected data on some 599 terrorists. This represents the most comprehensive information so far on the subject. Their conclusions are the same: that religious education has not driven acts of terror. Although neither Sageman nor Pape included acts of violence by Islamists in South Asia, the comprehensive nature of their studies provides a good hypothesis for the subcontinent. While the present paper does not pretend to be comprehensive, it offers substantial evidence to suggest that the Sageman-Pape hypothesis may indeed be relevant to the South Asian region.

---

² Marc Sageman, *Understanding Terror Networks* (Philadelphia: University of Pennsylvania Press, 2004), p.74. See also Peter Bergen and Swati Pandey, 'The *Madrassa* Scapegoat', in *The Washington Quarterly*, Vol.29, no.2 (Spring 2006), pp.117–25.
³ Sageman, *Understanding Terror Networks*, p.74.
⁴ *Ibid.*, p.75.
⁵ *Ibid.*, p.73.
⁶ Robert A. Pape, *Dying to Win: The Strategic Logic of Suicide Terrorism* (New York: Random House, 2005), pp.4, 203.
⁷ *Ibid.*, p.4 (emphasis added).
⁸ *Ibid.*
⁹ *Ibid.*, p.210.
¹⁰ *Ibid.*, p.215, Chart 14.
¹¹ *Ibid.*, pp.214–5.

The Mumbai Bombings of 1993

The thirteen bomb blasts which damaged various buildings and hutments near the Mumbai Stock Exchange, the Air India building, theatres, markets, hotels and one fishing enclave in India's most cosmopolitan city on 12 March 1993 killed 257 and injured 713.[12] It has been described by one commentator as 'the greatest act of terrorism in the world' after 9/11.[13] Damage to buildings and infrastructure has been estimated at $US6 million.[14] A wide range of explosive material and ammunition was smuggled into coastal western India—including no less than 5,000 kilograms of the highly damaging RDX.[15] According to the charges laid by the Central Bureau of Investigation (CBI) the bombings were carried out by Indians but orchestrated by Pakistan's Inter-Services Intelligence system (ISI) to avenge the destruction by Hindu fundamentalists of the Babri Masjid in the north Indian town of Ayodhya.[16]

By contrast, the international press has reported that the chief factor behind the bombings was the large number of Muslims killed in the communal riots[17] that followed the demolition of the Babri Masjid on 6 December 1992.[18] The Shiv Sena, an ultra-Right-wing Hindu chauvinist party, had stirred troubled and encouraged a violent putting down of Mumbai's Muslims in December 1992. Some of the defendants referred to this in their defence before the court. Some Indian reporters have been more cynical in pointing out that Mumbai's dominant crime syndicate, Dawood Ibrahim Kaksar's 'D-company', became involved in Pakistan's plots to destabilise India when their other smuggling business was in trouble: '...the

---

[12] CBI (Central Bureau of Investigation), 'CBI Moves US for Handing Over Bombay Bomb Blast Accused' (New Delhi: CBI, 5 Jan. 2007) [http://cbi.ni.in, accessed 11 Jan. 2007].

[13] Gilbert King, *The Most Dangerous Man in the World: Dawood Ibrahim* (New York: Chamberlain Bros., 2004), p.3.

[14] '1993 Blasts: A Month On, 39 Guilty, 15 Acquitted', *Hindustan Times.com* (12 Oct. 2006) [http://hindustantimes.com, accessed 13 Jan. 2007].

[15] 'A Low-Down on how Mumbai was Bombed', *The Times of India* (21 Sept. 2006) [http://timesofindia.indiatimes.com, accessed 10 Jan. 2007]. RDX is an explosive which is 150 percent more powerful than TNT and is easy to make. It is a white crystalline compound that can be readily stored. In Mumbai RDX was called 'black soap'.

[16] 'Day 1 of 1993 Judgment Day: Four Memon Family Guilty', *The Indian Express* (13 Sept. 2006) [http://www.indianexpress.com, accessed 9 Jan. 2007].

[17] BBC News, 'Profile: India's Fugitive Gangster', *BBC News* (12 Sept. 2006) [http://news.bbc.co.uk, accessed 10 Jan. 2007]; and Government of Maharashtra, *Srikrishna Report* (Mumbai: Government of Maharashtra, 1998), Vol.1, para. 1.30. In commenting on the origins of the Mumbai blasts of March 1993, the *Srikrishna Report* noted that 'the Muslims perhaps felt that the Government and police, instead of protecting their interests, had actually acted against their interests by joining hands with communal elements which took a lead in the riots'. *Ibid.*, Chap.6.

[18] The destruction of the mosque of Ayodhya was, in the words of the Srikrishna Commission, 'orchestrated' by the Bharatiya Janata Party which wanted to replace the mosque with a temple. The disputed site was, for Hindu fundamentalists, the birthplace of Lord Shri Rama. On 6 December 1992 the mosque was pulled down and the first lot of.countrywide riots followed; they continued for five days to 10 December 1992. A further 15 days of rioting occurred in 1993 from 6 to 20 January. *Ibid.*, Vol.1, paras. 1.1, 2.4.

mafia just had no choice. By the early 1990s, the decontrol of gold and silver brought the prices of these commodities tumbling down, stripping smugglers of their principal business'.[19] This view has it that Dawood found himself working for Pakistan's ISI by smuggling first heroin and then explosives, ultimately using his networks to plant bombs in Mumbai.[20] Another view is that the bombings were part of a power struggle in which Dawood, the 'Don' of Mumbai, was being challenged by his subordinate 'Tiger' Memon for control of Mumbai's crime world. It is said that 'Tiger' Memon, head of the Memon family—aware of misgivings in the underworld over Dawood's lack of response to the Mumbai riots of 1992–1993—was hoping to project himself as someone dedicated to revenging injustices.[21] The power struggle was a good match because 'Tiger' allegedly had the support of Pakistani gangsters, while Dawood had the backing of Pakistan's intelligence and military community. If there was a power struggle, then in that particular round Dawood managed to hold on to his control of Mumbai's underworld.

'Tiger' has neither confirmed nor denied these suppositions. However a key suspect, 'Tiger''s brother Yaqub Memon, suggested that 'The lack of justice produced terrorists...had the findings of the Srikrishna commission been acted on. . . . Then there will be no justification for (terrorists) to do any such wrong thing'.[22] Yaqub was referring to the Maharahstra government's Srikrishna Commission established to investigate the origin of the riots and why the Mumbai police could not control the situation. Amongst other evidence, the commission heard how the Mumbai police were divided along communal lines and how Hindu policemen stood by and not only tolerated but sometimes actively encouraged and participated in the riots.[23] Indeed 'Tiger' Memon himself had been a victim of these riots. In the words of Justice B.N. Srikrishna: "Tiger' Memon, the key figure in the serial bomb blasts case and his family had suffered extensively during the riots and therefore can be said to have had deep rooted motives for revenge'.[24]

---

[19] 'The Spreading Tentacles of Terror', *The Hindu* (31 Aug. 2003) [http://www.hinduonnet.com, accessed 11 Jan. 2007].

[20] Praveen Swami, 'India's Most Wanted', *Frontline* (19 Jan.–1 Feb. 2002) [http:www/hinduonnet.com, accessed 10 Jan. 2007]. Gilbert King reverses the relationship, arguing that Dawood has been funding the ISI at an annual cost of $US 1 billion. See King, *The Most Dangerous Man in the World: Dawood Ibrahim*, p.59.

[21] 'Blasts Linked to Power Struggle', *The Times of India Online* (18 Sept. 2006) [http://www.timesofindia.indiatimes.com, accessed 12 Jan.2007].

[22] Yakub Memon quoted in Swati Deshpande, 'Yakub Refers to Delay in Riot Cases', *The Times of India Online* (16. Sept. 2006) [http://timesofindia.indiatimes.com, accessed 12 Jan. 2007]. The medium- to long-term consequences of.anti-Muslim riots is only now beginning to be measured. See for example the account of this process in Ahmedabad. and Delhi by Imran Ali and Yoginder Sikand, 'Ghettoisation of Muslims in India', in *Countercurrents* [http://www.countercurrents.org, accessed 21 Jan. 2007].

[23] Government of Maharashtra, *Srikrishna Report,* Vol.1, para.1.30 and Chap.6.

[24] Government of Maharashtra, *Srikrishna Report,* Term No. (VII).

Whatever the motives behind the Mumbai bombings, the trial that started in 1995 was a massive affair: for security reasons the court sat inside the Arthur Road jail in Mumbai;[25] 123 people were charged, six of them women, and 100 were convicted.[26] The first convictions were read on 12 September 2006 followed by the final six on 4 December 2006. Of the 100 convictions, 48 were for conspiracy.[27] The sentences will be announced by early March 2007. Many of the convicted have pleaded for leniency for personal reasons (they say they have needy aged relatives or lovers who have waited for years to marry them) or on the basis that the Muslim communities of Mumbai had suffered extreme provocation by Hindu fundamentalists (as the *Srikrishna Report* documented).[28]

The Mumbai 1993 bombings trial will go down in history as one of the most spectacular criminal cases of the twentieth century in India. One hundred convictions 'are the highest in a single criminal trial in Indian judicial history';[29] 686 witnesses appeared in court; their evidence is contained in 35,000 pages of documents[30] which are yet to be released to the public. As a supreme example of the 'pathology' of the Indian legal system, the legal proceedings took so long—thirteen years—that perhaps up to 14 of the accused died during the protracted trial process.[31]

Once the trial ended the *Hindustan Times,* among other Indian newspapers, published a list of the 100 persons who were convicted for various offences ranging from 'possessing arms' to 'conspiracy'.[32] Who were these 100 convicted people? Which classes did they come from, what kind of education and employment did they have, what were their religious affiliations and motivations? A systematic analysis of the biographies of the 100 convicted cannot be undertaken until the documents are released and this will occur at some time after the sentences are passed. But a scan of the major Indian English-language newspapers that reported the trials

---

[25] '93 Blasts Verdict: Sentencing in Jan', *Hindustan Times.com* (5 Dec. 2006) [http://hindustantimes.com, accessed 13 Jan. 2007]. The first presiding judge was J.N. Patel who was succeeded by Judge P.K. Kode after 12 February 1996.
[26] Swati Deshpande, 'Tada Judge Hits a Six, Reaches 100', *The Times of India Online* (5 Dec. 2006) [http://timesofindia.indiatimes.com, accessed 10 Jan. 2007].
[27] *Ibid.*
[28] PTI (Press Trust of India), ''93 Blast: Convicts Rely on Srikrishna Commission Report', *Hindustan Times.com* (11. Dec. 2006) [http://hindustantimes.com, accessed 13 Jan. 2007].
[29] The Special Public Prosecutor quoted in Deshpande, 'Tada Judge Hits a Six, Reaches 100'.
[30] BBC News, 'Four Guilty of 1993 Mumbai Blasts' (12 Sept. 2006) [http://newsvote.bbc.co.uk, accessed 10 Jan. 2007].
[31] *Ibid.* One report stated that 'two passed away in police custody, 10 were killed in gang wars and one was gunned down in a police encounter'. See '1993 Blast Verdict Today', *Central Chronicle* (10 Aug. 2006) [http://www.centralchronicle.com, accessed 31 Jan. 2007].
[32] This list appears as an online 'popup' titled ''93 Blasts Verdict Out, Fates Sealed', *Hindustan Times.com* (19 Dec. 2006) [http://www.hindustantimes.com/news/61 1_0,001302410000.htm, accessed 13 Jan. 2007].

throws up a good deal of information that basically confirms the Sageman-Pape hypothesis discussed at the start of this paper. These conclusions are, of course, subject to revision once the full biographies become available and have been scrutinised. At this stage of my analysis, I have examined the available socioeconomic data for *all* the convicted individuals, not merely those accused of conspiracy and murder.[33] Many of the accused were convicted of lesser crimes such as possessing illegal firearms and/or aiding and abetting the plotters. When better access to the court records is obtained, a more focused study of the conspirators or terrorists will be possible. Over time, there is also the possibility that some of the key organisers of the bombings will be brought to trial.

What were they key characteristics of the Mumbai bombings?

First, the large quantity of ammunition and 5,000 kilograms of RDX explosive[34] cost a lot of money and had to be smuggled into India along the western coastline in Raigad district. This could only have been achieved with the support of the local police and customs' officials. The result is that the Mumbai trials have thrown up a great deal of information about how the smuggling networks operate in this part of the subcontinent. Many of the convicted were in fact police and customs' department employees.

Second, the people who owned, smuggled, collected, transported, stored, planted or used the ammunition and explosives were not the poor, unemployed and down-and-outs who characterise the street life of any Indian city. Rather they were working-class or middle-class persons; Sanjay Dutt was an exception, being a member of the Mumbai elite. Here are some examples of the people who were amongst the 100 convicted and for whom we have some job descriptions:

- Sanjay Dutt, one of Bollywood's best-known film stars. He attended the elite Lawrence School at Sanawar in Himachal Pradesh (established by the British in

---

[33] Readers wishing to see what the specific convictions were can do so by checking the references cited in this paper including the list generated by the South Asia Terrorist Portal, 'The Terrorist and Disruptive Activities (Prevention) Act Courts Judgment on the 1993 Serial Bomb Blasts in Mumbai' (New Delhi: 2007) [http://www.satp.org/satporgtp/countries/india/database/mumbai_blasts_judgement.htm, accessed 30 Jan. 2007].

[34] For a description of the smuggling of this material see 'A Low-Down on How Mumbai was Bombed'. For various reasons there remains uncertainty about the exact volume of RDX smuggled into Mumbai, including the notion that the Mumbai bombings were not originally planned for 12 March 1993 but as part of a larger series of bombings designed to go off on 1 May. One lot of RDX found by the Mumbai police in March 1993 'after a tip-off weighed 1,500 kg. See 'A Happy Moment for Mumbai Police', *The Hindu* (13 Sept. 2006) [http://www.hinduonnet.com, accessed 13 Jan. 2007]. According to Farhana Shah (lawyer for the defence for 80 of the accused) the Mumbai police collected about 59 bags of RDX each containing between five and 10 kg. of explosives. Interview with Farhana Shah, Mumbai, 28 Jan. 2007. According to Advocate Shubash Kanse, assistant to Majid Memon (lawyer for the Memon family) the exact chain of events that brought the RDX into western India has not been established. Interview with Shubash Kanse, Mumbai, 31 Jan. 2007.

1847). Dutt is named as no. 88 on the *Hindustan Times* list.[35] He is rumoured by some Maharashtrians to identify himself as a 'Muslim' presumably because his famous film star mother (Nargis) was a Muslim. But his father was a Hindu and there is no evidence to suggest that Dutt considers himself a Muslim. According to his defence lawyer, Dutt is very fond of Ganesh.[36] During the trial Dutt wanted to go to Pune to worship at the Balaji Temple and the Dagdu Seth Ganesh Temple but the CBI rejected the request.[37] Again in December 2006 Dutt spent four hours praying at the Siddhivinayak Temple, Mumbai, in the hope of extending his bail.[38] Of course, many see these acts as a sign not of his devotion, but rather as a pragmatic strategy to avoid a heavy sentence by seeking sympathy from the Hindu majority of the Indian public.

- A manufacturer of spare parts and friend of Sanjay Dutt, Rusi Mulla (a Parsi).[39]
- The proprietor of a driving school, Ibrahim Chauhan, and also a friend of Sanjay Dutt.[40]
- The owner of the Magnum video company, Sameer Hingoria, also a friend of Sanjay Dutt.[41]
- A builder, Noor Mohammed Khan.[42]
- Another builder and one of 'Tiger' Memon's aides, Liaqat Ali Khan.[43]
- A salesman, Shoaib Kasam Ghansar, who worked at the Heera Panna shopping centre[44] near the Haji Ali tomb and lived in the well-to-do Mumbai suburb of Andheri with his elderly mother and sister. He was one of the convicted who asked for leniency in sentencing because his girlfriend had already been waiting for him for more than a decade.[45] Ghansar, a cousin of Asgar Yusuf Mukadam

---

[35] "93 Blasts Verdict Out, Fates Sealed'.
[36] Interview with Farhana Shah, Mumbai, 28 Jan. 2007.
[37] Swati Deshpande, 'Dutt Postpones Trip to Temples as CBI Objects', *The Times of India Online* (16 Sept. 2006) [http://timesofindia.indiatimes.com, accessed 12 Jan. 2007].
[38] 'Sanjay Dutt Seeks Divine Intervention', *Hindustan Times. com*(17 Dec. 2006) [http://www.hindustantimes.com, accessed 13 Jan. 2007]. According to the head of the temple, Dutt undertook 'one of the difficult yajnas' that required no less than 15 priests.
[39] Mustafa Plumber, '1993 Blasts: 3 Held Guilty for Aiding Dutt', *Hindustan Times.com* (29 Nov. 2006) [http://hindustantimes.com, accessed 13 Jan. 2007].
[40] *Ibid.*
[41] *Ibid.* The video company Magnum has been described as 'one of the largest players in the distribution of Hindi movies in West Asia, Europe and the United States'. See Molly Charles, K.S. Nair, Gabriel Britto and A.A. Das, 'The Bombay Underworld: A Descriptive Account and its Role in Drug Trade', in UNESCO, *Globalisation, Drugs and Criminalisation: Final Research Report on Brazil, China, India and Mexico* (Geneva: UNESCO/MOST Secretariat, 2002), p.27 [http://unesdoc.unesco.org/images/0012/001276/127644e.pdf].
[42] 'Blasts: Mumbai Builder Guilty', *Dance with Shadows* (23 Nov. 2006) [http://www.dancewithshadows.com, accessed 10 Jan. 2007].
[43] *Ibid.*
[44] Swati Deshpande, 'Bomb Planter Convicted', *The Times of India Online* (15 Sept. 2006) [http://timesofindia.indiatimes.com, accessed 12 Jan. 2007].
[45] Swati Deshpande, 'My Girl's Been Waiting for 13 Years', *The Times of India Online* (16 Sept. 2006) [http://timesofindia.indiatimes.com, accessed 12 Jan. 2007; and Deshpande, 'Tada Judge Hits a Six'.

(see below), was convicted despite rejecting his own confession because it had been extracted by force.[46]
- The manager of a shop in the Heera Panna shopping centre,[47] Asgar Yusuf Mukadam, who also lived in Andheri (at the Nagnath Society flats, Seven Bungalows) with his aged aunt and uncle.[48] The family owned another apartment in the same area and his brother, recently returned from Qatar, had opened a factory in Belasis Road, Mumbai.[49] Asgar also worked as a manager/accountant for 'Tiger' Memon.[50]
- A butcher, Shahnawaz Abdul Kadar Qureshi, who had followed his father's trade, and lived in the slum of Bandra.[51] His only education was as an apprentice at the.abattoir in Deonar.[52] He was recruited to Dubai and Pakistan with the promise of a new job which he subsequently discovered involved weapons training in Pakistan.[53] He said he had been brainwashed by 'Tiger' Memon, but he was clearly. open to persuasion because 'my house was set ablaze during the riots'. Before. Memon's influence he claimed to have been an 'ordinary boy from a village in.Nasik district'[54] who had no innate hatred of Hindus. In fact, he had married a Maharahstrian' (which term presumably means a Hindu woman).[55]
- An electrician, Bashir Ahmed Usman Ghani Khairullah, who undertook terrorist. training in Sandheri, Raigad district, Maharashtra.[56] Bashir appears to have.panicked as he ran home with the grenades intended for the Hindu residents of a fishing village in Mahim.
- An unemployed man (no further details) named Zakir Hussain Noor Mohammad. Shaikh, a co-accused with Bashir.[57] He was clearly literate because he had written. a book in prison with a colleague entitled 'Prevention of Terrorism or Religious. Intolerance'.

---

[46] Deshpande, 'Bomb Planter Convicted'.
[47] Swati Deshpande, 'Plaza Bombers Guilty, Face Death Penalty', *The Times of India Online* (19 Sept. 2006) [http://timesofindia.indiatimes.com, accessed 12 Jan. 2007].
[48] Nitasha Natu, 'Family Lost in a Void', *The Times of India Online* (19 Sept. 2006) [http://timesofindia.indiatimes.com, accessed 12 Jan. 2007].
[49] *Ibid.*
[50] 'Pak-Trained Bomber Found Guilty', *The Telegraph* (19 Sept. 2006) [http://www.telegraphindia.com, accessed 13 Jan. 2007].
[51] Deshpande, 'Plaza Bombers Guilty, Face Death Penalty'.
[52] Swati Deshpande, 'Plaza Bombers; Traitors or Trapped?', *The Times of India Online* (19 Sept. 2006) [http://timesofindia.indiatimes.com, accessed 12 Jan. 2007].
[53] 'Two "Tiger" Memon Aides Held Guilty in Theatre Blast', *The Indian Express* (19 Sept. 2006) [http://www.indiaexpress.com, accessed 10 Jan. 2007].
[54] Shahnawaz Qureshi quoted in 'Plaza Cinema Bombers Plead for Leniency', *The Times of India Online* (19 Sept. 2006) [http://timesofindia.indiatimes.com, accessed 12 Jan. 2007].
[55] Deshpande, 'Plaza Bombers: Traitors Or Trapped?'.
[56] Mustafa Plumber, ''93 Blasts Case: Six Memon Aides Held Guilty', *Hindustan Times.com* (4 Dec. 2006) [http://hindustantimes.com, accessed 13 Jan. 2007].
[57] *Ibid.*

- A clothes vendor, Abdul Akhtar Khan, who lived in the Bandra reclamation area and had received terrorist training in Pakistan. He was the 3rd co-accused with Bashir.[58]
- A well-to-do unemployed man, Feroz Amani Mallik, who lived in Pathanwadi, Malad, the 4th co-accused with Bashir.[59]
- A 17-year-old youth, Moin Qureshi,[60] the 5th co-accused with the above four men. He pleaded that he had been a minor in 1993, even though he had received weapons training in Pakistan.
- A private driver, Salim Rahim Shaikh, resident of Mahim, who had also received terrorist training in Pakistan. He was the 6th co-accused with the above five men.[61]
- Abdul Ghani Ismail Turk, 'Tiger' Memon's private driver and otherwise an ordinary Mumbai taxi driver.[62] He had met 'Tiger' Memon while working in Saudi Arabia. The Bombay court found him guilty of the worst bombing incident which killed 120 people.[63]
- Memon's landing agent/smuggler Dawood Mohammed Phanse (alias Dawood Takla).[64]
- A Memon aide/smuggler Sharif Abdul Gafoor Parkar (alias Dadabhai).[65]
- 'Tiger' Memon's aide, Parvez Nasir Ahmed Shaikh.[66]
- A mechanic and aide to 'Tiger' Memon, Mohammed Iqbal Yusuf Shaikh.[67]
- A watchman of a 'high security microwave tower', Tulsiram Dhondu Surve.[68]
- A financier and financial advisor to 'Tiger' Memon, Mulchand Shah.[69]
- A civil contractor, Shahwali Khan.[70]
- A travel agent, Altaf Ali Sayed.[71]

---

[58] *Ibid.*
[59] *Ibid.*
[60] *Ibid.*
[61] *Ibid.*
[62] Deshpande, 'Tada Judge Hits a Six'; Kartikeya, 'Century Bazaar Bomber was a Taxi Driver', *The Times of India Online* (18 Sept. 2006) [http://timesofindia.indiatimes.com/articleshow/2000710.cms, accessed 12 Jan. 2007].
[63] Swati Deshpande, ''93 Blasts: Deadliest Bomber Found Guilty', *The Times of India Online* (20 Sept. 2006) [http://www.timesofindia.indiatimes.com, accessed 12 Jan. 2007].
[64] Sheela Bhatt, 'TADA Court Accepts Dawood's Role in 1993 Mumbai Blasts', *Rediff.com* (22 Sept. 2006) [http://www.rediff.com, accessed 31 Jan. 2007]; and Shahid Raza Burney, 'Two Smugglers Found Guilty in Blasts Case', *Arab News* (23 Sept. 2006) [http://www.arabnews.com, accessed 1 Feb 2007].
[65] *Ibid.*
[66] '1993 Mumbai Blasts "Tiger" Memon Aide Convicted', *The Times of India Online* (21 Sept. 2006) [http://timesofindia.indiatimes.com, accessed 10 Jan. 2007].
[67] South Asia Terrorist Portal, 'The Terrorist and Disruptive Activities (Prevention) Act Courts Judgement on the 1993 Serial Bomb Blasts in Mumbai'.
[68] *Ibid.*
[69] *Ibid.*
[70] *Ibid.*
[71] *Ibid.*

Of these 24 men, only Zakir Hussain Noor Mohammad Shaikh and Moin Qureshi cannot be ascribed to any socioeconomic group because we do not have enough information about them. The remaining 22 men, or about 92 percent of those convicted about whom we have some data from newspaper reports, were all in employment and hardly poor—at least not by Indian standards. We do not have educational details at this stage, but given the international focus on *madrassas* since 9/11, if any of these men had been a product of a *madrassa* that information would certainly have been dredged up in court. It was not. The butcher, Shahnawaz Abdul Kadar Qureshi, stands out as the only illiterate and the only occupant of a really dirty, working-class job.

A fully reliable account of the socioeconomic status of the 100 convicted persons must wait until the court records are released to the public, and no doubt some newspaper reports will turn out to be only partially accurate. Of special interest will be the individuals who received weapons training in Pakistan. According to Farhana Shah, the lawyer for a large number of the defendants, 47 of the 100 convicted persons were declared guilty of conspiracy. Farhana Shah represented 37 of the 47 'conspirators' and of these 37, about 15 or 40 percent had received weapons training in Pakistan. None of these 15 had any prior criminal conviction or record of any kind including non-cognisable complaints; none of them belonged to any criminal gangs; all of them were aged between 21 and 23; and all of them were working-class youths who had been enticed to Dubai on the promise of better jobs. From Dubai they were taken to Pakistan where they had no means of leaving because their passports had been taken by those who had 'recruited them' for the training program.[72] In other words, the Sageman-Pape hypothesis will need to be adjusted to account for various levels of hierarchy amongst those convicted in the Mumbai trials. In this case, the baseline operators who received training in Pakistan were working-class youths in contrast to their middle-class criminal masters. This relates to the next set of observations.

Third, the higher up we go in this Mumbai hierarchy of terror, the wealthier the accused turn out to be. The key coordinators on the ground were the four members of the Memon family (Yakub, Yusuf, Essa and Rubeena—wife of Suleiman[73]—who were all convicted of conspiracy during the trials) plus the

---

[72] Interview with Farhana Shah, Mumbai, 28 Jan. 2007.

[73] Suleiman was a Non Resident Indian (NRI) living in Dubai; he spent five years in a Mumbai prison but was eventually acquitted by Judge Kode. His wife, however, was convicted. Her car was one of the vehicles used in the bombings. Although she lived in Dubai with her husband, the car was still registered in her name. Interview with Shubash Kanse, Mumbai, 31 Jan. 2007; and 'The Acquitted', *The Indian Express* (3 Dec. 2006) [http: //www.indianexpress.-com, accessed 2 Feb. 2007].

'mastermind'[74] Mohammed Yusuf Shah Memon (or 'Tiger' Memon) who had left Mumbai the day before the blasts. 'Tiger' Memon, his brother Ayub Memon, both of their wives, Dawood Ibrahim (see below), Anis Ibrahim (Dawood's brother) and Mohammed Dosa are all on the court's list of 29 accused who could not be brought to trial as they had 'absconded'.[75] Another accused, Feroz Abdul Rashid Khan, is a fugitive currently living in the US—again clearly not a poor man.[76] Abdul Razzak Memon, father of 'Tiger', was one of the accused who died during the trials.

The Memons are a middle-class Mumbai family of Kutchi Gujaratis who attracted a lot of social attention when one of the sons married at the Islam Gymkhana in south Mumbai.[77] After 'Tiger' Memon, the most 'talented' brother is Yakub, who has been described as a highly-educated, very articulate chartered accountant.[78] It was Yakub who lectured the court and judge about the injustices suffered by Muslims, insisted on his innocence (based on his willingness to return to Mumbai with his whole family) and implied that the 1993 bombings were justified given the appalling violence inflicted by Hindu fundamentalists on Muslims in the weeks following the demolition of the Babri Masjid. The car laden with explosives had not been his but his deceased father's.[79] He also demanded leniency for Rubeena, the wife of his brother Suleiman Memon, because there was no-one to look after the children and her mother-in-law.[80] 'Tiger''s two younger brothers are disabled in various ways: Yusuf is a schizophrenic; and Essa has a brain tumour.[81] Yusuf pleaded that he had no idea who was travelling to Pakistan on the tickets he was asked to buy (allegedly in order to train some of the conspirators in Pakistan), and Essa pointed out that his Mahim office had been destroyed in the riots of 1992–1993.

Not much is yet known about the Memon family and how the brothers became involved in Mumbai's crime world. But crime is no doubt a source of their

---

[74] In Mumbai, the term 'mastermind' is reserved for 'Tiger' Memon as he was the person in charge of operationalising the Mumbai bombings; Dawood Ibrahim is locally described as the 'brains' behind the operation. Interview with Shubash Kanse, Mumbai, 31 Jan. 2007.
[75] 'Day 1 of 1993 Judgement Day: Four of Memon Family Guilty', *The Indian Express* (13 Sept. 2006) [http://www.indianexpress.com/story/12563.html, accessed 10 Jan. 2007]; and 'Four of Memon Family Found Guilty', *The Hindu* (13 Sept. 2006) [http://www.hindonnet.com, accessed 10 Jan. 2007].
[76] CBI, 'CBI Moves US for Handing Over Bombay Bomb Blast'.
[77] Swami, 'India's Most Wanted'; and interview with Shubash Kanse, Mumbai, 31 Jan. 2007. Kanse describes the family as 'middle-class'.
[78] Swati Deshpande, 'Hang Three Memon Brothers: CBI', *The Times of India Online* (15 Sept. 2006) [http: //timesofindia.indiatimes.com, accessed 12 Jan. 2007].
[79] Deshpande, 'Yakub Refers to Delay in Riot Cases'.
[80] 'Day 1 of 1993 Judgement Day: Four of Memon Family Found Guilty'.
[81] Deshpande, 'Hang Three Memon Brothers: CBI'. According to Kanse, these illnesses only emerged after the Mumbai bombings and so do not change the circumstances in which the Memon family was involved in the Mumbai blasts. Interview with Shubash Kanse, Mumbai, 31 Jan. 2007.

wealth, although Yakub disingenuously asserted in court that he had no idea that his older brother, 'Tiger' Memon, was one of Mumbai's big crime bosses. More likely, Yakub knew about his hot-headed brother's criminal life but had no idea that 'Tiger' was involved in planning any bombings in Mumbai.[82] Another gangster convicted in Mumbai in 2006 was Ejaz Pathan,[83] formerly a member of Dawood Ibrahim's syndicate. Pathan was a specialist in smuggling narcotics. His assistant, Dawood Khan, was also convicted.[84] However, compared to Dawood Ibrahim, these criminals were not at the top of the tree.

Fourth, at the apex of this hierarchy of terror stands Dawood Ibrahim, Mumbai's 'Don'. He is now living with his brother and accomplice, Anis Ibrahim, in Pakistan.[85] It is important to stress that although the Indian government alleged as early as April 1993 that the Mumbai blasts were engineered by Dawood Ibrahim,[86] it was not until the Mumbai trials that the evidence for a direct link between Dawood and the bombings emerged. That piece of critical evidence rests on the confession of one of the co-accused in the Mumbai trials—'Tiger' Memon's 82-year-old 'landing agent' Dawood Mohammed Phanse.[87] Phanse wrote in his confession that he had met Dawood Ibrahim and 'Tiger' Memon in Dubai where the Mumbai blasts had been planned.[88] It is important to note that Phanse, like most of the other accused, never withdrew his confession and that the court accepted it fully. In the words of Rakesh Maria, the senior investigating police officer:

> Dawood Phanse's conviction proves that our investigation was on the right path. It proves Dawood Ibrahim's complicity in the 1993 bomb blasts. He was an integral part of the conspiracy that led to the blasts.[89]

Rakesh Maria's certainty is not shared by all. Majid Memon, lawyer for the Memon brothers, notes that '.. .the prime accused Dawood Ibrahim and "Tiger" Memon are not going to be convicted...because they have not stood trial in

---

[82] This is the view of one prominent Indian journalist familiar with the circumstances surrounding the 1992–1993 Mumbai blasts. He wishes to remain anonymous. Interview with Indian journalist, New Delhi, 28 Jan. 2007.
[83] Mustafa Plumber, ''93 Blasts Verdict: Two More Convicted', *Hindustan Times.com* (20 November 2006) [http://hindustantimes.com, accessed 13 Jan. 2007].
[84] *Ibid.*
[85] BBC News, 'Profile: India's Fugitive Gangster'.
[86] Statement by the Minister of Home Affairs, Shri S.B. Chavan, on the 'Investigation by the Bombay Police in Regard to Bomb Explosions in Bombay on March 12, 1993' (New Delhi: Indian Parliament, 21 April 1993) [http://www.parliamentofindia.nic.in, accessed 31 Jan. 2007].
[87] Phanse was arrested soon after the bombings and along with 28 other accused has been in prison for 13 years awaiting trial. Burney, 'Two Smugglers Found Guilty in Blasts Case'. In the event that some of these accused receive a sentence of less than 13 years, they will be in a position to demand compensation.
[88] Bhatt, 'TADA Court Accepts Dawood's Role in 1993 Mumbai Blasts'.
[89] *Ibid.*

court'.[90] With the exception of Phanse's confession, other trial documents do not refer to Dawood's involvement in the bombings.[91] In the meantime, the 'small fry' have been tried.[92] Moreover, all the convicted have the right to appeal to the Supreme Court of India. For the moment the 78 confessions which the TADA court[93] accepted appear reasonable (there were a total of 88 confessions; ten were rejected).[94] But there is no predicting what might happen on appeal to the Supreme Court. Confessions are notoriously unreliable as sources of information, and the methods by which confessions are obtained can jeopardise their legal standing. At least two of the original accused have withdrawn their confessions citing coercion. Despite this, the confessions are the primary documents which led to the 100 convictions,[95] followed by circumstantial evidence[96] and the evidence supplied by accused persons who became witnesses for the prosecution (called 'approvers' in the trial reports).[97] These caveats need to be stated when considering the cases of each of the 100 convicted persons, and of those who have eluded the legal system up until now including Dawood Ibrahim.

Given the consensus that Dawood Ibrahim conceived the Mumbai bombings, who is he? Dawood began his infamous career at the age of 19 when he dropped out of the Ahmad Sailor English Medium School and started robbing banks. His first bank robbery was uncovered by his own father, a Mumbai policeman.[98] Dawood's gang hoped to relieve the Metropolitan Bank of half a million rupees. He went on from this to the leadership of a group of Konkani Muslim thugs from the Ratnagiri area; then he worked for various local crime bosses. Finally, with his brother Anis in tow, he graduated into an influential smuggler of bullion and a mob leader in Mumbai's world of prostitution, narcotics, gambling, and even Bollywood.[99]

---

[90] Sheela Bhatt, 'Dawood, 'Tiger' Memon Can't be Convicted', *Rediff.com* (9 Aug. 2006) [http://www.rediff.com, accessed 1 Feb. 2007].
[91] *Ibid.*
[92] *Ibid.*, quoting Adhik Shirodkar, a criminal lawyer.
[93] TADA is the law under which the accused were arrested and tried, namely the Terrorism and Disruptive (Prevention) Activities Act, 1987. For a discussion of the history of this and related legislation see Oliver Mendelsohn, 'The Legal Response of India, Malaysia, Singapore and Australia to 9/11', in Marika Vicziany (ed.), *Controlling Arms and Terror in the Asia Pacific: After Bali and Baghdad* (Cheltenham, UK and Northampton, MA: Edward Elgar, 2007), pp.60–83.
[94] Interview with Shubash Kanse, Mumbai, 31 Jan. 2007.
[95] *Ibid.*
[96] Interview with Farhana Shah, Mumbai, 28 Jan. 2007.
[97] At least two 'approvers' have been named by the Mumbai press: Mohammed Khatlab and Mohammed Usman Jan Khan. The latter accused a further 33 persons of complicity in the plot. See '1993 Blast Verdict Today'.
[98] 'How Don Made it to the Crime World?', *Central Chronicle* (27 Feb. 2006) [http://www.centralchronicle.com, accessed 10 Jan. 2007]; and BBC News, 'Profile: India's Fugitive Gangster'.
[99] BBC News, 'Profile: India's Fugitive Gangster'; and 'Blasts Linked to Power Struggle'. The only relatively comprehensive biography of Dawood is that by King, *The Most Dangerous Man in the World: Dawood Ibrahim*. But

Not until he fled to Karachi did Dawood become interested in religion, probably because the city of Karachi is a complex mixture of political, ethnic and religious tensions[100]—the tensions between various Islamic sects is especially dire. In these conditions, Dawood may have become involved with the Barelvi sect which leans towards Sufism. The Barelvis are involved in deadly competition with other Islamic sects in Pakistan, especially the puritanical Deobandis and Wahhabis. The Barelvis do not condone the latter's strict moral code. They oppose *jihad* and other manifestations of religious fundamentalism. They are the liberal alternative within Islamic consciousness. Sectarian conflict in Pakistan cuts very deep and Dawood could have become caught up in it. For example, he refused to help free Maulana Masood Azhar from detention in India because 'he is a Deobandi'.[101] The problem with placing Dawood into the context of the Barelvi sect of Karachi is that the Barelvi is not compatible with his alleged funding of Lashkar-e-Taiba which adheres to the Ahl-e-Hadith sect, an even more puritanical movement than the Deobandis. On the other hand, perhaps Dawood was comfortable with Lashkar-e-Taiba because they represent a newly-emerging technocratic elite?

The US Department of the Treasury view, however, is quite different from the one offered above. It holds that in the 1990s Dawood became involved with Osama bin Laden, and that 'successful routes established. . .by Ibrahim's syndicate have been subsequently utilised by bin Laden.' The treasury account also alleges that in the late 1990s Ibrahim travelled to Afghanistan under the protection of the Taliban.[102] These allegations cannot, however, be proven—as Shahzad has noted. Dawood's men have not participated in any international terrorist act and his D-company syndicate is 'nothing' compared to the outfits of Chinese and other Asian crime mobsters.[103] Indeed, given Dawood's Sufi leanings, there is nothing ideologically compatible between him and al-Qaida, Jemaah Islamiah or the other Salafi terrorists. If Dawood occasionally drew close to Osama bin Laden it may have been to further develop trade

---

King has no data about Dawood's early life or private life today. It is widely believed in Mumbai that Dawood was a victim of child abuse.

[100] The information in this paragraph is drawn from Syed Saleem Shahzad, 'Dawood: "War on Terror" Takes a Strange Turn', *Asia Times Online* (22 Oct. 2003) [http://www.atimes.com/atimes/South_Asia/EJ22Df07.html, accessed 13 Jan. 2007].

[101] *Ibid.* Azhar achieved international fame when the Indian government released him from prison in January 2000 as part of a deal to end the hijacking of Indian Airlines Flight IC-814. He subsequently set up Jaish-e-Mohammed, a terrorist outfit noted for its 'innovative' suicide missions in Kashmir. See 'Maulana Masood Azhar', *Kashmir Herald* (Jan. 2002) [http://kashmirherald.com/profiles/masoodazhar.html, accessed 2 Feb. 2007].

[102] US Department of the Treasury quoted in BBC News, 'Profile: India's Fugitive Gangster'.

[103] Shahzad, 'Dawood: "War on Terror" Takes a Strange Turn'. For a contrary position that supports the US Treasury view rather uncritically, see B. Raman, 'Dawood Ibrahim: The Global Terrorist', *South Asia Analysis Group*, Paper no.818 (19 Oct. 2003) [http://www.saag.org/papers9/paper818.html, accessed 13 Jan. 2007].

routes for his illegal shipments of narcotics and guns.[104] If Dawood's ideological affiliations remain ambiguous, less so is his involvement with Pakistan's ISI. The general view in India is summed up by Vir Sanghvi when he writes that in exchange for the right to live in Pakistan without harassment, and continue his smuggling business in peace, 'Dawood offered up the services of his gang in acts of terrorism'.[105]

Fifth, in none of the trial proceedings is there any evidence to suggest that religious fanaticism, pan-Islam, *shariat* law, the desire to set up an Islamic state or indoctrination by *madrassas* played any role in recruiting the 100 convicted persons. The Mumbai bombings of March 1993 are best seen as an act of community retribution against Hindu fundamentalists who had inflicted so much damage in the events surrounding the demolition of the Babri Masjid. None of the accused spoke about the need to defend Islam or the Prophet; rather they spoke of revenge and justice. Nor did the convicted have any known association with *madrassas*. Moreover, amongst the convicted, ten percent were Hindus! They included five customs' officers and five police officers, who will be sentenced not for conspiracy, but for smuggling and transporting explosives and taking bribes.[106]

The most prominent Hindu convicted was Sanjay Dutt. The charge of conspiracy was quashed but Dutt now faces sentencing for possession of illegal firearms, which he says were kept in his house to 'protect his family'.[107] During the Mumbai communal riots, Sanjay's father had helped many Muslims and for this the family had been threatened by Hindu fundamentalists. The lighter conviction came as a great relief to his sister Priya, a member of the Lok Sabha (lower house) of the national parliament in New Delhi.[108] The local Congress committees were also pleased, given the patronage that the Dutt family has traditionally extended to the Congress Party of India.

---

[104] Gilbert King again reverses this relationship: it was Dawood's smuggling circuits that enabled Osama bin Laden to escape the US at the fall of the Taliban. Since then Dawood has also been allegedly funding both Osama bin Laden and Lashkar-e-Taiba. See King, *The Most Dangerous Man in the World: Dawood Ibrahim*, p. 17.

[105] Vir Sanghvi, 'Godfather III: The Terrorist', *The Hindustan Times.com* (12 Nov. 2005) [http://hindustantimes.com, accessed 13 Jan. 2007]. See also 'A Godfather's Lethal Mix of Business and Politics', *US News & World Report* (12 May 2005) [http://www.usnews.com, accessed 13 Jan. 2007].

[106] Imtiaz Ahmed cites Shiv Visvanathan's evidence suggesting that Custom's former Assistant Collector R.K. Singh negotiated on behalf of his staff a pay-off of Rs7–8 lakh 'per landing': 'Such a price was high, for the normal customs rate for landing smuggled goods was in the Rs3 lakh range. This indicated that the customs officials were aware that what was landing was something different, even lethal, and not just textiles, silver, watches or gold'. Shiv Visvanathan, 'Notes on the Bombay Blast', in Shiv Visvanathan and Harsh Sethi (eds), *Foul Play: Chronicles of Corruption* (New Delhi: Banyan Books, 1998), p.121 cited in Imtiaz Ahmed, 'South Asia without SAARC', in *Seminar*, Vol.517 (Sept. 2002) (http://www.india-seminar.com/2002/517, accessed 21 Jan. 2007).

[107] BBC News, 'Star Guilty in Mumbai Bomb Trial', *BBC News* (28 Nov. 2006) [http://news.bbc.co.uk, accessed 11 Jan. 2007].

[108] Dharmendra Jore, 'Cong[ress] Relieved at Verdict on Sanjay Dutt', *Hindustan Times.com* (28 Nov. 2006) [http://hindustantimes.com, accessed 13 Jan. 2007]. See also 'Biographical Sketch, Member of Parliament, 14th Lok Sabha

If the Mumbai bombings of 1993 had been mainly a religious affair, why did they involve Hindus? Clearly the evidence points to the essential prerequisite for the bombings—namely the extent and depth of Mumbai's criminal underworld. Sanjay Dutt's links to the criminals who supplied the arms to the Memon plot also supports this—even if Dutt had no idea what he was getting caught up in. Bollywood has for many decades been an avenue for numerous money-laundering operations. Indeed the city's criminals are among the film industry's top investors. In the case of the Mumbai bombings, it was Dawood Ibrahim's D-company crime syndicate that was the critical facilitator for the damage inflicted on the city. The syndicate itself consisted of both Muslim and Hindu thugs; the inter-faith nature of Dawood's gang and of other gangs has probably not changed despite the communal tensions of 1992–1993.[109] The nature of these criminal interests is considered next.

Although the compulsion behind the March 1993 bombings was revenge for the destructiveness of Hindu fundamentalism in late 1992, the logistical framework that made the thirteen bombings possible was the smuggling/crime syndicates that Dawood Ibrahim and 'Tiger' Memon, amongst others, had built up over many decades in Mumbai. Leadership of the syndicates involved in the Mumbai bombings was in the hands of Muslim criminals who in their determination to avenge the marginalised and victimised Muslim communities of India had increasingly been drawn into the orbit of terror organised by Pakistan's ISI and by privately-organised Islamic terrorist organisations such as the Lashkar-e-Taiba. Dawood Ibrahim and 'Tiger' Memon became caught up in these eddies and not surprisingly a number of the bombers who brought havoc to Mumbai in March 1993 had been to Pakistan for special training in terrorist tactics. Dawood and his close associates were all wealthy men, living on their ill-gotten gains and buying their way into respectable South Asian families.[110]

The balance of evidence reviewed above emphasises the home-grown nature of the Mumbai blasts of March 1993 and the wide diversity of accused persons pulled in by the Mumbai police. Amongst the 100 convicted persons there were distinctive

---

for Mumbai North West (Maharashtra), elected November 2005' [http://164.100.24.208/ls/lsmember/biodata.asp?mpsno=4210, accessed 15 Jan. 2007].

[109] Gilbert King argues against this, saying that the Mumbai bombings created a division between Dawood Ibrahim and Chhota Rajan along communal lines, with the Muslim thugs siding with the former and the Hindu with the latter. He adds that this bifurcation then changed into a situation where the ISI's backing of Dawood was matched by Indian intelligence backing of Rajan. See King, *The Most Dangerous Man in the World: Dawood Ibrahim*, pp.45–55. This scenario is questioned, however, by well-informed journalists such as Maseeh Rahman who reported at length on the 1992–1993 Mumbai riots. Also see Charles *et al*, 'The Bombay Underworld', p.39.

[110] Dawood's daughter married the son of the famous Pakistani cricketer Javed Miandad. See BBC News, 'Profile: India's Fugitive Gangster'.

groups, not all of whom were conspirators or terrorists. In the words of Swati Deshpande:

> While 100 seems a huge figure, less than 50% of those convicted— 48—have been held guilty of conspiring to cause the blasts. Most of the others have been convicted either for abetment in the attacks or for smuggling in arms and explosives, or for undergoing training in Pakistan in anticipation of further strikes. They include a former policeman, customs officials, a hawala agent and youths recruited for the job. More than ten, including actor Sanjay Dutt, have been held guilty for mere possession of weapons.[111]

Sanjay Dutt was caught up in the net because he was found in possession of illegal firearms. And the way he acquired these was also illegal and may have involved individuals who played a role in the Mumbai bombings. Then there were the usual smugglers, operators, and corrupt customs and police officials who were merely doing business as usual—i.e. facilitating the importation of smuggled goods without necessarily realising what these were or what they were intended for. The third group consisted of young men caught up in this general web of illegal activity, servicing the needs of their masters—Dawood and 'Tiger'—in pursuit of better employment opportunities in both India and Dubai. And there were quite a few very old men who had been loyal servants of the criminal Dons for a long time. A fourth group were those members of the Memon family who lived close to the centre of the storm—namely 'Tiger' Memon—but had no inkling of the fires that were raging and became caught in the maelstrom. And finally there were the master criminals, determined to avenge the injustices inflicted on Indian Muslims in the aftermath of the demolition of the Babri Masjid. All of these people were in employment, many of them doing very well owing to their ill-gotten gains. All the Memon brothers except 'Tiger' were college-educated, and Yakub Memon held more than one degree. The only group in this mixed lot that comes close to being relatively weak in terms of socioeconomic status was the third—in particular the 15 young men who ended up in Pakistan on a weapons training program largely, they claim, against their will. In other words, only 15 percent of the 100 persons convicted in the Mumbai bombing trials appear to have come from insecure personal circumstances and most of these were not poor by Mumbai standards. The remaining 85 percent seem to confirm the Sageman-Pape hypothesis.[112]

---

[111] Deshpande, 'Tada Judge Hits a Six'.
[112] These conclusions will be refined in the next paper on the subject of the Mumbai trials once the sentences have been announced and the trial papers made available. With this more detailed information it will be possible to undertake a close review of the socioeconomic backgrounds of the 100 convicted persons subdivided into the five groups noted above.

The home-grown origins of the Mumbai blasts of 12 March 1993 is beyond dispute, yet because Dawood continues to live in Pakistan under the protection of the ISI, it is important to examine whether there were any links between Dawood and Lashkar-e-Taiba before 1993. Lashkar-e-Taiba comes into these calculations because Dawood has allegedly developed a close association with this terrorist group, which is also protected by the ISI. Lashkar-e-Taiba has also been suspected of playing a major role in various terrorist incidents inside India. Most recently, it is alleged to have planted the seven bombs that blew up various Mumbai trains on 11 July 2006 killing about 200 people and injuring hundreds more. Earlier, it was associated with the response to the pogrom in Gujarat where about 2,000 Muslims[113] were killed in February–March 2002 in the lead-up to the state elections.[114] If the *madrassa* factor was absent from the lives of the Indians convicted in the Mumbai trials of late 2006, could Pakistani *madrassas* have played a role in the 1993 bombings? The nature of Lashkar-e-Taiba and its parent body, Jamaat-ul-Dawa, suggests not.

Jamaat-ul-Dawa and Lashkar-e-Taiba

Exactly when Dawood Ibrahim fled India is not known, although a widely-cited date is 1986.[115] At first he lived in Dubai, but after the 1993 Mumbai bombings relocated to Karachi. In moving to Karachi he was joined by Chota Shakeel and Jamal Memon.[116] It is alleged that the bombings of 1993 were orchestrated by Dawood from the safety of the United Arab Emirates. For Pakistan to offer him protection after the carnage in Mumbai suggests a much earlier relationship between Dawood and the ISI and Dawood and Lashkar-e-Taiba. The US Treasury, better informed about international terrorism and money-laundering that any other body in the world, has stated that Dawood and Lashkar-e-Taiba began working together in the autumn of 1992, at least six months before the March 1993 blasts, with Dawood financing Lashkar-e-Taiba.[117] The relationship has continued since then, fuelled in part by the growing insecurity of Indian Muslims caused by the anti-Muslim riots that have been churned up by Right-wing Hindu fundamentalist

---

[113] The official death toll by May 2002 was 950 compared to the unofficial estimate which exceeded 2,000. See People's Union for Democratic Rights, *State, Society, and Communalism in Gujarat* (Delhi: May 2002), p.1.
[114] The South Asia Terrorist Portal run by the Institute of Conflict Management in New Delhi (http://www.satp.org/satporgtp/icm/index.html) provides a list which starts with the 1996 article 'Incidents Involving Lashkar-e-Toiba', and runs up to the present. See http://www.satp.org/satporgtp/countries/india/states/jandk/terrorist_outfits/lashkar_e_toiba_lt.htm.
[115] BBC News, 'Profile: India's Fugitive Gangster'; and US Department of the Treasury, 'Fact Sheet: Dadwood Ebrahim' [http://www.ustreas.gov/press/releases/reports/fact_sheet.pdf, accessed 21 Jan. 2007].
[116] Ghulam Hasnain, 'Karachi's Gang Wars', *Newsline* (Sept. 2001) [http://www.newsline.com.pk/News Sept2001/coverstory1.htm, accessed 21 Jan. 2007].
[117] BBC News, 'Profile: India's Fugitive Gangster'.

parties. In October 2003 the US declared Dawood Ibrahim to be a terrorist and put pressure on international agencies to close down all his bank accounts.[118]

The history of violent revenge by Muslims against Hindus dates from at least 1985, when Hindu fundamentalists attacked the Muslim community of Bhiwandi, a troubled textile town in Maharashtra,[119] and has increasingly come to rely on external support, mainly from Pakistan's Lashkar-e-Taiba. Some argue that 'the foundations for this independent jihadi infrastructure were laid in 1985', with Lashkar units starting up in various provinces including Gujarat, Maharashtra and Andhra Pradesh.[120] A frequently-cited example of how successful Lashkar-e-Taiba has been in India is the case of Jalees Ansari, 'the kingpin' in no less than 50 bomb blasts across India exactly one year after the destruction of the Babri Masjid.[121] Ansari came from a poor labouring family. His father, a migrant from Uttar Pradesh, worked in a Mumbai textile factory. Ansari was the first in his family to graduate—from the Maratha College, Nagpara. Then he studied at the Sion Medical College in Mumbai and graduated as a doctor.[122] Lashkar-e-Taiba has had no difficulty in recruiting intelligent, middle-class and angry men like Ansari who are also enthusiastic supporters of the same Islamic sect as Lashkar-e-Taiba—namely Ahl-e-Hadith. The explosions that Ansari was responsible for are regarded by some as constituting Lashkar-e-Taiba's first attack inside India.[123] But another report suggests that Ansari was behind bombs planted in the late 1980s.[124] Allegations arising from the trial of the Mumbai bombings in March 1993 also indicate that Lashkar-e-Taiba may have already been active before late 1993 via the criminal networks of western India. Many of the Indians it recruited in 1992–1993 were sent for military training to Pakistan—including some of those convicted in the 1993 Mumbai bombings trials. These deeply-alienated Indian Muslims were bolstered by Pakistani nationals such as Mohammed Salim Junaid (also known as Mohammed Ishtiaq), a fully-trained Lashkar-e-Taiba operator. Junaid married into a Hyderabadi family under the cover of running a transport business and assumed a 'normal' life in central India.[125]

---

[118] Praveen Swami, 'Terrorist Dawood, a Symbolic Label', *The Hindu* (18 Oct. 2003) [http://www.hinduonnet.com, accessed 21 Jan. 2007].
[119] Bhiwandi continues to be a scene of violence with the recent killing of two policemen over arguments about whether a new police station should be built next one of the town's mosques. See '2 Policemen Stabbed to Death in Bhiwandhi', *The Hindu* (7 July 2006) [http://www.hindu.com, accessed 16 Jan. 2007].
[120] 'The Spreading Tentacles of Terror'.
[121] *Ibid.*
[122] Praveen Swami, 'Harnessing Hate', *Frontline,* Vol.23, no.15 (29 July–11 Aug. 2006) [http://hinduonnet.com, accessed 13 Jan. 2007].
[123] *Ibid.*
[124] Chitrangada Choudhurym, 'Decade after Dr Jalees Ansari went to Jail, a Family is still Seething', *Mumbai Newsline* (2 Mar.2004) [http://cities.expressindia.com/fullstory.php?newsid=77579, accessed 10 Feb.2007].
[125] Swami, 'Harnessing Hate'.

So Who or What is Lashkar-e-Taiba?

Lashkar-e-Taiba is the military wing of Jamaat-ul-Dawa, one of the largest, most popular and rapidly-growing charity organisations in Pakistan. It was formed in the mid 1980s by Hafiz Mohammed Saeed, a former professor of engineering at the University of Punjab, as a voluntary army to support the anti-Indian insurgency in Kashmir. Afterwards he set up the Centre for Preaching (Markaz Dawa ul-Irshad) with the aim of taking up social work and also to provide a respectable umbrella for Lashkar-e-Taiba. The Centre for Preaching was subsequently renamed Jamaat-ul-Dawa, but the division of labour remained the same. Both Jamaat-ul-Dawa and Lashkar-e-Taiba have their headquarters near Lahore in the town of Muridke. The Centre quickly developed a reputation for talking tough about *jihad* and attracted huge numbers to its annual meetings (crowds of up to 100,000 were reported). At first Lashkar-e-Taiba was funded through modest means such as public collection boxes,[126] but today ordinary Pakistanis believe that it is funded largely by Saudi Arabian money.

Despite this rabble-rousing history, though, neither organisation fits the Western stereotype of what the Islamic revolution is supposed to represent—beards for instance.[127] In particular, many of its members are technocrats who are less concerned with sporting beards than with learning about modern technologies. They are modernists with 'hidden beards' who support, amongst other things, the professional women's movement in Pakistan[128] and the use of modern technology (whether for communication purposes, engineering projects or warfare). Islamic fundamentalists in the North Western Frontier Provinces and Baluchistan, by contrast, are Luddites in their destruction of television sets, video equipment, musical instruments and sound systems in a supreme effort to cleanse Islam of the various instruments which 'pleasure the flesh'.[129] Jamaat-ul-Dawa does not tolerate music either, but it provides more than just a critique of the West. Given that *madrassas* are supposedly the *jihadi* factories

---

[126] BBC News, 'Profile: Lashkar-e-Toiba', *BBC News* (17 Mar. 2006) [http://www.bbc.co.uk, accessed 22 Jan. 2007].

[127] See for example 'The Future Looks Bearded', *The Economist* (6 July 2006) [http://www.economist.com/index.htmleconomist.com, accessed 16 Jan. 2007].

[128] For example the Jamaat-ul-Dawa website has a link to al-Huda International. See http://www.jamatdawah.org/pages.php?action=menu&id=93, accessed 4 Nov. 2006. Al-Huda is an international women's movement based in Pakistan but active across the globe. It attracts upwardly-mobile, young professional women in an effort to increase their commitment to Islam. For an account of this movement, see Aneela Babar, 'Living Room Seminaries: Negotiating Religious Networks, Gendered Selves and Inter-Communal Relationships within the Pakistani Diaspora', unpublished PhD thesis, Centre for Cultural Research, University of Western Sydney, 2006.

[129] See for example the special issue of *The Herald* (Karachi) (June 2006), 'Flashpoint Frontier: Religious Extremists are Pushing their Agenda across Large Swathes of the NWFP', pp.60–71.

of Pakistan, are there links between Jamaat-ul-Dawa's social work and the *madrassas*?

Jamaat-ul-Dawa does indeed undertake a wide range of educational programs which includes schooling from primary to tertiary levels. According to the organisation's website,[130] Jamaat-ul-Dawa has six special functions: missionary work (including links to al-Huda International that recruits young, middle-class professional women to its cause); media outreach; social service to the community; professional outreach; welfare work amongst youth and women; and education. These functions are spread across thirteen separate departments of which the Department of Education is the largest and best-organised. It looks after a vast number of institutions which are part of Pakistan's private school system.

Yet government schools in Pakistan dominate education, accounting for about 65 percent of all enrolments. Despite all the scaremongering, the *madrassas* that provide a very traditional Islamic education account for a mere 12 percent of all students.[131] Moreover, the schools and colleges of Jamaat-ul-Dawa, like other private institutions, are distinguished from *madrassas* by providing a modern professional education which leads to employment opportunities in the modern sector.[132] In particular they have:

- Excellent teaching infrastructure including computer and other labs;
- International links to the Pakistani diaspora;
- Well-managed international websites based in the US (San Francisco); and
- International financial support for 'charitable' work.

Despite their modernity, the educational institutes of Jamaat-ul-Dawa practise a religious austerity that reflects the organisation's adherence to the Ahl-e-Hadith sect of Islam.[133] The values inculcated are those that can be broadly described as sacrificing the interests and comforts of the self for the cause of Islam. Despite their modern equipment, the buildings constructed by Jamaat-ul-Dawa—whether in the elite suburbs of Karachi or the earthquake-devastated parts of Pakistani

---

[130] Jamaat-ul-Dawa website [http://www.jamatdawah.org/pages.php?action=menu&id=71, accessed 15 Sept. 2006].
[131] These estimates are based on a review of a wide range of relevant sources by Marika Vicziany and Aneela Babar, *A Literature Review on Madrassahs in Pakistan* (Canberra: Ausaid, November 2006).
[132] The Jamaat-ul-Dawa Education Department manages '2000 model schools, two science colleges and eleven madrassas' according to Mohammed Amir Rana, *Gateway to Terrorism* (London: New Millenium Publication, 2003), p.340. 'Madrassas' in this instance refers to seminaries. Plans have also been developed for the establishment of specialist colleges for training engineers and doctors.
[133] *Ibid.*, p.331. The Ahl-e-Hadith emerged in South Asia in the 1830s. It aimed at religious reform *(islah)*, criticizing many existing religious practices as 'unlawful innovations' *(bida)*. It emphasises the original principles of Islam as against the interpretations of the four orthodox Sunni religious schools of interpretation.

Kashmir[134]—are simple, functional and devoid of distracting decorations. Moreover, many graduates service the needs of the system when they complete their education—either as professional workers attached to the organisation and engaged in charity work at low wages, or by holding highly-paid jobs and donating a sizeable proportion of their wages back to Jamaat-ul-Dawa. In other words, the culture of Jamaat-ul-Dawa educational institutions is informed by religious values but not in a manner that sacrifices modernity.

It is the prospect of receiving a modern professional education that attracts the Pakistan public to Jamaat-ul-Dawa schools and colleges. The students tend to come from middle-class or upwardly-mobile socioeconomic groups. Religious education is not ignored, but the system provides much more. For its clients Jamaat-ul-Dawa is not simply a *madrassa*. A *madrassa* in Pakistan is, strictly speaking, a school that provides religious education. The children who are sent there are not necessarily poor, but come from families who feel that at least one of their children should receive a proper religious upbringing. The desire for such an education reflects a view that such instruction is in itself virtuous.[135] (One thinks here of Catholic parents encouraging one of their offspring to go to a seminary with the intention of becoming a priest or nun.)

The curricula of *madrassas* continue to rely on traditional Arabic sources[136] and rote-learning methods; today there is great debate throughout South Asia about

---

[134] Lashkar-e-Taiba was the first relief group to arrive in Muzaffarabad after the earthquake of Oct. 2005: it pulled the living and the dead from the rubble and provided help before any other Pakistani or foreign agency. It had the capacity to do this because it is well-managed, well-funded, and highly-trained. In Muzaffarabad it set up a network of '. . .350 of itsjihadi members connected with wireless phones; 16 ambulances and mobile X-ray machines/ operation theatres; kitchens to feed 3,000 people daily; motorboats to rescue people from inaccessible areas; an orthopaedic unit under the supervision of Dr. Amir Aziz (who was arrested after the 9/11 for treating bin Laden and later acquitted by the Supreme Court)'. See Mohammed Shehzad, 'Pakistan—The State Fails, the Jihadi Prevails', in *South Asia Intelligence Review* (7 Nov. 2005) [http://www.satp.org, accessed 10 Jan. 2007]. See also Declan Walsh, 'Extremist Measures', *Guardian Unlimited* (18 Oct. 2006) [http://www.guardian.co.uk, accessed 3 Nov. 2006].

[135] There is growing evidence to reject the stereotypical view that *madrassas* only cater to the needs of extremely poor and illiterate families: recent fieldwork by Aneela Babar in Pakistan has confirmed the importance of religious motivations. See also Masooda Bano, 'Beyond Politics: The Reality of a Deobandi Madrasa in Pakistan', in *Journal of Islamic Studies,* Vol.18, no.1 (January 2007), pp.43–68 [http://intl-jis.oxfordjournals.org/current.dtl, p.15]. The work of Mumtaz Ahmad also rejects the link between poverty and *madrassas*. A 2000 survey showed that the dominant socioeconomic group represented in *madrassas* was 'peasant families and petty traders (55%) followed by those working in the "lower level private sector" (35%)'. See Mumtaz Ahmad, 'Madrassa Education in Pakistan and Bangladesh', in Satu P. Limaye, Robert Wirsing and Mohan Malik (eds), *Religious Radicalism and Security in South Asia* (Honolulu: Asia Pacific Centre for Security Studies, 2004), p. 108.

[136] Most reports stress that the medieval Arabic curriculum as taught today has shrunk and typically excludes the scientific subjects that used to be taught in the past. See Arif Jamal, 'The Dars Today', *The News on Sunday* (7 Aug. 2005), p.24. Moreover, there is no common curriculum: the various sects promote the works of their own leaders.

whether and how to reform them. However there is little evidence that *madrassas* in Pakistan are *jihadhi* factories. Instead the fuel for *jihad* in Pakistan comes from modern professional schools of the kind provided by Jamaat-ul-Dawa—an organisation that subscribes not to a fundamentalist Islam bogged down in textual disputes about medieval Arabic texts, but to a modernist constructed ideology of the sort that Meghnad Desai has eloquently described.[137]

To summarise, Lashkar-e-Taiba, which has been implicated in a number of violent bombings in India including the 1993 Mumbai blasts and more recently the Mumbai train bombings in July 2006,[138] is an unusual organisation that does not fit the stereotype of what an Islamic terrorist group should look like: it has tried to avoid sectarian conflict; it does not have strong links with *madrassas;* it upholds modern professional values and technologies; it appeals to upwardly-mobile and middle-class female professionals; and it is quintessentially a middle-class movement determined to right the perceived wrongs of the Muslims of South Asia. And it seeks to do all this without ignoring the need to increase Islamic consciousness. The hardest thing to explain about Lashkar-e-Taiba is why it exists as a terrorist organisation at all. Its social reform wing is a charitable organisation and Lashkar-e-Taiba itself is often the first organisation on the ground when Pakistan experiences a natural calamity such as the earthquake in late 2005. Understanding terrorism in Mumbai, for all these reasons, requires us to find the sources for a unique religious-military nexus that has emerged in Pakistan since the late 1970s when President Zia ul-Haq decided to marry state sponsorship of social organisations (including *madrassas)* with the inculcation of military values throughout society.

The Origins of *Jihad* and Militarism in Pakistan

Pakistan's *jihadi*-militaristic program did not begin with Lashkar-e-Taiba and its associated charity Jamaat-ul-Dawa. That agenda was developed—and continues to be maintained—by a succession of military governments who, lacking any other legitimacy, have created a special warrior culture that provides the basic fuel for ter-rorist organisations. Those warrior values have now thoroughly permeated Pakistan's religious organisations. Thus, as Babar notes, the country's religious leaders no longer need to find Islamic texts to justify violence. Such textual validation is superfluous; raw power has become a virtue of its own regardless of whether it is wielded by the state or religious organisations. Quoting the former *Amir* (head) of

---

[137] Meghnad Desai, *Rethinking Islamism: The Ideology of the New Terror* (London: I.B. Taurus, 2006).

[138] It is also suspected of having encouraged and funded a conspiracy in the UK to blow up ten passenger jets. The plot was intercepted and 23 suspects taken into custody. See Joshua Partlow and Kamran Khan, 'Charity Funds Said to Provide Clues to Alleged Terrorist Plot: Officials Say Money for Attacks Came from Earthquake Relief', *Washingtonpost.com* (15 Aug. 2006) [http://www.washingtonpost.com, accessed 3 Nov. 2006].

Jamaat-e-Islami based in Mansoorah, Babar writes: '.. if we have to use power or force to convince the people, it is justified. We have been instructed to put our lives in the path of God as it is the cause of truth'.[139]

As these words suggest, Pakistan's warrior culture has been conflated with religious idealism, a transition made possible by converting the professional soldier into a military hero. This transmogrification was essential because the economic diversification of the Pakistan economy created desirable employment opportunities in new industries such as IT, a process which devalued the traditional attractions of a military career. To compensate for the military's diminished prestige, the 'Soldier as Religious Hero' was born. Quoting Maulana A. Saleemi, one of Pakistan's most influential religious politicians,[140] Babar notes:

> The Pakistan military is competing against a country of *kafirs* (non-believers). So...I would say the soldier is a *ghazi* (martyr). We are taking his time and effort so we have to pay him.[141]

The Pakistan military has in recent times blatantly played on the religious sensitivities of the Pakistan people, including the use, in a highly selective manner, of 'The Sayings of the Holy Prophet' ('Sahee Bukhari Hadees') in its recruitment campaigns:

> And it has been said, to stay awake for one night in this war is better than to spend a thousand nights in prayer, and to stand steadfast in this war for one day is better than to spend sixty years in prayer, the fires of Hell have been banned on the eyes that stay awake in this war, the feet that have grown dusty in this war have been promised that they will never be dragged into the fires of Hell. Along with this, the people who have escaped war to stay at home and have hesitated at the call of war have been admonished in the sternest tone.[142]

The general public has also been subjected to the glorification of war in countless mundane ways. Military icons have, for example, entered into the public spaces of Pakistani cities where beautification programs have involved placing tanks and

---

[139] Aneela Babar, personal conversation with Amir Chaudhry Tufail at Mansoorah, April 1999, cited in Vicziany and Babar, *A Literature Review on Madrassahs in Pakistan*.
[140] Aneela Babar, personal conversation with Maulana A. Saleemi *(Naib Amir* or Deputy Head of Jamaat-e-Islami) at Mansoorah, April 1999, cited in Vicziany and Babar, *A Literature Review on Madrassahs in Pakistan*.
[141] A. Babar, *Texts of War: The Religio-Military Nexus in Pakistan and India* (Bangkok: Monograph 11, Gender Studies, Asian Institute of Technology, 2001), p.26.
[142] *Ibid.,* p.30.

missiles at important public intersections.¹⁴³ When residents of one neighbourhood objected to the sudden appearance of unsightly military hardware as urban decoration, the tanks were painted pink to make them more cheerful. But urban icons and military recruitment campaigns would be an insufficient basis for the generalised militarism that Pakistan manifests today. To understand the basic fuel of militarism and xenophobia, we need to turn to the curriculum of Pakistan's government schools.

The *Jihadi* Curricula of Pakistan's State Schools

The most pernicious aspect of the state-inspired militarism has been the manner in which the Curriculum Wing of the Ministry of Education has produced textbooks and curricula that promote (1) narrow views about who can legitimately be called a Pakistani Muslim, (2) hatred of all non-Muslims despite the religious complexity of Pakistan,¹⁴⁴ (3) hatred of India and Hindus, and (4) *jihad* and martyrdom and the virtues of war.¹⁴⁵ War Studies in particular forms an important sequence in the state's curricula and textbooks for Years XI and XII.¹⁴⁶ Typically, the lessons draw on a range of illustrations about Islamic heroes, Islamic teachers, Islamic history and Islamic literature of the narrowest and most distorted kind. True history begins with the arrival of Islam in Pakistan, and the evolution of society thereafter occurs in a vacuum that is unrelated to regional or global events. And the narratives of historical and cultural change are fraught with inaccuracies and deliberate distortions designed to serve the needs of the state and its beneficiaries.¹⁴⁷ One Punjab textbook for Class IV says: 'The religion of the Hindus did not teach them good things—Hindus did not respect women'.¹⁴⁸ The Social Studies textbook for Class VI reports: 'The people of the sub-continent used to live in dark and small houses before the arrival of the Muslims'.¹⁴⁹ And the end of the Indus Valley Civilisation for Class V students is described as a process by which Hindus '. . .treated the ancient population of the Indus Valley very badly. . .they set fire to their houses and butchered them'.¹⁵⁰ There is no mention here of the rich scholarly

---

¹⁴³ *Ibid.*, see various photographs.
¹⁴⁴ A.H. Nayyar, 'Insensitivity to the Religious Diversity of the Nation', in A.H. Nayyar and Ahmad Salim (comp.), *The Subtle Subversion: The State of Curricula and Textbooks in Pakistan (Urdu, English, Social Studies and Civics)* (Islamabad: SDPI Publications, 2003), pp.9–63.
¹⁴⁵ A.H. Nayyar and Ahmad Salim, 'Glorification of War and the Military', in A.H. Nayyar and Ahmad Salim (comp.), *The Subtle Subversion: The State of Curricula and Textbooks in Pakistan (Urdu, English, Social Studies and Civics)* (Islamabad: SDPI Publications, 2003), pp.79–91.
¹⁴⁶ *Ibid.*, pp.80–1. Paradoxically, it was Prime Minister Ali Bhutto who first introduced the War Studies program.
¹⁴⁷ Ahmad Salim, 'Historical Falsehoods and Inaccuracies', in A.H. Nayyar and Ahmad Salim (comp.), *The Subtle Subversion: The State of Curricula and Textbooks in Pakistan (Urdu, English, Social Studies and Civics)* (Islamabad: SDPI Publications, 2003), pp.63–73.
¹⁴⁸ Nayyar and Salim, 'Glorification of War and the Military', p.81.
¹⁴⁹ *Ibid.*, p.82.
¹⁵⁰ *Ibid.* Unfortunately the rise of Hindu fundamentalism in India over the last twenty years has seen the emergence there of similar concerns about the rewriting of textbooks to a serve narrow fundamentalist political agenda. See for

debates about the decline of the Indus Valley Civilisation; nor is there any hint of the complex process by which Hinduism eventually evolved over many thousands of year (after the decline of the Indus Valley) or the many intellectual questions about who the Indus people were and what replaced them.

In this manner, the state has sought to forge the ideal Pakistani citizen. No effort has been made to cultivate tolerance of ethnic or religious minorities, promote peaceful co-existence with neighbouring countries or the synergistic aspects of daily life in modern Pakistan. Aneela Babar, a participant of this system, remembers how unfavourable references to non-Muslims caused her classmates to shoot furtive, meaningful stares at any Christian or Ahmadiyya students who sat amongst them.[151] Pervez Hoodbhoy, one of the earliest critics of government education, notes that the standard of good citizenship promoted in Pakistan places a high value on respecting only authoritarian leadership and *jihad*.[152]

Ironically, it is these *government* texts that are imported into the *madrassas* and private schools of Pakistan by *reform-minded* teachers wanting to expand the curriculum in *modern* directions. As numerous studies have stressed, so long as the *madrassas* used only the arcane books of Arabic discourse, they lacked any ideological bias in favour of militarism or *jihad*—this because the old texts were the works of scholars who lived within Muslim-majority states where the pre-modern intelligentsia was not threatened by non-Muslims, and who thus were confident and comfortable with their cultural dominance and wrote texts from positions of strength. These were people who did not *need* to resort to *jihadi* terminology or the language of martyrdom. In the words of Mumtaz Ahmad, the study of Islamic law required careful attention to 'the problem of menstruation...and other legal hairsplitting rather than on political or jihadic issues'.[153] Today, the *jihadi* rhetoric of the military and educational authorities is amplified by input from the clergy, whose chief role is to ensure that the curriculum does not have any secular leanings. Not even iconic military leaders have been spared from attack—for example, General Ayub Khan has been criticised for introducing 'un-Islamic' family laws.[154] So: have the *madrassas*, via the modern state school curricula, been converted into recruiting centres for terrorism?

---

example Mushirul Hasan, 'The BJP's Intellectual Agenda: Textbooks and Imagined History', in *South Asia*, Vol.XXV, no.3 (Dec. 2002), pp. 187–209, and also published in John McGuire and Ian Copland (eds), *Hindu Nationalism and Governance* (New Delhi: Oxford University Press, 2007), pp.226–52.

[151] A special thanks to Dr. Aneela Babar, Honorary Research Fellow, Monash Asia Institute, for sharing this experience with me.

[152] Pervez Hoodbhoy, 'Deconstructing Muslim Terrorism', in Marika Vicziany (ed.), *Controlling Arms and Terror in the Asia Pacific: After Bali and Baghdad* (Cheltenham, UK and Northampton, MA: Edward Elgar, 2007), pp.117–29.

[153] Ahmad, 'Madrassa Education in Pakistan and Bangladesh', p. 114.

[154] Yvette Claire Rosser, 'Curriculum as Destiny: Forging National Identity in India, Pakistan and Bangladesh', unpublished PhD. thesis, The University of Texas at Austin, August 2003, p. 106.

The *Madrassas* and Terrorism

There can be no doubt that *some* Pakistan *madrassas* have been corrupted in this way. In particular, *madrassas* in Pakistan's border regions have been used to recruit 'warriors' for Afgahanistan and Kashmir. This is not surprising, since many of these border *madrassas* cater specifically to displaced people from Afghanistan.[155] Another reason is that when the Afghan militia fled across the border into Pakistan during the Soviet occupation, they set up military camps which they called *madrassas* to give them some kind of respectability.[156] Thirdly, in this part of Pakistan most of the *madrassas* are Deobandi, a tendency which, as noted above, is friendly to *jihad*.[157] In other words, regional culture is certainly a factor to consider when analysing the relationship between *madrassas* and terrorism. Similarly, *madrassas* in Punjab have provided a fertile recruitment ground for terrorists willing to be exported to Kashmir. By these standards, the Binori Town *madrassa* in central Karachi is an exception, as Karachi is not at the cross-roads of any international borders. Yet it is an extreme Deobandi centre with a long involvement with local sectarianism; its also boasts about its special links with Afghanistan's Taliban and home-grown extremists such as Maulana Masood Azhar who studied there.[158]

Despite this, the *madrassa* system as a whole has little direct association with transnational terrorism. Rather, the *madrassas* are busy fighting each other for students, teachers, leadership, funds and—above all—religious authority.[159] The consequences of this culture of violence have been devastating, and the worst-affected have been Pakistani citizens. Since independence, each decade has seen an escalation of sectarian conflict in Pakistan, the worst of it between the four Islamic sects, the Deobandi, Barelvi, Ahl-e-Hadith and Shia, that continue to carve up the

---

[155] Muhammad Qasim Zaman, *The Ulama in Contemporary Islam: Custodians of Change* (Princeton and Oxford: Princeton University Press, 2002), pp. 137–9. As Zaman notes, these *madrassas* gained a lot of prestige within Pakistan with the rise of the Taliban. *Ibid.*, pp.141–3.

[156] Ahmad is right to stress that these *madrassas* began as camps of war, not educational centres. As such they are very different from the typical South Asian *madrassa*. See Ahmad, 'Madrassa Education in Pakistan and Bangladesh', p. 115.

[157] Bano, 'Beyond Politics: The Reality of a Deobandi Madrasa in Pakistan', pp.8–9.

[158] See for example Farhana Ali, 'Pakistan's Madrassas Provide Safe Haven for al-Qaeda Militants', *Terrorism Focus* (14 March 2006) [http://jamestown.org/terrorism/news, accessed 4 Feb. 2007]; and Yahya Durrani, 'The Binori Town Madrassah: Vanguard of the Jihad', *Rediff.com* (16 Jan. 2000) [http://www.paklinks.com. accessed 4 Oct. 2007]. Google has 10,600 internet references to 'Binori Town Madrassa'. The Binori Town *madrassa's* image has been blended with the general reputation of violence in Karachi which includes the murder of journalist Daniel Pearl. See Justin Huggler, 'Karachi: A City of Violence, Murder and Islamic Militancy', *The Indepdendent* (19 July 2005) [http://news.independent.co.uk, accessed 4 Feb. 2007].

[159] There is new evidence to suggest that in parts of Pakistan, south Punjab for instance, the sectarian conflict may be hiding a deeper economic struggle between feudal Shia landlords and peasants belonging especially to the Deobandi sect. See Saleem H. Ali, 'Islamic Education and Conflict: Understanding the Madrassahs of Pakistan', (paper presented at the US Institute of Peace, 24 June 2005), MS of August 2005, pp.59, 80–82. It is too soon, however, to generalise from this case to the rest of Pakistan

community. The state of Punjab has been particularly caught up in this turmoil as Table 1 shows. In the six years between 2000 and 2005 almost 900 people are said to have been killed, and some 1,600 injured, in a total of 295 incidents. Moreover these are certainly underestimates because of the difficulty of determining the cause of death in rural areas. In a meticulous study of Ahmedpur district in Punjab, Saleem Ali has calculated that 80 percent of Deobandi *madrassas* have been involved in sectarian violence, followed by Shia *madrassas* (70 percent), Barelvi (25 percent) and Ahl-e-Hadith (14 percent).[160]

These four major Islamic sects have been both the cause and victims of their xenophobic teachings. The Deobandi, Barelvi, Ahl-e-Hadith and Shia hate each other as much as they despise Christians and Hindus. Small children are taught that people belonging to the 'other' schools are their enemies. In this way, Pakistani society has been slowly but relentlessly gnawing at itself, dissolving the fabric of social cohesion. Meanwhile, the sects have thrown up their own political parties which have, in turn, spawned militant adjuncts. These military units are widely recognised

Table 1
Incidence of Sectarian Violence in the Punjab: 2000 to 2005[161]

Year	Incidents	Killings	Injuries
2000	19	46	61
2001	102	211	320
2002	44	84	115
2003	39	126	185
2004	20	218	638
2005	71	207	330
Total	295	892	1649

Source: Ali Waqar, 'Another Attempt to Curb Sectarianism', *Friday Times* (Lahore) (1–7 Sept. 2006), p.4 [http://watandost.blogspot.com/2006_09_01_ archive.html, accessed 5 Feb. 2007].

---

[160] *Ibid.*, p.56.
[161] According to Amir Mir between 1989 and 2005 there were 1,866 sectarian events causing 4,279 injuries and 1,784 deaths. Cited in *Ibid.*, p.70.

as terrorist groups and they include the SSP (Sunni), SMP (Shia), and JUP (Barelvi). These cancerous growths have done inestimable damage to Pakistan since the first Shia–Sunni riots of the 1950s.[162]

Explaining the rise of sectarianism in Pakistan brings us back to the role of the state in engineering the post-independence political scenarios. As Rais has argued in the present volume, the separate political electorates that existed until 2002 when General Musharraf decided to re-introduce joint political electorates, provided an electioneering calculus that was divisive. Sectarian fanaticism was also fuelled by the decision to disinherit the Ahmadiyyas by changing the Pakistani constitution in 1973. Suddenly Pakistani society was filled with internal traitors. And the genuine non-Muslim minorities fared even worse thanks to the introduction of anti-blasphemy laws. Thus the ground was laid for violent sectarianism which, Professor Rais suggests, escalated as the capacities of the state declined.

Declining state capacity is, however, an insufficient factor to explain why Pakistani society began to implode. For one thing, the violence itself was largely the result of state action: through the educational system; through military recruitment; and through its co-option of religious leaders to support the ideology of extreme militarism that Islamabad had appropriated to define modern Pakistan. For another, sectarian differences alone could hardly have generated the level of social turmoil illustrated in Table 1. A few years ago Yoginder Sikand interviewed a fourteen-year-old Deobandi student in India. The young man said that his 'mission in life' was to 'combat un-Islamic ideologies'. That combat needed to focus on

> . . .all those groups that claim to be Muslim but are actually Zionist creations designed to destroy Islam from within. These include the followers of Maududi, Qadianis, the so-called Shi'as, the Barelwis and so on. . .they are all agents of the Devil.[163]

A Deobandi student in Pakistan would express himself in identical language, but the difference is that in Pakistan the existence of sectarian political parties, militias and terrorist adjuncts greatly increases the risk of an ideological dispute morphing into physical violence. The culture of the religious military hero may well have been initially directed at infidels, but in the peculiar circumstances of Pakistan it soon turned inwards and began to seek out 'soft' targets inside the country.

---

[162] S. Irfani, '[Pakistan] Religious Extremism: Fringe or Mainstream?', Parts 1 & 2, *Daily Times* (27 Aug. 2004 & 3 Sept. 2004) [http://www.dailytimes.com.pk/default.asp?page= story _27-8-2004_pg3_2, accessed 5 Feb. 2007].
[163] Yoginder Sikand, *Bastions of the Believers: Madrasas and Islamic Education in India* (New Delhi: Penguin India, 2005), p. 105.

Conclusion

The *madrassas* of India played no role in the March 1993 Mumbai bombings. The destruction inflicted on Mumbai by the explosions and related violence was a home-grown affair led by angry, disillusioned Muslims who felt that it would be cowardly not to respond to the war drums beaten by India's Hindu fundamentalists. Avenging the killing of Indian Muslims did not, however, make this into an instance of religious conflict. The leaders behind the Mumbai bombings were criminal syndicates that had flourished in the city for decades. The most powerful syndicate, Dawood Ibrahim's D-company, incorporated both Muslim and Hindu thugs. Dawood Ibrahim has not yet been brought to trial and so evidential links between him and the bombings remains uncertain. The operational brain behind the Mumbai blasts appears to have been 'Tiger' Memon—another Mumbai criminal. But like Dawood Ibrahim, he has not been brought to trial either. Instead members of his family have been convicted, as part of a mixed group of some 100 convictions. Moreover, the extensive bribery needed to bring explosives and ammunition into Mumbai required the support of Indian police and customs authorities, the bulk of whom were Hindu.

The 100 persons convicted for the violence that hit Mumbai city on 12 March 1993 were not mainly poor, desperate, or unemployed Muslims or Hindus. With few exceptions, nor do they appear to have been illiterate. Evidence thus far confirms the Sageman-Pape hypothesis stated at the start of this paper, although closer study of the particular groups involved in the bombings may reveal that the individuals who had received weapons training in Pakistan were of a much lower socioeco-nomic status than the 'masterminds'. One important caveat remains to be repeated in this conclusion: the evidence on which these 100 persons have been convicted remains beyond the reach of the public. Final conclusions about the Mumbai bombings are not, therefore, possible until the vast body of data has been systematically analysed. In particular, it is necessary to sift those who unintentionally were caught up in this conspiracy from those who were recruited, willingly or unwillingly, to target the commercial heart of India. This paper, therefore, has the status of an interim survey. Despite this, there is no whisper of any *madrassa* involvement— not in India or in Pakistan.

The notion that Pakistani *madrassas* may have been involved derives from the alleged links that Dawood Ibrahim has with the ISI and Lashkar-e-Taiba. The former protected Dawood Ibrahim from the Indian authorities, and the latter may well have provided the weapons training that some of convicted Mumbai citizens received in Pakistan. At the moment, exactly who provided that training is unknown. Nevertheless, the alleged complicity of Lashkar-e-Taiba in the Mumbai bombings provides one with an opportunity to explore the nature of the educational training providing by Jamaat-ul-Dawa, Pakistan's largest charity, and one that was established by Lashkar-e-Taiba.

Therefore, the second part of the paper addressed the question of whether Pakistani *madrassas* are central to our understanding of the Mumbai bombings. The findings are fairly unequivocal in this regard. They do not bear out the conventional view of what supports terrorism in Pakistan. Jamaat-ul-Dawa represents a modern technocratic approach to education. It attracts mainly middle-class Pakistanis and belongs more to the private school system than to the *madrassa* system whose curricula are based on arcane Arabic texts. But whether we look at the old Arabic curricula or the new technocratic curricula of Jamaat-ul-Dawa, we will not find the basis for teachings that inspire hate and international terrorism. The search for the origin of Pakistan's 'hate campaigns' takes us rather to the *government* curricula that have been developed in the first instance for government schools. During the last three decades, these curricula have assiduously promoted military values and *jihad*. In raising religious-military heroism to national prominence, the government-controlled school curricula of Pakistan have created their own communal monster which increasingly is directing its energy against internal enemies rather than India. The significance of these government texts needs to be appreciated if we are to develop policies that effectively respond to the growing violence inside Pakistan and on its borders.

In the hierarchy of terror, the *madrassas* of South Asia rank low in importance; in the case of the March 1993 bombings in Mumbai they were off the radar. In understanding those blasts, described by some observers as a terrorist attack that heralded 9/11, we need to come to grips with how various factors coalesced to bring about the destruction of so many people and so much property: criminal gangs; corrupt Hindu officials; angry and victimised local Muslims; the ISI and Lashkar-e-Taiba in Pakistan; the religious-military values promoted by Pakistan's leaders and politicians; and the Pakistan state school text books that propagate hatred and intolerance of the non-righteous 'Other'.

Force and Compromise: India's Counter-Insurgency Grand Strategy

Rajesh Rajagopalan

The Indian Union has one of the world's most successful records in fighting insurgencies. It has not yet lost a counter-insurgency campaign within the country; its only unsuccessful campaign was the one it fought against the Liberation Tigers of Tamil Eelam (LTTE) guerrillas in Sri Lanka in the late 1980s. Victory and loss in insurgency campaigns is, of course, relative, as expressed in the general belief among military professionals that a counter-insurgency campaign can only be lost, not won. This would find support in the Indian record: most of India's domestic insurgencies continue, though the Indian Army and other security forces have managed to contain their intensity to very low levels. Only the Mizo insurgency can be considered to have been resolved (though even in Mizoram some insurgent activity does continue). Punjab, which can be seen as one major victory, is not considered here because it never managed to progress from a terrorist movement to a fully-fledged insurgency—and the Punjab Police rather than the Indian Army was the primary force fighting it.

The Indian success in counter-insurgency campaigns owes a lot to its very political approach to counter-insurgency. The Indian state has always seen counter-insurgency as a political rather than a military problem, and it has insisted that the Indian Army accept it as such. Even more creditably, the Indian Army has accepted such a characterisation and now, typically, assimilates this value and all that it encompasses much more rigorously than its civilian masters.[1] That the Indian Army has had its own organisational–cultural reasons for accepting such

---

[1] Rajesh Rajagopalan, '"Restoring Normalcy": The Evolution of the Indian Army's Counter-Insurgency Doctrine', in *Small Wars and Insurgencies*, Vol.XI, no.1 (Spring 2000), pp.44–68.

a characterisation should not in any way take credit away from the army on this count.

The Indian approach has also been relatively 'soft' when considered against the universe of such campaigns. I must hasten to add that this is not to suggest that there have not been humanitarian and human rights problems associated with them.[2] Counter-insurgency campaigns are always particularly ugly because both sides use and abuse the non-combatants for whose support they vie. But the Indian Army has deliberately adopted a less violent approach to counter-insurgency than most other armies of the world—abjuring, for example, the use of artillery and air support in such operations. Thus the intensity of violence has remained *relatively* lower than in other counter-insurgency campaigns, which has made it easier for the opposing sides to compromise in pursuit of a political resolution—which is of course the idea behind imposing limitations on violence.

This essay looks first at the theory of counter-insurgency warfare in order to situate the Indian approach. I argue that conventional forces tend to have difficulty fighting counter-insurgency campaigns because the most effective and appropriate method to fight such wars, which requires dispersal of forces and small unit operations, are also the most difficult for conventional forces to adopt because the latter tend to emphasise the opposite: concentration of forces and large-scale operations.[3] The second part of the essay looks at some of the major counter-insurgency campaigns that the Indian Army has been engaged in since independence. The final part looks at some broad conclusions that can be drawn from the Indian experience.

Counter-Insurgency Theory and Conventional Forces

Despite the Indian Army's long experience with counter-insurgency, it is not a task that the army is comfortable with. Even today, the army would be happier if it were confined to what it considers to be the more glorious and unambiguous task of defending the borders against foreign threats rather than fighting fellow citizens. Such sentiments are not helped by the belief of many in the army that the insurgents have legitimate grievances against a corrupt and uncaring political elite.[4] But such discomfort in fighting these campaigns is not peculiar to the Indian Army. They lie in the nature of such campaigns.

---

[2] Even accounts by army officers reveal cases of the abuse of human rights. See for example Shyamol Kumar Sinha, *A Soldier Recalls* (New Delhi: Lancer International, 1992), pp.214–6.

[3] Rajagopalan, '"Restoring Normalcy"', pp.48–68.

[4] See for example Col. R.D. Palsokar, 'Essentials of Guerrilla War,' in *USI Journal*, Vol.103 (January–March 1973), p.39.

The reason for such attitudes is that most conventional armies have great difficulty in adapting themselves to the task of counter-insurgency. Conventional armies are designed to fight positional wars with other conventional armies. Even when they fight guerrilla wars, they adopt counter-insurgency doctrines that have a positional-war bias. This leads them to fight as they do in conventional positional wars and makes them increasingly frustrated when their efforts result in little success. Andrew Krepinevich argues that the US Army, despite paying lip service to the need for a distinct counter-insurgency doctrine, continued to apply the 'Army Concept'—a conventional, positional-war approach designed to deal with a Soviet invasion of central Europe—in fighting the Viet Cong guerrillas.[5] Similarly, in Afghanistan, the Soviet Union strategy emphasised large-scale use of air power and artillery, along with an emphasis on holding territory. In both cases, though these armies adopted counter-insurgency doctrines, their counter-insurgency doctrines had a positional-war bias.

It is understandable that conventional armies will apply existing positional-war doctrines, even when faced with counter-insurgency war. Even the (eventually) successful British effort in the Boer War (1899–1902) began with the British Army using positional-war-oriented doctrines, which emphasised traditional large unit operations and heavy artillery. On the other hand, when the traditional approach failed, the British Army successfully innovated smaller units with greater mobility and less reliance on heavy artillery, and isolated the civilian population in concentration camps away from the rebels.[6] The above case, however, is an exception. Most conventional armies find it difficult to adopt counter-insurgency doctrines that are not afflicted with the positional-war bias. This difficulty can be traced to the nature of insurgencies and the tasks that face an army in a counter-insurgency operation.

Though terms such as 'insurgency' and 'guerrilla' are sometimes used interchangeably, an insurgency can be characterised as an armed rebellion that seeks to replace existing political authority.[7] Guerrilla war, its most common synonym, simply describes one military stage in an insurgency in which the rebels adopt a strategy of hit-and-run attacks by small armed bands against the larger forces of the state.

Insurgencies go through various political and military stages. Very broadly these can be divided into the political-preparatory stage, the guerrilla war stage and the

---

[5] Andrew F. Krepinevich, *The Army and Vietnam* (Baltimore: Johns Hopkins University Press, 1986), pp.4–7.
[6] Thomas Pakenham, *The Scramble for Africa* (London: Abacus, 1991), pp.572–80.
[7] Julian Paget, *Counter-Insurgency Operations: Techniques of Guerrilla Warfare* (New York: Walker and Company, 1967), pp.14–15.

conventional war stage.[8] Most armies get into counter-insurgency operations during the second (guerrilla) stage of an insurgency. In this stage, rebels conduct hit-and-run operations designed to harass the superior government forces and cut the lines of communication between strongholds such as cities.[9] As the relative capabilities of the opposing forces shift in favour of the rebels, they conduct larger-scale operations and begin to hold territory. Eventually, when the rebel forces are strong enough, they form a conventional army with large units and heavy weapons such as tanks and artillery and engage government forces in set piece, positional battles designed to deliver the final blow. This 'war of movement' represents the third stage of the insur[10]gency. In theory, at this stage the rebels will be strong enough to defeat the government's forces on the battlefield. On the other hand, for the rebels, knowing when to make this transition to positional war can be critical and difficult.[11] If the transition is made too hastily, they can be defeated on the battlefield, derailing the entire insurgency. Just such a premature transition was responsible for the decimation of the communist forces in southern China in 1930.[12] In Sri Lanka, similarly, the Tamil Tigers paid a heavy price for attempting to hold Jaffna city against superior Indian forces in the early stages of the Indian operations there. Of course, insurgencies can differ from this broad template. What is common to all insurgencies, however, is the guerrilla war stage.[13]

Guerrilla strategy is determined by the weakness of the guerrillas in relation to the military forces of the state. This weakness precludes a direct trial of strength with the state. The guerrillas therefore follow a strategy of denial, of progressively weakening and ultimately denying the government control over its territory and population which leads to a corresponding rise in the strength of the insurgency. In other words, the guerrilla stage of an insurgency is aimed at the progressive reversal

---

[8] These are my characterisations. Every writer on guerrilla war suggests some variation of this pattern. See in particular Douglas S. Blaufarb, *The Counter-Insurgency Era: U.S. Doctrine and Performance, 1950 to the Present* (New York: The Free Press, 1977), pp.3–11; Robert Thompson, *Defeating Communist Insurgencies: Experiences from Malaysia and Vietnam* (New York: Walker and Company, 1967), Ch. 3; Baljit Singh and Ko-Wang Mei, *Theory and Practice of Modern Guerrilla Warfare* (Bombay: Asia Publishing House, 1971), Ch.3; and David Galula, *Counter-Insurgency Warfare: Theory and Practice* (New York: Frederick A. Praeger Publishers, 1964), Ch.3.
[9] Galula, *Counter-Insurgency Warfare*, pp.48–53. The specifics of these tactics are detailed by Mao in his pamphlet *On Guerrilla Warfare* published in 1937. See Mao Tse-tung, *On Guerrilla Warfare* (trans. and ed. Brig.-Gen. Samuel B. Griffiths II) (New York: Praeger Publishers, 1961), pp.46–7.
[10] Blaufarb, *The Counter-Insurgency Era*, p.5; Galula, *Counter-Insurgency Warfare*, pp.53–8; and Thompson, *Defeating Communist Insurgencies*, pp.42–3.
[11] Of course, all these are pure categories. In reality, these stages might be mixed, and it is not always possible for contemporary observers to decide what stage the insurgency is at.
[12] Edward R. Rice, *Wars of the Third Kind: Conflict in Under developed Countries* (Berkeley CA: University of California Press, 1988), pp.82–3, 88; and Thompson, *Defeating Communist Insurgencies*, pp.42–3. See also Gerard Chaliand, *Terrorism: From Popular Struggle to Media Spectacle* (London: Saqi Books, 1987), pp.58–9.
[13] Heilbrunn provides the best account of guerrilla operations, which he calls 'partisan warfare'. See Otto Heilbrunn, *Partisan Warfare* (New York: Frederick A. Praeger Publishers, 1962), Ch.4 & 5.

of the balance of power between the insurgents and the government, which allows the former to turn into an orthodox, conventional military force that can defeat the government in a direct confrontation.[14] A strategy of denial, by definition, does not require the guerrillas to control either the territory or the population; all that is required is for the guerrillas to use their limited capability to prise away the government's control over its population. This denial strategy is accomplished by selective attacks and ambushes on isolated outposts and lines of communications which expose the vulnerability of the government's military forces. The purpose of these attacks is not to defeat the state forces, or even to eliminate the unit that is targeted, but to force persistent vulnerability on the army and force it to into defensive passivity. Mao Tse-tung argued that in 'protracted war' it is vitally important for the guerrillas to maintain their own initiative and force the enemy into passivity: 'Passivity is...always disadvantageous and one must try to get out of it by all means'.[15]

This strategy of denial is supported by a guerrilla military doctrine which stresses three basic principles: secrecy, surprise, and speed.[16] Secrecy is possible as the guerrillas gain the support of the people and conversely, as the government can no longer depend on the population for intelligence and information. Surprise is the result of careful preparation before operations and is essential because of the weakness of the guerrillas. Speed is a function of the mobility of the guerrillas, who generally carry only light equipment.

Another fundamental principle of guerrilla military doctrine is pragmatism in operations. In practice, this means that the guerrillas maintain the engagement only as long as they have the advantage, and break off contact when the advantage shifts to the enemy.[17] The Viet Minh manual on guerrilla warfare, for example, suggests withdrawal in the face of a superior enemy and warns against obstinacy in pressing home attacks unless victory is assured.[18] The point is to make government forces vulnerable, even without winning every engagement. When attacking weakly-protected convoys or isolated military posts, the guerrillas may press their attacks because they enjoy the necessary superiority to eliminate the enemy.

---

[14] Mao, *On Guerrilla Warfare*, pp.56–7.

[15] Mao Tse-tung, 'On Protracted War', in *Selected Works, Vol.II* (London: 1954), p.211, as cited in Heilbrunn, *Partisan Warfare*, p.56. Of course, if the chance does present itself, the guerrillas will attempt to eliminate the unit that they have attacked.

[16] Heilbrunn, *Partisan Warfare*, p.92, citing the Viet Minh manual. In Sri Lanka, an Indian journalist recounts a Tamil Tiger commander's instructions to his 'boys' before sending them into battle: 'stealth, speed and surprise'. See Shyam Tekwani, 'Sri Lanka: In the Tiger's Den', *India Today* (15 Nov. 1987), p.32.

[17] Paget, *Counter-Insurgency Operations*, p.25. Mao, for example, suggests: 'When the guerrillas engage a stronger enemy, they withdraw when he advances; harass him when he stops; strike him when he is weary; pursue him when he withdraws'. Mao, *On Guerrilla Warfare*, p.46.

[18] Heilbrunn, *Partisan Warfare*, pp.78–9.

On the other hand, because the purpose is harassment rather than victory, the attack can be broken off quickly and guerrillas withdrawn and dispersed when they have caused enough damage or when the battle begins to turn against them.[19]

The guerrilla strategy of isolated but sharp and frequent attacks presents the government with a dilemma. In order to maintain its control over territory and population, the ruling regime is forced to deploy its forces in a widely-dispersed pattern which stretches them thin. Moreover, maintaining such a pattern of deployment requires extended lines of communications, which are vulnerable to attack. If such attacks increase, the government may be prompted to withdraw its more exposed and vulnerable forces and consolidate them in stronger positions. This reduces the problem of vulnerability of the deployed forces and also shortens the lines of communications. On the other hand, it leaves vast stretches of territory under the control of the guerrillas. Guerrilla strategy succeeds by denying the government control over its territory and population.

Effective Counter-Insurgency Warfare

What are the appropriate objectives for the government in counter-insurgency warfare and how do these affect counter-insurgency military strategy and doctrine?[20] Successful counter-insurgency efforts aim at preventing insurgents from replacing state authority. If significant territorial control has been lost, efforts must aim not just at regaining it but, more importantly, at retaining such control. But retaining authority over all parts of the country simultaneously requires spreading governmental forces thinly across the territory, despite the above-mentioned vulnerability of such diluted and dispersed deployment, because success and failure in an insurgency is determined by who controls the most population and territory, not by which side wins more engagements.

The US Army in Vietnam clearly won more engagements, killed more enemy soldiers, and proved its superiority in military capabilities but still lost the war.[21]

---

[19] The Viet Minh manual suggests two types of operations that aim at the annihilation of the enemy, the 'surprise attack' and the 'commando raid'. However, both assume superiority of the guerrillas at the point of engagement. Heilbrunn, *Partisan Warfare*, pp.94–5.

[20] Counter-guerrilla war is a more accurate description of this type of warfare than counter-insurgency. However, counter-insurgency is the more widely accepted and used term. Besides, military counter-guerrilla operations form a component of a larger political–military counter-insurgency strategy. Making a distinction between the broader counter-insurgency policies and the specific military counter-guerrilla strategies may be useful in other instances, but is unnecessarily cumbersome for the purposes of this essay. In addition, for the military itself, there is little distinction between counter-insurgency and counter-guerrilla war. Rather, the distinction is between these types of war and conventional war. So counter-insurgency is as appropriate a term as counter-guerrilla to describe these kinds of war. What is lost in accuracy will hopefully be compensated for by the convenience of the usage.

[21] Harry G. Summers, *On Strategy: A Critical Analysis of the Vietnam War* (Novato, CA: Presidio, 1982), p.1.

This is because the American forces were deployed mainly in well-protected bases, rather than dispersed among the population in rural areas.[22] Similarly, the success of the British counter-insurgency effort in Malaya was at least partly the consequence of the British refusal to withdraw from rural areas after the Malayan People's Anti-British Army (MPABA), the military wing of the Malayan Communist Party (MCP), began the insurgency in 1948. Instead, the British put up defensive systems around population centres operated by the civilian Special Constabulary, which thwarted the objectives of the insurgents.[23] Likewise, the French instituted a 'quadrillage' or grid system in Algeria, which emphasised holding on to population centres. The system was effective, especially during the early stages of the insurgency.[24] This advantage was wasted, however, because of indiscriminate French military violence against Algeria's civilian population, both through retaliatory killings and the use of torture as a semi-official policy.[25]

Reasserting control over the territory and population can be accomplished through a number of different strategies. Which strategy is adopted will be determined by the situation and the capability of the military commanders. Specific strategies to retake and retain government control over territory and population include the resettlement of vulnerable populations to isolate them from the guerrillas; various types of clear and hold strategies such as the 'outward blockade', which the British Army used during the Boer War and the Japanese Army used in the north China plains during World War II; and the 'oil-spot' strategy, in which the military spreads outwards like an expanding oil spot, to bring more and more territory under government control.[26] All these strategies have the same objective: reasserting control over territory and population. Of course, once territory is retaken, the government has to maintain its control over this territory. This requires diluted and dispersed deployment of forces. Counter-insurgency military doctrines must reflect this requirement by emphasising such deployment patterns and prescribing methods for conducting such operations.

In addition—as a corollary to retaining control over the newly-recovered territory and population—the government has to aim at keeping the insurgents on the

---

[22] The major exceptions to this pattern were the Combat Action Platoons (CAPs) of the Marines, which were deployed in small units in villages and which were relatively successful. See Michael E. Peterson, *The Combined Action Platoons: The U.S. Marines' Other War in Vietnam* (New York: Praeger, 1989).

[23] Edgar O'Ballance, *Malaya: The Communist Insurgent War, 1948–60* (Hamden: Archon Books, 1966), pp.82–4. To some extent, the British were aided by the sheer incompetence of the MPABA during the early stages of this struggle.

[24] Edgar O'Ballance, *The Algerian Insurrection, 1954–62* (Hamden, Con.: Archon Books, 1967), pp.64–6; and Alistair Horne, *A Savage War of Peace: Algeria 1954–1962* (New York: The Viking Press, 1977), pp.165–9.

[25] Horne, *A Savage War of Peace*, pp.195–207.

[26] Rice, *Wars of the Third Kind*, pp.92–103; Thompson, *Defeating Communist Insurgencies*, pp.111–17; and Heilbrunn, *Partisan Warfare*, pp.66–7.

defensive and away from population and economic centres. Forcing the guerrillas on the defensive requires the military to seek out the guerrillas and deprive them of the capability to concentrate their forces unmolested. However, large-scale operations designed to clear guerrillas from specific areas—the classic 'search-and-destroy' mission—will be unsuccessful because guerrilla forces can easily detect and avoid such cumbersome assaults. Most successful counter-guerrilla operations have used offensive patrolling units which emulate the guerrillas in being small and highly mobile. This imitative strategy was used with great effectiveness by the German Army Jagdkommando (commando hunters) units in Russia during World War II and by the British 'ferret force' in Malaya.[27]

Counter-insurgency strategies of this type can allow a government to deny guerrillas control over rural areas even if it is unable, itself, to maintain a continuous and permanent presence there. The small size of such units also prevents them from being betrayed when operating among hostile populations, as was the case with the Jagdkommandos in Russia. In addition, such operations allow the state forces to gain much-needed intelligence, and decrease the vulnerability of state forces that are deployed in fixed positions. In short, a successful counter-insurgency strategy hinges on the use of small-unit rather than large-unit operations.

Counter-insurgency military doctrines have to reflect the prominent, if not the exclusive, use of small-unit rather than large-unit operations. Such operations emphasise different skills, weapons, and even attitudes. Counter-insurgency military doctrines must reflect this also.[28] Yet the doctrinal requirements of the dilution and dispersal of forces across a broad theatre of operations, as well as the conduct of small-unit offensives against guerrillas, present difficulties for conventional armies. Diluted deployment of forces contradicts a fundamental principle of positional war, the principle of mass, which is deeply ingrained in military minds.[29] Though military theorists

---

[27] Heilbrunn, *Partisan Warfare*, pp.65–9; and O'Ballance, *Malaya*, pp.87–8.

[28] Though small-unit operations are most prominent, larger-scale operations might sometimes be useful. If large concentrations of insurgents are located, the government forces can use large units in encirclement operations. However, such operations are difficult to coordinate and are only rarely successful. At best, such operations provide the government temporary relief by dislocating the insurgents from their base areas. Examples of such encirclement operations include the Russian operations in the Caucasus against the forces of Imam Shamyl in the 1850s, the Chinese Nationalist offensives against Mao's Red Army bases in Jiangxi Province, especially the Fifth Offensive, and various German and Italian offensives against Tito's forces in occupied Yugoslavia during the Second World War. See Rice, *Wars of the Third Kind*, pp.98–9; and Heilbrunn, *Partisan Warfare*, pp.66–7. I do not include these operations in studying counter-insurgency wars, both because such operations are neither prominent nor useful, and because they reflect conventional doctrinal influences.

[29] The principle of mass is also sometimes referred to as the principle of concentration. Maj.-Gen. D.K. Palit, *The Essentials of Military Knowledge* (London: C. Hurst, 1968), pp.128–31; Julian Lider, *Military Theory: Concept, Structure, Problems* (New York: St. Martin's Press, 1983), p.222; Hew Strachan, *European Armies and the Conduct of War* (London: George Allen and Unwin, 1983), pp.1–2, 73; and J.F.C. Fuller, *The Conduct of War,1789–1961* (New Brunswick: Rutgers University Press, 1961).

emphasise that all principles, including that of mass, are meant only as guidelines, conventional armies habitually prefer to concentrate their forces. In addition, the principle of mass only refers to the application of maximum force at the point of decision, and thus should be as applicable to guerrilla war as to conventional positional war.[30] However conventional armies have generally interpreted this principle to mean consolidation of forces in large units. Inevitably, the counter-insur-gency doctrines adopted by conventional armies also tend to stress large-unit operations. This has led to an emphasis on ineffective large-unit operations when such conventional armies engage in guerrilla wars.

On the other hand, such a deployment pattern may be unavoidable in a conventional positional war. Diluted-deployment when facing a conventional enemy can lead to military disaster because thinly-deployed forces are highly vulnerable to conventional adversaries. Two instances from recent South Asian military history can illustrate this. In 1962 the Indian Army was sparsely deployed along the Himalayan border with China, responding to a political imperative of maintaining a presence along that disputed frontier. When the Chinese Army attacked, it quickly overpowered and penetrated the weak Indian line, routing the Indian Army.[31] Similarly, in 1971 the Pakistan Army was thinly deployed along the India–East Pakistan border to defeat what was expected to be a limited Indian probe. The Indian Army took advantage of this light deployment to carry out a *blitzkrieg* that netted more than 90,000 prisoners of war and dismembered the eastern wing of Pakistan to form the new state of Bangladesh.[32] Thus, though it is inappropriate in guerrilla war, the principle of mass is not easy for conventional armies to ignore.

To summarise, the objectives of counter-insurgency war require dispersal and dilution of forces. Such a pattern of deployment contradicts one of the fundamental principles of positional war, the principle of mass, which is the basis of the organisation of conventional forces. Thus, most conventional armies tend to adopt counter-insurgency doctrines that exhibit a positional-war bias by emphasising concentration of forces and large-unit operations. Counter-insurgency doctrines with such positional-war bias lead to the defeat of conventional armies in guerrilla wars.

---

[30] In fact, Mao's writings as well as the Viet Minh manual stress the concentration of superior forces against the enemy during combat. Mao, *On Guerrilla Warfare*, pp.102–3; and Heilbrunn, *Partisan Warfare*, pp.56–7, and esp. pp.96–7.
[31] Brig. J.S. Dalvi, *Himalayan Blunder: The Curtain Raiser to the Sino–Indian War of 1962* (Bombay: Thacker and Company, 1969); Sita Ram Johri, *Chinese Invasion of Ladakh* (Lucknow: Himalayan Publications, 1968); and Lorne J. Kavic, *India's Quest for Security: Defence Policies, 1947–1965* (Berkeley: University of California Press, 1967).
[32] Pran Chopra, *India's Second Liberation* (Cambridge, Mass.: The MIT Press, 1974); and K. Subramanyam and Mohammad Ayoob, *The Liberation War* (New Delhi: S. Chand, 1984).

The Indian Experience

India's counter-insurgency efforts employed both political measures and military force. Though each iteration of these combinations of efforts looks messy and *suigeneris*, there is a common underlying grand strategy. On the other hand, it is difficult to say whether this is a conscious strategy or whether it has evolved out of the deep background of Indian strategic culture. The essence of this strategy is the willingness to compromise with rebellious sub-nationalities on all issues with one exception: secession is taboo. In order to permit such compromises, it was essential that military force be kept carefully limited—though force *was* used, and frequently. This grand strategy was evident in all the major counter-insurgency campaigns, and it has been effective in avoiding defeat, a major objective in guerrilla wars. The following section first looks at the Naga and Mizo campaigns.

The Naga and the Mizo territories were among the last to be brought under Britain's colonial administration in India. The term 'administration' is used loosely here, because the primary objective of the colonial government was to ensure that the Nagas and the Mizos were sufficiently pacified to ensure tranquillity along the plains that bordered these regions, which had been subject to frequent raids by both the Nagas and the Mizos. Both areas were categorised as 'Excluded Areas', which limited their contact with the rest of India and, as a consequence, isolated them from political developments in the rest of India including the Indian independence movement. Although, with independence, these areas became part of the Indian Union, both the Naga and the Mizo territories were given a special administrative status that allowed them a substantial degree of autonomy.

This arrangement, however, did not satisfy all Nagas and Mizos: some, especially among the Nagas, demanded total independence.[33] Under the leadership of Angami Zapu Phizo, they began an armed rebellion in 1955, which led to the induction of the Indian Army into the Naga Hills in 1956. Unfamiliar with both the terrain and the populace, the Indian Army faced a number of difficulties in its initial operations, including inadequate intelligence. Most Nagas lived in an autonomous Naga Hills District in the state of Assam; but some also lived in the Tuensang Frontier Division of the North-East Frontier Agency (NEFA), which was directly administered by the central government. In response to demands from moderate Nagas, New Delhi formed a new administrative unit called the Naga Hills–Tuensang Area (NHTA) in December 1957, carving out the Naga Hills District

---

[33] Though difficult to state with any degree of precision, more Nagas appeared dissatisfied with the arrangements than do Mizos. For example the Nagas, in response to the call of secessionist leaders, boycotted the local assembly elections in 1951 and national elections in 1952. The Mizos, on the other hand, consistently and overwhelmingly supported the Mizo Union, a political party which advocated staying in India, as opposed to the United Mizo Freedom Organisation which advocated secession.

from Assam and placing it directly under central administration. When this concession did not satisfy all the insurgents, and in order to further strengthen the moderate faction within the Naga elite, a new state called 'Nagaland' with a local legislature was created in 1963 to replace the NHTA.

At the same time, the Indian government continued pressure through the army. This was the Indian army's first counter-insurgency experience, and careful control was exercised by the centre in respect of the quantity of force used. For example, air power, despite army demands, was not permitted in support of counter-insurgency operations,[34] with the result that army officers frequently complained of the restrictions that forced them to fight with 'one arm tied behind their backs', as it were.[35] Nevertheless, India's use of force was helped, at least in the early days, by the Naga tendency to fight a conventional rather than a guerrilla campaign, a consequence of the Naga experience in the British Army. Even after the Nagas switched to guerrilla tactics, the Indian Army's carefully modulated use of force prevented complete Naga alienation from India, and helped the effort to begin ceasefire negotiations.

In September 1964 a ceasefire came into force to allow negotiations between the government and the Naga rebels. (At one point Indira Gandhi, the Indian prime minister, actually negotiated directly with leaders of the Naga rebels.) But the latter were unwilling to accept anything short of complete independence, which New Delhi refused to concede. Despite several further rounds of negotiations, no final settlement could be reached, and as the years dragged on the Indian authorities became increasingly frustrated by Naga procrastination—which they interpreted as a delaying tactic designed to give the Nagas time to improve their military capability. Moreover reports started to come in of the Nagas seeking—and apparently receiving—assistance from Pakistan and China, India's regional adversaries. Citing violations of the ceasefire agreement by the Naga rebels, the Indian government ended the ceasefire in September 1972. But further negotiations led to a breakthrough and the signing of the Shillong Accord of November 1975 under which most Naga rebels accepted being bound by the Indian constitution.

The Accord marked a victory for the Indian government's bottom-line strategy: that no secession would be permitted, but that everything else, including the political rehabilitation of former rebel leaders and cadres, was open to negotiation. In the event a Naga regiment was formed within the Indian Army, while another group

---

[34] Sarvepalli Gopal, *Jawaharlal Nehru: A Biography,Vol.2, 1947–1956* (Cambridge, Mass.: Harvard University Press, 1979), p.211.
[35] P.D. Stracey, *Nagaland Nightmares* (New Delhi: Allied Publishers, 1968), p.114.

of Naga fighters who had rebelled against the Naga high command and surrendered to the Indian Army were inducted into the Border Security Force (BSF).[36]

Even so, a small number of Nagas insisting on full secession stubbornly continued the fight. At first their relative weakness prevented them from posing a serious challenge to the Army, and Nagaland enjoyed more than a decade of peace. But in the late 1980s a combination of official incompetence and corruption led to increased popular frustration and reinvigorated the insurgency. Meanwhile the rebels had split. The original Naga Federal Army (NFA) was displaced by the National Socialist Council of Nagaland (NSCN), formed in 1980 by dissidents from the NFA led by Isak Chishi Swu and Thuingaleng Muivah. In the late 1980s, tribal differences within the NSCN led to a further split, with S.S. Khaplang, a Myanmarese Naga leader, forming his own distinct group called the NSCN-K (as distinguished from the original group, now known as the NSCN-IM. Differences between these groups remain fierce: in April 1988 an attack by NSCN-K forces on the NSCNIM guerillas resulted in more than one hundred cadres of the latter being killed.[37]

The Naga insurgency also became complicated in the 1990s by the intermixing of various ethnic conflicts. Not only are the Nagas themselves divided along tribal lines, they are also involved in inter-tribal conflicts with, among others, the Kukis. This process was accelerated when the Naga insurgency spread into the neighbouring Manipur state, which is home not only to a large population of Nagas but also to ethnic groups such as the Meitis (the majority group in Manipur), the Kukis, the Paites, and the Vaiphies. Almost every one of these groups has its own militant organisation, and the Kukis, the strongest of them, are bent on securing a separate 'Kukiland'. Despite rumours that the Kukis were given arms by the central government in a bid to counter the Naga threat, the army has not escaped Kuki wrath either.[38]

A cease-fire between the NSCN-IM and the central government began in August 1997, and has been continually renewed. But the cease-fire has not been very effective—partly because it was limited to Nagaland, while the main field of NSCN-IM operations was Manipur, and partly because it originally excluded the NSCN-K, the dominant Naga militant group operating in Nagaland. Though the NSCN-K has since joined the cease-fire, it has not been extended to Manipur because of Manipuri fears that such an extension would legitimise Naga claims to 'Greater Nagaland' which include Naga areas of Manipur.

---

[36] Lt. Col. Vivek Chadha, *Low Intensity Conflictsin India: An Analysis* (New Delhi: United Service Institution of India and Sage Publications, 2005), p.97. The rebel leader who had defected was made a commander within the BSF.
[37] *Ibid.*, pp.298–9.
[38] 'State of Anarchy', *Hindustan Times* (8 Dec. 1997), p.8.

Though a final settlement continues to elude the two parties, the Naga struggle for secession is probably over. The Indian strategy of limited use of force plus political concessions to most of the Naga demands short of secession has taken much of the support out of the Naga militant cause.

The Mizo case is another good example of a successful political resolution of an insurgency. Led by Laldenga, the leader of the Mizo National Front (MNF), the Mizo struggle began in 1966 as a consequence of the poor response by the Assam government to a famine in the Mizo Hills in 1959–60 and the attempt to impose Assamese as the official language. The initial rebel attack, called Operation Jericho, took the Indian Army and administration completely by surprise, and the rebels managed to gain control over a couple of towns as well as a good part of Aizawl, the provincial capital. Indian forces reacted quickly, however, and managed to drive the rebels out. Incidentally, this particular counter-insurgency operation is the only instance of the Indian Air Force (IAF) being used to attack rebel forces. The IAF was used to strafe and bomb parts of the rebel defences within Aizawl, which was the first town to be relieved by the Indian forces. The Indian Army was also beginning to learn how to fight such campaigns, a guerrilla warfare school having been opened in 1968 in Vairengte in Mizoram to train troops destined for affected areas.

Nevertheless, there were also mis-steps. A serious one was the attempt to set up a 'village-grouping' scheme in Mizoram similar to the ones employed by the British in Malaya and by the US in Vietnam. As we have seen the idea in such cases was to isolate the guerrillas from the general populace. But such schemes are difficult to implement in domestic insurgencies, where the government is responsible to the populace it is supposedly defending by such measures. As with the similar pilot scheme tried earlier in Nagaland, the Mizoram experiment proved counterproductive, alienating the local people. Following a legal challenge by human rights activists, the project was abandoned, clearing the way for a resumption of political initiatives which were welcomed by the moderate Mizo leaders.

Again, the government of India showed a willingness to make concessions. In 1972 it separated the Mizo Hills area from Assam, and constituted it as a Union Territory with its own legislature. It established a North Eastern Council to look into persistent local complaints of neglect and maladministration. Responding to these overtures, in 1976 Laldenga signed an agreement with the government of India, accepting Mizoram as an integral part of India—although a final agreement to end the insurgency was not concluded until 1986.[39]

---

[39] Unlike the situation in Nagaland, this agreement was accepted by the entire rebel movement, ending the insurgency completely.

Under the 1986 agreement, Mizoram became a full-fledged Union state. A year later the MNF competed in, and won, the inaugural state elections, whereupon Laldenga became the first chief minister. Thus, notwithstanding some recent rumblings, Mizoram can be counted as a genuinely successful case of counter-insurgency. As in Nagaland, it was the government's willingness to impose limitations on the use of force by its troops and its willingness to make political compromises short of secession that produced this successful outcome.

Aside from Nagaland and Mizoram, the most notable Indian counter-insurgency effort has been in Sri Lanka, where the Indian Army deployed several divisions as peace-keepers in the late 1980s. Sri Lanka had long been suffering simmering tensions between the majority Sinhalese and the minority Tamil populations. In the late 1970s, a section of the Tamil minority in Sri Lanka undertook an armed rebellion against the Sinhalese-dominated government of Sri Lanka with the objective of creating a homeland for the Tamils called Tamil Eelam,[40] which received material assistance from the Tamil population in neighbouring India and some moral blessing from the government of India.[41] The Sri Lankan government sought to put down the rebellion by force, which exacerbated the conflict. The use of force also complicated relations with India, because the Sri Lankan government sought logistical help from other countries such as Pakistan, Israel and the United States, which India perceived as being inimical to its interests in the region.

In July 1987 the government of India persuaded the Sri Lankan government and the Liberation Tigers of Tamil Eelam (LTTE), the dominant Tamil rebel group, to agree to a peaceful settlement of the conflict.[42] Neither the Sri Lankan government nor the Tamils were particularly satisfied with the terms of the deal, but they acquiesced because there seemed little alternative. In order to create the climate necessary for this political agreement to work, the Tamils agreed to give up their armed struggle and surrender their weapons, and the Sri Lankan Army undertook to withdraw from Tamil-dominated areas, or confine itself to its bases. A specially-constituted force from the Indian Army, called the Indian Peace Keeping Force (IPKF), was given the responsibility for implementing the military aspects

---

[40] For a brief overview of the development of the crisis, see Shantha K. Hennayake, 'The Peace Accord and the Tamils in Sri Lanka', in *Asian Survey*, Vol.29, no.4 (Apr. 1989), pp.401–15.
[41] Jeyaratnam Wilson, *The Break Up of Sri Lanka: The Sinhalese–Tamil Conflict* (London: Orient Longman, 1988), Ch.7.
[42] The LTTE was not the only Tamil group fighting the Sri Lankan Army; it was, however, the strongest. On the relations between India and the various Tamil groups, see Dagmar Hellmann-Rajanayagam, 'The Tamil Militants: Before the Accord and After', in *Pacific Affairs*, Vol.61, no.4 (1988–89), pp.603–19.

of the accord, such as collecting weapons from the Tamils and providing general law and order.[43] In particular, the Indian Army was to function as a buffer force between the Tamils and the Sri Lankan Army.

Despite some early successes, the agreement soon faltered. The LTTE was reluctant to trust either the Indian or the Sri Lankan governments. On 3 October 1987 some members of the LTTE were captured by the Sri Lankan Navy. The Indian government intervened to have them released, but Colombo refused, and the prisoners— as they had threatened—committed suicide. The LTTE blamed India for their deaths. This incident effectively marked the end of the fragile cease-fire. The LTTE resumed its military campaign, this time attacking the IPKF. The IPKF, which was responsible for disarming the Tamil militants under the peace agreement, responded with force.

The war between the IPKF and the LTTE proceeded in two stages. The first stage, in which the LTTE attempted to conduct a conventional defensive war against the IPKF, lasted through most of the October of 1987. The Indian Army had underestimated the capabilities of the LTTE and therefore took longer than expected to fulfil its objectives. However, with time, it was able to dislodge the LTTE from its base in the city of Jaffna and establish IPKF control there. This in itself demonstrates the importance of military doctrines in understanding the consequences of armed confrontations: despite strong morale, prepared positional defences, outstanding and unmatched tactical intelligence, and a supportive population, the LTTE was unable to withstand the IPKF's assault, despite the fact that the IPKF did not use heavy fire-power or close air support, and despite the IPKF strength not even being significantly larger than that of the LTTE. The LTTE's attempt to stay and fight for Jaffna was foolish, and ultimately unsuccessful.

The next stage, however, proved more difficult for the IPKF as the LTTE changed strategy and began a guerrilla war.[44] For two frustrating years, the IPKF conducted counter-insurgency operations against the LTTE with only limited success.[45] Though the IPKF managed to contain the LTTE, it was not able to completely defeat it despite massive reinforcements that eventually pushed the strength of the IPKF above 100,000,[46] according to some

---

[43] Ralph R. Premdas and S.W.R. de A. Samarasinghe, 'Sri Lanka's Ethnic Conflict: The Indo–Lanka Peace Accord', in *Asian Survey*, Vol.28, no.6 (June 1988), pp.676–90.
[44] Shankar Bhaduri and Afsir Karim, *The Sri Lanka Crisis* (New Delhi: Lancer, 1990).
[45] Rajesh Kadian, *India's Sri Lanka Fiasco: Peace Keepers at War* (New Delhi: Vision Books, 1990).
[45] The IPKF had originally constituted about only 8,000 troops.

estimates.[47] Indeed, this increase in strength did not make the IPKF any more effective.[48]

Moreover, many of the difficulties that the Indian Army faced in domestic counter-insurgency operations also resurfaced in Sri Lanka, and with even more negative consequences. For example, the Indian Army's penchant for conducting large-scale cordon-and-search operations, of doubtful military utility, continued in the operations against the LTTE. Similarly, the army's focus on controlling the populated areas, while only occasionally foraying in strength into rural areas, was in evidence in Sri Lanka too. Some Indian units did perform well; in particular, Indian para-commandos did well, especially when they imitated guerrilla tactics. But these were the exceptions: by and large, the Indian Army's propensity to blanket an area with troops to smother rather than defeat guerrillas continued in these operations too. Indeed, after the IPKF operations were finished, there is little indication that there was any subsequent attempt to learn the lessons from the operation for future counter-insurgency campaigns.

Though the IPKF's operations were by and large less dependent on heavy firepower, it nevertheless did lead to civilian casualties, which further eroded support for the IPKF among the Sri Lankan Tamils and further strengthened that of the LTTE.[49] But the most important difficulty that the IPKF faced was that though it was able to bottle up significant elements of the LTTE guerrilla force in the Vanni jungles south of the Jaffna peninsula, it was never able to deliver a knock-out blow to the 'Tiger' forces. The LTTE focused its energies on surviving and outlasting the IPKF. Thus the standard Indian counter-insurgency 'Grand Strategy' which emphasised long-term political solutions with a good dose of compromise could not work in Sri Lanka. In dealing with domestic Indian rebels, the Indian government's greatest advantage was time: this was a luxury that was not available when fighting in a foreign land. Political changes within Sri Lanka, where a portion of the Sinhalese political elite saw the Indian force as a bigger threat than the Tamil rebels, led to a temporary alliance between Colombo and the LTTE leadership, with both interested in expelling the IPKF. Without political support, the IPKF's mission became untenable. In March 1990, the IPKF was withdrawn from Sri Lanka with its objectives unrealised.

---

[47] There is some dispute about the peak strength of the IPKF in Sri Lanka, with the Indian government and Army routinely providing a figure around 50,000 while independent sources in India suggest that upward of 100,000 troops were dispatched. See, 'Comments: Sri Lanka', in *Indian Defence Review*, Vol.1 (Jan. 1988), pp.19–22. See also similar high estimates in Marshall R. Singer, 'Sri Lanka in 1990: The Ethnic Strife Continues', in *Asian Survey*, Vol.31, no.2 (Feb. 1991), pp.140–5.

[48] Edgar O'Ballance, *The Cyanide War: Tamil Insurrection in Sri Lanka 1973–88* (London: Brassey's, 1989).

[49] For a first-hand account of the human rights violations by the various sides in this conflict, see William McGowan, *Only Man is Vile: The Tragedy of Sri Lanka* (New York: Farrar, Straus and Giroux, 1992), Ch.12 & 16.

The Indian failure in Sri Lanka also illustrates a disadvantage of India's political approach to counter-insurgency. The approach requires great patience and commitment. In Sri Lanka, though the IPKF managed to effectively sideline the LTTE and push it into the Vanni jungles, reducing its clout as a military force, it was not able to defeat the LTTE. The LTTE, by managing to stay alive and avoid defeat, was able to eventually outwait the IPKF. In other words, the LTTE won by *avoiding defeat*. A strategy that was effective against domestic insurgents failed in a foreign war because time, generally on the side of the incumbent government in a domestic context, was an adversary in a foreign land.

Conclusions

The Indian counter-insurgency experience suggests two broad conclusions. First, though military force is a necessary ingredient in counter-insurgency campaigns, such use of force needs to be carefully modulated for it to be effective. The Indian political elite appears to have understood, almost instinctively, the need to reach an eventual political settlement with rebels and hence the need to limit the level of violence used in counter-insurgency campaigns. India's strong tradition of civilian control over the military made it possible for India's civilian decision-makers to make the country's military elite accept these restrictions, albeit initially reluctantly.

Second, it is clear from the Indian experience that patience and a long-term perspective are essential attitudinal requirements in fighting counter-insurgency campaigns. What is not so clear is whether New Delhi chose patience from foresight, or whether it simply preferred to ignore difficult situations until, with the fullness of time, they resolved themselves. Probably it was more the latter than the former, for there is little evidence that Indian decision-makers ever systematically thought through the issue, and plenty to suggest that patience often masked policy drift. In the four decades since first Prime Minister Jawaharlal Nehru's death, despite a wide array of domestic upheavals in various parts of the country, the only conceptual Indian government template that exists for understanding and dealing with internal rebellions remains Nehru's thinking on these issues in the 1950s.[50] Nehru's strategy of political compromise and limited use of force has become a 'default' strategy, implemented by rote. But even if by accident and inaction, the Indian reluctance to hurry through or devise a 'victory' strategy has had beneficial effects on its counter-insurgency grand strategy.

---

[50] On Nehru's views about fighting deomestic insurgents and the influence of his thinking on Indian Army doctrine, see Rajagopalan, "'Resoring Normalcy'", pp.47–50.

Ethno-Nationalism and the Politics of Terror in India's Northeast

Wasbir Hussain

India's north-eastern frontier is one of South Asia's hottest trouble spots. With as many as 30 armed insurgent organisations[1] currently operating there and pushing demands ranging from secession to autonomy and the right of self-determination, and a plethora of ethnic groups clamouring for their rights and distinct identity—at times not just fighting the Indian state but engaged in internecine turf wars—the region has all the ingredients that make for and sustain tension and turmoil. Moreover, the location of the eight north-eastern Indian states[2] itself goes to explain why it has always been a hotbed of militancy with trans-border ramifications. This region spreading over 263,000 square kilometres shares a highly porous and sensitive frontier with China to the north, Myanmar to the east, Bangladesh to the southwest and Bhutan to the northwest.[3]

Moreover the region is connected to the Indian mainland by a tenuous 22 kilometre-long land corridor passing through Siliguri in the eastern state of West Bengal, fancifully described as the 'Chicken's Neck'. This is the region where India's longest-running insurgency is located—spearheaded by the Naga tribal separatists who have been clamouring for an independent homeland ever since India attained independence from the British in 1947. And in four of the eight north-eastern

---

[1] The Indian Ministry of Home Affairs' Annual Report for 2003–2004 lists 18 active insurgent groups in the north-eastern states (there are several dormant ones). In the chapter titled 'Security Scenario in the North East', the report states: 'The North-Eastern States have been affected by insurgency for quite some time now. Militant activities of various underground groups and ethnic divisions have kept the conditions disturbed in several areas of Assam, Manipur, Nagaland and Tripura, as well as in some areas of Meghalaya and Arunachal Pradesh'. See Ministry of Home Affairs, *Ministry of Home Affairs Annual Report, 2003–2004* (New Delhi: Ministry of Home Affairs, Government of India, 2004), pp.2 & 33 [http://mha.nic.in/Annual-Reports/ar0304-Eng.pdf].

[2] The state of Sikkim has recently been formally bracketed under 'Northeast' after it was included in the North Eastern Council (NEC), the region's apex funding and development agency. The other seven states of the Northeast are Arunachal Pradesh, Assam, Manipur, Meghalaya, Mizoram, Nagaland and Tripura.

[3] It is located at longitude 89.46 degrees E to 97.30 degrees E and latitude 21.57 degrees N to 29.30 degrees N.

Indian states, namely Assam, Manipur, Nagaland and Tripura, the violence has reached a level that can justifiably be categorised as Low Intensity Warfare—that level of conflict in which fatalities are over 100 but less than 1000 per annum.[4] Between 1992 and 2002, there have been 12,175 fatalities due to insurgency or other types of armed conflict in India's Northeast.[5]

The region is an ethnic minefield, as it comprises around 160 Scheduled Tribes,[6] besides an estimated 400 other tribal or sub-tribal communities and groups. Turbulence in India's Northeast is, therefore, not caused just by armed separatist groups representing different ethnic communities fighting the federal or local governments or their proxies to press for some form of autonomy, but also by the recurring battles for territorial supremacy among the different ethnic groups. If the faction of the National Socialist Council of Nagaland headed by Isak Chishi Swu and Thuingaleng Muivah (NSCN-IM) has been pushing ahead with its demand for an independent Naga homeland to be carved out of India, the Naga and the Kuki ethnic groups in the state of Manipur, and the Bodo and Santhal tribespeople in western Assam have been struggling no less fiercely to retain control of their ancestral lands and thereby preserve their identity and rights.

What the Northeast of India is witnessing is essentially an ethno-national push by these groups to further their sub-national aspirations. For instance, the movement for greater autonomy by the Bodos, Assam's largest plains tribal community, led to the group securing a new politico-administrative structure within the existing state of Assam following a memorandum of understanding (MoU) with the central government on 10 February 2003. The Bodo-majority areas came under the Bodoland Territorial Council (BTC), a 40-member elective body that would run the day-to-day administration of the areas under it and undertake developmental projects to improve the condition of the community and the areas which they inhabit with funds allocated to it by the federal government, and the state governments.[7] The BTC—run initially by an interim team of administrators—held its first elections on 13 May 2005. The 2003 MoU was reached between the government and the Bodo Liberation Tigers (BLT), the insurgent group spearheading the autonomy

---

[4] Ajai Sahni, 'Survey of Conflicts and Resolution in India's Northeast', in *Faultlines: Writings On Conflict and Resolution*, Vol.12 (May 2002), p.39.

[5] South Asia Terrorism Portal [http//www.satp.org, accessed 27 Jan. 2004].

[6] Those tribes or tribal communities that are recognised under Article 342 of the Indian Constitution.

[7] The MoU with the BTC, signed on 10 February 2003, reads: 'In order to accelerate the development of the region and to meet the aspirations of the people, the Government of India will provide financial assistance of Rs100 crores per annum for 5 years for projects to develop the socio-economic infrastructure in BTC areas over and above the normal plan assistance to the state of Assam'. For the full text see South Asia Terrorism Portal [http://www.satp.org/satporgtp/countries/india/states/assam/documents/papers/memorandum_feb02.htm, accessed 16 Feb. 2004].

movement. Thus it was not a surprise to find the BLT-floated political party, the Bodo People's Progressive Front headed by the BLT chief-turned-politician Hagrama Mahilary, winning the polls and coming to run affairs at the Council. The BTC Accord is seen as a fulfilment of the sub-national aspirations of the Bodos of Assam.

Similarly, the six-year-long anti-foreigner uprising spearheaded by the All Assam Students' Union (AASU), the state's apex student body, from 1979 to 1985, was triggered by the indigenous Assamese community's fear of being overwhelmed by the ongoing influx of illegal Bangladeshi migrants from across the porous border. The anti-foreigner stir—perhaps among the biggest mass uprising in India since the country's freedom struggle—ended with the signing of an agreement, popularly called the Assam Accord, between the federal and state governments and the AASU on 15 August 1985. As far as the illegal foreign migrants were concerned, the Accord fixed the arrival date of 25 March 1971 as the cut-off for their detection and expulsion from the state.

The region has been caught in a vicious cycle of inadequate economic development and insufficient job opportunities, causing unrest and militancy, and then militancy and violence—which has, ironically, further retarded economic growth.[8] For instance, the plan for industrial investment in the region between August 1991 and December 1994 involved a mere Rs2,224 crore, whereas in a single state like Maharashtra, the figure for the corresponding period was Rs67,978 crore.[9] As for the employment scenario, in Assam (total population 26,655,528 according to 2001 census, the largest state in northeast India), the number of total job seekers registered with the state-government-run employment exchanges stood at 1,521,966 at the end of December 2002.[10] This has resulted in the region's various ethnic groups and communities finding it rather easy to press their respective demands through agitation—for they have a bank of aggrieved constituents to draw upon for foot soldiers.

Another dimension to the problem is that underground armed insurgent groups, overground socio-political groupings representing ethnic communities, and influential students' outfits based in these communities, are more often than not striving to achieve the same goal, namely to protect the rights of their respective communities.

---

[8] For specific indicators demonstrating the economic under-development of India's Northeast, see Wasbir Hussain, 'Contemporary North-East India: Problems and Prospects,' in J.P. Singh (ed.), *Trends in Social Sciences and Humanities in North East India (1947–97)* (New Delhi: Regency Publications, 1998), pp.129–36.
[9] *Ibid.*
[10] Directorate of Economics and Statistics, *Economic Survey: Assam, 2003–2004* (Guwahati: Directorate of Economics and Statistics, Government of Assam, 2004), p.83.

The Nagas' Homeland Dream and its Impact

Insurgency is by far the most extreme form of any ethno-political stirring, and the Nagas epitomised armed insurrection in the Northeast. Comprising about 17 major tribes and more than 20 sub-tribes, the Nagas have always considered themselves to be an independent nation. 'We are Nagas by birth, Indians by accident', is a common refrain among these indigenous tribal people.

The roots of Naga separatism precede India's Independence. As far back as 1929, under the banner of the 'Naga Club', the Nagas petitioned the Simon Commission, which was examining the feasibility of future self-governance in India, that they be left alone to determine their own future as they had in the past, and not be forced to be ruled by Indians who had 'never conquered them'.[11] By 1946 what had started as a political movement for the assertion of Naga identity was turning into an insurrection. Angami Zapu Phizo, regarded as the father-figure of the Naga insurgency, met Mahatma Gandhi on 19 July 1947. Two years later he became the president of the Naga National Council (NNC). Gandhi assured the delegation headed by Phizo that under no circumstances would force be used against the Nagas who were free to stay out of the Indian Union if they so desired.[12]

Emboldened by this, on 14 August 1947, the eve of Indian Independence, the Nagas took the Indian National Congress leadership by surprise and declared their 'independence'. In May 1951 more than 99 percent of the Naga population endorsed this stand in a plebiscite.[13] Anxious lest the same spirit started engulfing other tribal groups in the Northeast, in 1953 the Indian government moved troops in large numbers into the Naga Hills and launched a crackdown on the NNC. In March 1956 Phizo created an underground government called the Naga Federal Government (NFG) and a Naga Federal Army. In December Phizo left the Naga Hills for Switzerland and London and began to campaign from exile for an independent Naga homeland. He never returned, dying in London in April 1990. His daughter Adinno Phizo, who succeeded him as NNC president, is still pursuing Phizo's dream from the family home in London.[14]

Meanwhile in 1972, New Delhi proscribed the NNC as an unlawful organisation under the Unlawful Activities (Prevention) Act of 1967 and launched a massive counter-insurgency offensive. Cornered, and faced with reverses, the insurgents

---

[11] Wasbir Hussain, 'Peace in Naga Country: New Delhi's Challenges in the Far-Eastern Frontier', paper presented at a seminar on Peace Initiatives in South Asia organised by the Delhi Policy Group and Friedrich Ebert Stiftung at the United Services Institute, New Delhi, 28–29 November 2001.
[12] Hokishe Sema, *Emergence of Nagaland* (New Delhi: Vikas Publishing House Pvt. Ltd, 1986), p.160.
[13] Rev. V.K. Nuh, *Nagaland: Church and Politics* (Kohima: V. Nuh & Bro., 1986), p.131.
[14] Wasbir Hussain, 'Father's Daughter', *The Sentinel, Melange (Sunday Magazine)* (31 Aug. 2003), pp.22–9.

agreed to hold peace talks with the Union Government. This led to the signing of the controversial Shillong Accord on 11 November 1975 between a section of the NNC and its 'underground government', the Naga Federal Government (NFG), and the Union Government.[15] The signatories to this agreement accepted the Indian Constitution and agreed to surrender their weapons and join the Indian national mainstream.[16]

A group of around 140 NNC cadres, however, repudiated the Shillong Accord and refused to surrender. They formed a new insurgent group called the National Socialist Council of Nagaland (NSCN) under the leadership of Thuingaleng Muivah, Isak Chishi Swu and S.S. Khaplang. The significant point to be noted is that this new group, formed in 1980, took shape and was launched from this faction's bases inside Myanmar.[17] With the passage of time, the NSCN emerged as the most radical and powerful insurgent group fighting for the Naga cause. But clannish divisions among the Nagas (between the Konyak and Tangkhul tribes) resulted in a split of the NSCN in 1988. The Konyaks took the lead in forming the NSCN-K (Khaplang) under the leadership of Khole Konyak and S.S. Khaplang. The other faction—led mostly by the Tangkhuls under the leadership of Swu and Muivah—came to be known as NSCN-IM. After fighting a prolonged guerrilla war with the Indian security forces, the NSCN-IM signed a ceasefire agreement that came into effect on 1 August 1997. Ever since, the NSCN-IM and the Indian government have been engaged in peace negotiations aimed at arriving at an 'acceptable solution' to the Naga problem.

Before it made up its mind to enter into peace negotiations with New Delhi, the NSCN-IM may have concluded that it would work on a compromise formula. After all the rebel leadership—in the wake of several previous failed peace initiatives—must have realised the futility of sticking to a demand for nothing less than total independence. If one analyses the progress of the peace negotiations between the NSCN-IM and the Indian government during the past decade, it appears that the rebels may be willing to give up their demand for an independent Naga homeland but not, under any circumstances, their dream of the different Naga tribes to 'live together in one land as one family'.[18] It would like to deny it, but the NSCN-IM wants something like a 'Greater Nagaland' to be formed by the merger of

---

[15] For the complete text of the Shillong Accord, see Nuh, *Nagaland: Church & Politics*, pp.158–60.
[16] Hussain, 'Peace in Naga Country'.
[17] *Ibid.*
[18] 'Unified Naga Homeland; Foundation of Any Political Settlement', *Nagalim.NL News* (9 September 2005) [http://www.nagalim.nl/news/00000138.htm].

Naga-inhabited areas in the adjoining states of Manipur, Assam and Arunachal Pradesh, and if possible those in Myanmar, into the present state of Nagaland.[19]

Indeed the NSCN-IM has made it clear, through a careful play of words, that it has an expansionist agenda. In an interview in 2002, the NSCN-IM General Secretary Muivah said that his group is not campaigning for a greater Nagaland or a smaller Nagaland, but added that the 'division drawn on the Naga territories had been done by the British colonialists and the Government of India, not by the Nagas'.[20] This means that the present territorial boundaries of the states in the Northeast are not acceptable to the NSCN-IM. 'Besides, Muivah has said that the Nagas are not claiming land belonging to others and that the areas where the Nagas are living (in states like Manipur, Assam and Arunachal Pradesh, apart from Nagaland) belong to them. All these go to reinforce the fact that the NSCN-IM is bent on uniting the Naga areas in the Northeast, transgressing the present state boundaries. And, here lies the problem'.[21] Such demands, however, elicit strong protests and opposition from these states as well as from different tribal groups that reside in the areas claimed by the Naga leadership.

During most of the peace dialogue between the NSCN-IM and New Delhi, the issue of resolving the dispute over the jurisdiction of the ceasefire area has dominated proceedings. The rebel leadership has been pressing for the truce to be extended to all the Naga-inhabited areas outside Nagaland; the Indian government has been reluctant. But at length, on 14 June 2001—after a two-day meeting in Bangkok with the NSCN-IM headed by General Secretary Muivah—New Delhi's peace envoy announced that the ceasefire would be extended for a further year, and that henceforth the truce would have no 'territorial limits'.[22]

The agreement triggered off the biggest-ever mass uprising of the majority Meiteis in the Imphal Valley in the adjoining state of Manipur, who feared that an extension of the ceasefire could lead to parts of Manipur being sliced off and merged into Nagaland as part of a deal with the NSCN-IM. Up to 50,000 Meiteis took to the streets in Imphal on 18 June 2001—four days after the extension of the ceasefire limits outside Nagaland was announced—to oppose the extension of the NSCN–New Delhi truce

---

[19] *Ibid.* See also Bibhu Prasad Routray, 'Manipur: The Siege Within', in *South Asia Intelligence Review*, Vol.4, no.1 (18 July 2005) [http://www.satp.org/satporgtp/sair/Archives/4_1.htm].
[20] Wasbir Hussain and Bibhu Prasad Routray, 'Naga Identity, Meitei Nationalism and Electoral Politics: Sub-Nationalism in Northeast India', in *Faultlines: Writings on Conflict and Resolution*, Vol.10 (Jan. 2002), p.128, [http://www.satp.org/satporgtp/publication/faultlines/volume10/Article8.htm].
[21] *Ibid.,* pp.128–9.
[22] The joint statement issued in Bangkok, for instance, said the ceasefire agreement was between the 'Government of India and the NSCN as two entities without territorial limits'. See 'Extension of Truce Beyond Nagaland Withdrawn', *The Hindu* (28 July 2001) [http://www.hindu.com/thehindu/2001/07/28/stories/01280001.htm].

to Manipur. A rampaging mob burnt the Manipur Legislative Assembly building and a dozen other government offices. Eighteen protestors were killed when security forces eventually opened fire to quell the frenzied mob. A massive civil disobedience movement followed and Imphal was placed under curfew for nearly a month. Finally, on 24 July, after a meeting with the chief ministers of the north-eastern states in New Delhi, Prime Minister Atal Behari Vajpayee announced that the cease-fire would once again be restricted only to the state of Nagaland. This concession eased the situation in the Imphal Valley.

However it did not satisfy the Nagas. The NSCN-IM accused New Delhi of going back on its Bangkok agreement of 14 June 2001 and questioned the sincerity of the Union Government. Nevertheless contrary to speculation, the NSCN-IM did not call off the ceasefire and resume its guerrilla war, although several of the group's top leaders, including V.S. Atem, its former military chief, threatened to resume the campaign if the jurisdiction of the truce did not cover all the Naga-inhabited areas in the region. Why? Firstly, the NSCN-IM was under tremendous pressure from Naga NGOs not to take any hasty steps. This was because there was a general mood for peace among the civilian population in Nagaland, and prominent civil society groups were at the forefront of the peace move. Secondly, it could have been a tactical ploy on the part of the NSCN-IM not to over-react on the ceasefire jurisdiction issue, and instead pursue the Naga unification plan in a more systematic manner. For its part, the government was apprehensive that an extension of the ceasefire to all Naga-inhabited areas would have meant recognising the NSCN's claim to all Naga-inhabited areas in the Northeast, including those outside the present state of Nagaland.

In fact, signs of a systematic campaign were obvious. On 26 October 2001 the United Naga Council, Manipur (UNC), which purports to represent Naga opinion in Manipur, met Prime Minister Vajpayee in New Delhi and submitted a memorandum demanding the integration of the Naga areas in Manipur with Nagaland. In the words of K.S. Paul Leo who led the UNC delegation:

> Historically, Nagas have been wanting to live as one people, under one political roof. Therefore, we want that all Naga inhabited areas in Manipur be merged with Nagaland as an immediate interim arrangement pending a final settlement of the Naga problem so that the community's distinct culture and identity can be protected.[23]

In support of this merger, the memorandum cited Jawaharlal Nehru's letter dated 13 May 1956 to then-Assam Chief Minister Bishnu Ram Medhi:

---

[23] Interview with K.S. Paul Leo in Guwahati on 5 November 2001.

> One of their [the Nagas'] grievances is that under our Constitution we split them up in different political areas. Whether it is possible or desirable to bring them together again is for us to consider. Also what measure of autonomy we should give them so that they can lead their own lives without any sensation of interference. . . .[24]

Although the NSCN-IM is engaged in bitter inter-group rivalry with the Khaplang faction of the NSCN as well as the Naga National Council, all these groups are in direct confrontation with the Indian nation-state. 'Internal conflicts in India's Northeast are overwhelmingly conceptualised within the framework of unique ethnic identities that are threatened by, and in confrontation with, the nationalist state, which is often seen as a representative of an inchoate cultural mainstream'.[25] That is the primary reason why the rebels, who enjoy the backing of a sizeable section of the Nagas, are determined to unify all the Naga-populated areas in the region under a single administrative set-up. Both the Naga's aspirations for a unified homeland and the Meitei's fears of having to lose territory to the Nagas are grounded in the absolute determination of these groups to preserve their identities.

Inter-Ethnic Feuds: Battle of One-Upmanship

New Delhi appears to have been convinced that an integrationist policy in holding the Northeast together with the national mainstream was not a correct approach in view of the diverse nature of the region's demographic profile. The Union has ceased to present itself in the region as a 'homogenising state', and now takes into account the unique differences and distinct identities of the region's ethnic groups and communities. But this change of vision has opened a Pandora's box, encouraging a proliferation of movements aimed at economic and political liberation on ethnic lines, and thereby sparking feuds between the ethnic groups located in different parts of the Northeast over territorial supremacy.

Prior to the 10 February 2003 agreement between New Delhi and the leaders of Assam's Bodo ethnic group, another Bodo Accord had been signed in February 1993 that led to the creation of a Bodoland Autonomous Council (BAC).[26] The BAC was a non-starter as the government could not arrive at a consensus

---

[24] Letter no.1116-PMH/56 cited in the UNC memorandum to the prime minister dated 26 October 2001. See Hussain and Routray 'Naga Identity, Meitei Nationalism and Electoral Politics: Sub-Nationalism in Northeast India.
[25] Sahni, 'Survey of Conflicts and Resolution in India's Northeast', p.46.
[26] For the text of the Bodoland Autonomous Council Agreement 1993 see Chandana Bhattacharjee, *Ethnicity and Autonomy Movement: Case of Bodo-Kacharis of Assam* (New Delhi: Vikas Publishing House Pvt. Ltd., 1996), pp.347–83. For the Memorandum of Settlement on the Bodoland Territorial Council signed on 10 February 2003, see http://www.satp.org/satporgtp/countries/india/states/assam/documents/papers/memorandum_feb02.htm.

over the territorial boundary of this Council. Nonetheless, the set of modalities that it put in place to fix the Council's boundary triggered off a violent ethnic cleansing in western Assam.

What triggered the inter-ethnic violence? In the summer of 1996, the Bodos clashed with the Santhals, another ethnic group that cohabited around the principal district town of Kokrajhar, 250 kilometres west of Guwahati, Assam's capital. More than 300,000 people belonging to both communities were displaced, and around 250 people killed in the ethnic riots that began in May 1996 and continued sporadically until the end of the year.[27] As of February 2004 an estimated 130,000 people belonging to both communities were still living in the so-called relief camps set up by the government.[28] Although a relative calm now prevails in the area, the schism between these two groups has widened.

Both communities, Bodos and Santhals, have been living in the area for decades. But after the Bodo Accord of 1993, the Union government came up with a formula whereby only those villages with a Bodo population of 50 percent or more were to be included into the proposed BAC. This provision—which sought to preserve the non-Bodo population—resulted in a section of Bodos, including armed militant groups, launching an ethnic cleansing drive—which saw vast stretches of territory turned into Bodo-majority areas ripe for inclusion in the proposed Bodo Council.[29]

Radical elements in the Santhal population responded by forming a raft of ragtag armed groups with menacing names such as the Adivasi Cobra Militants of Assam. The Cobra rebels soon started snatching arms from the police and paramilitary, and if they can transform themselves into a more organised outfit the chances of peace in Assam's Bodo tribal heartland—also home to the Santhals— will be remote.[30]

The Kuki–Naga riots that rocked the state of Manipur during the mid 1990s, and especially in 1992–93, led to the deaths of hundreds of people.[31] Both the Nagas and the Kukis are fighting for separate homelands and their territorial demands

---

[27] Wasbir Hussain, 'Our Land, Our Refugees', *The Hindu* (26 May 2000).
[28] Interview with Dr. A.K. Bhutani, Deputy Commissioner, Kokrajhar, 26 February 2004.
[29] *Ibid.*
[30] Wasbir Hussain, 'Meeting the Challenges of Insurgency in NE: The Centre's Responsibility', paper presented at a national seminar organised by the Indian Council of Social Science Research on Terrorism: An Unending Malaise, New Delhi, 2–3 March 2000.
[31] According to one estimate 750 Kukis lost their lives and a total of 114,300 others belonging to both Naga and Kuki communities were displaced during the conflict. See Bhagat Oinam, 'Patterns of Ethnic Conflicts in the Northeast: A Study on Manipur', *Imphal Free Press* (26 June 2003).

overlap. Members of the two groups have frequently clashed in the past for control of the lucrative heroin trade route through Moreh, an Indian outpost close to the border with Myanmar. The key factor that has prompted Kuki–Naga clashes include the desire of the Nagas' rebel elements to ease out the Kukis from the four hill-tribe-dominated districts in Manipur. Faced with this threat, the Kukis formed insurgent groups of their own to defend their community in remote hill-top hamlets. But they have struggled to hold their ground. Now the Nagas in Manipur, led by the United Naga Council, Manipur, are openly seeking the merger of the Naga areas in Manipur with the adjoining state of Nagaland.

The armed insurgent groups in the region may be fighting the Indian state, but when it comes to protecting their own homeland cause, they do not hesitate to lock horns with other rebel groups or forces within the region. For instance, the United Liberation Front of Asom (ULFA)—Assam's frontline rebel group which has been fighting since its formation in April 1979 for a 'sovereign, Socialist Assam'—openly came out against the designs of the NSCN-IM to unify the Naga-inhabited areas in the Northeast by merging Naga-dominated territories in states like Assam with the state of Nagaland.

On 17 July 2001 through its mouthpiece, *Freedom*, the ULFA ridiculed the idea of Nagalim or a 'greater' Naga homeland and observed that 'history should not be distorted only to satisfy the chauvinistic ego'.[32] Terming the decision to extend the ceasefire 'a suicidal act', the ULFA expressed the hope that the Naga leaders would 'review' their ambitions to extend 'Nagalim over others' territories'.[33] This has, of course, been one of those rare occasions when the ULFA chose to criticise its former ally, and was obviously aimed at playing to its Assamese constituents in the state.

The Battle Rages On

Homeland aspirations have affected other tribal communities of the region too. As the Indian state over the years has shown signs of listening only to the voices of people holding guns—which could be seen as a policy of rewarding terror—each passing day has added to the number of tribal communities threatening to wage war against the Indian state unless their demands for autonomy are addressed.

---

[32] Bibhu Prasad Routray, 'Naga Cease-Fire Extension: Clash of Imagined Homelands', *Institute of Peace and Conflict Studies* [http://www.ipcs.org/ipcs/issueIndex2.jsp?action=showView&kValue=812&issue=1014&status=article&mod=b, accessed 27 Jan. 2004].
[33] *Ibid.*

For instance, over the past decade or so 35,000 Reangs, also known as Brus, have been fighting for autonomy from the state of Mizoram from their base in relief camps in North Tripura. In October 1997 these tribals were forced leave Mizoram after the Mizos, led by the influential student organisations the Mizo Zirlai Pawl and the Young Mizo Association, allegedly burnt several Bru villages and killed and raped a number of Bru men and women.[34] Since then the Bru National Liberation Front (BNLF) has been negotiating the status of the refugees with the Mizoram state government. On 26 April 2005, the BNLF signed a Memorandum of Understanding (MoU) with the Mizoram government.[35] The MoU was supposed to have led to the repatriation of the estimated 40,000 Bru refugees from the six relief camps in North Tripura. But this has not happened yet. On 5 April 2006 the Mizoram government informed New Delhi that it would initiate repatriation of Bru refugees only after the Bru Liberation Front of Mizoram (BLFM)—believed to be a breakaway faction of the BNLF which wanted to negotiate its own separate peace deal—laid down its arms and eschewed violence.[36] Up until the first half of 2006, the Mizoram government remained adamant about not negotiating with the BLFM, perhaps because it did not attach much importance to this splinter group.

However 809 BLFM militants did surrender at Naisingpara relief camp in North Tripura on 23 October 2006. They deposited 70 firearms, including AK series rifles, grenades, a mortar and explosives. Mizoram Home Minister Tawnluia declared that the state government would provide Rs40,000 to each of these BLFM militants and free rations for one year in transit camps in Mizoram. But on 4 November Tripura Police Chief G.M. Srivastava disclosed that the surrender was a 'stage managed' affair and that those who had laid down their weapons were not really BLFM rebels at all but merely ordinary Bru youth from the relief camps.[37] Things remain hazy. While Mizoram sticks to its promise of taking back the displaced Bru,[38] the finality of an autonomous region for the tribal group hangs in the balance.

In Assam's southern districts of Karbi Anglong and North Cachar Hills, there has been a continuing push for an autonomous state since the mid 1980s. Both

---

[34] Syed Sajjad Ali, 'The Reang Refugees', in *Frontline*, Vol.15, no.15 (18–31 July 1998).
[35] 'Mizoram Assessment 2006', South Asia Terrorism Portal [http://www.satp.org/satporgtp/countries/india/states/Mizoram/index.html].
[36] See Bibhu Prasad Routray, 'Mizoram: Surrender Swindle', in *South Asia Intelligence Review*, Vol.5, no.21 (4 Dec. 2006) [http://satp.org/satporgtp/sair/Archives/5_21.htm#assessment2].
[37] *Ibid.*
[38] On 20 January 2004 Mizoram Chief Minister Zoramthanga met Prime Minister Atal Behari Vajpayee in New Delhi and assured him that that the Reang tribal refugees, sheltered in six North Tripura camps for over six years, would be taken back within two months. See 'Mizo Refugees to be Taken Back: Zoramthanga' [http://sify.com/news/othernews/fullstory.php?id=13369784, accessed 12 Feb. 2004].

these districts enjoy special protection under the Sixth Schedule of the Indian Constitution,[39] and have in place Autonomous District Councils to look after their administration. However, fear of being dominated by 'outsiders' (which means anyone not a local tribal) has generated a call for full statehood by the prosaically-named Autonomous State Demand Committee (ASDC).[40] Complicating this situation is the fact that the ASDC movement has split into two groups—the ASDC-United and the ASDC-Progressive—and that the Autonomous District Council is run by the Congress Party. The demand for an autonomous state, even though not dead as yet, has effectively been pushed onto the backburner.

Besides the political movement led by the ASDC factions, there are two fringe, yet violent and militant outfits, in these two districts, namely the United People's Democratic Solidarity (UPDS)[41] and the Dima Halam Daogah.[42] Even though negotiations are in progress with both groups, violence still has not ceased. Interestingly, the proposed homelands of both these outfits eat into the NSCN-IM's dream of a 'Greater Nagaland'.

Additionally, in Karbi Anglong itself, the Kuki population, the antecedents of whom remain a matter of speculation, are locked in a bitter conflict with the Karbis in general and the UPDS in particular. The Kuki demand for an autonomous region within Karbi Anglong has met with violent opposition from UPDS cadres—opposition which has enjoyed silent support from Karbi politicians who view the Kuki autonomy movement as a threat to their own aspirations for autonomy. In October–November 2003, a number of deaths were reported from Karbi Anglong as a result of militant attacks by the UPDS and the Kuki militant outfit, the Kuki Revolutionary Army.

Yet another struggle for autonomy involves the Hmar tribespeople. The Hmars live scattered in Mizoram, Manipur and Assam and have, since the mid 1980s, been demanding a homeland for themselves. Initially the Hmar People's Convention

---

[39] The Sixth Schedule of the Indian Constitution provides for the creation of autonomous district councils in exclusively tribal areas so they have an elected politico-administrative body of local representatives who can run their respective regions through powers vested in them. These councils are empowered to prepare their own annual budgets for the development of their regions, although the allocation of funds has to be ratified by the legislature in the respective states.

[40] For details see 'The Karbi Anglong and NC Hills Experience' [http://www.cpiml.org/PGS/polorreport/7.htm, accessed 27 Jan. 2004].

[41] For a profile of the United People's Democratic Solidarity, see South Asia Terrorism Portal [http://www.satp.org/satporgtp/countries/india/states/assam/terrorist_outfits/upds.htm, accessed 27 Jan. 2004].

[42] For a profile of the Dima Halam Daogah, see South Asia Terrorism Portal [http://www.satp.org/satporgtp/countries/india/states/assam/terrorist_outfits/dhd.htm, accessed 27 Jan. 2004].

(HPC) pressed for an administrative structure that conferred limited self-governance for the north and northeast of Mizoram:

> In 1992, HPC representatives and the Government of Mizoram mutually agreed to hold ministerial level talks. Consequent to nine rounds of such talks, a Memorandum of Settlement (MoS) was signed at the Mizoram capital Aizawl on 27 July 1994, for establishing the 'Sinlung Development Council' and subsequently 308 HPC militants surrendered along with their arms.[43]

However, that led to a hard-line section of HPC cadres parting ways with the movement and forming the HPC-Democracy (HPC-D) in 1995. The HPC-D has shown little sign of responding to calls for peace. In 2003 HPC-D militants fought with Dimasa tribals for a period of two months in Assam's Cachar and North Cachar districts—a conflict that claimed an estimated 60 lives.[44]

In Tripura, a bitter militancy has continued for three decades.[45] Over the years, new terrorist outfits have originated and violence continues to haunt the state. Currently three outfits—two factions of the National Liberation Front of Tripura[46] and the All-Tripura Tiger Force[47]—are locked in mortal combat with government security forces. Even though the demands of these three outfits are various—ranging from the expulsion of the immigrant Bengali population to the establishment of an independent homeland for the tribals—the pattern of violence resorted to by these organisations demonstrates that they have long given up their separatist ideology and have degenerated into criminal gangs. This pattern is unfortunately rather typical. Many insurgent outfits have gradually given up their ethnic nationalist pretensions and become overtly dependent on foreign support and/or guided by foreign elements.

Homeland Battles, Foreign Links

Trans-border links between Northeast Indian insurgent groups started developing less than a decade after India became independent in 1947. After the NSCN was

---

[43] 'Hmar People's Convention-Democracy', South Asia Terrorism Portal [http://www.satp.org/satporgtp/countries/india/states/mizoram/terrorist_outfits/HPC_D.htm, accessed 20 Feb. 2004].

[44] 'Dispur Needs to Apply Wise Counsel', *The Statesman* (Calcutta) (1 July 2003).

[45] The first organised militant grouping, the Sengkrak, was formed in the mid 1960s in opposition to non-tribals settling in the tribal reserve forest areas. See website of the Tripura State Police [http://tripurapolice.nic.in/amilitancy.htm, accessed 30 Jan. 2004].

[45] For a profile of the National Liberation Front of Tripura, see South Asia Terrorism Portal [http://www.satp.org/satporgtp/countries/india/states/tripura/terrorist_outfits/nlft.htm, accessed 27 Jan. 2004].

[47] For a profile of the All-Tripura Tiger Force, see South Asia Terrorism Portal [http://www.satp.org/satporgtp/countries/india/states/tripura/terrorist_outfits/attf.htm, accessed 27 Jan. 2004].

formed inside Myanmar and had established itself as a front-ranking insurgent group in the Northeast, it began providing arms training and other logistical support to newer rebel outfits such as the ULFA. The ULFA in turn sent its cadres for advanced 'military training' at the hands of the Kachin Independence Army (KIA), who have been fighting the Burma government since 1948. Surrendered or captured ULFA rebels interviewed by this writer have confirmed that they received such arms training.[48] And American author Shelby Tucker testifies to having met ULFA chairman Arabinda Rajkhowa at the Pajau Bum headquarters of the Kachin Independence Organisation, the political wing of the KIA, around 1989.[49] Former ULFA rebels say the group's commander-in-chief, Paresh Barua, was also in Myanmar's Kachin Hills around that time.

Such trips were among the first attempts by rebels from Assam to forge strategic alliances with militant groups located in neighbouring countries like Myanmar. In 1985 the ULFA opened operations in Bangladesh by setting up safe houses at Damai village in Moulvi Bazar district bordering the north-eastern Indian state of Meghalaya.[50] By 1990, the ULFA had its Pakistani contacts in place, thanks to the efforts of Munin Nobis (since surrendered) and other leaders. Nobis told this writer in October 2002 that the Pakistanis had facilitated the cross-over of a number of ULFA leaders, including Paresh Barua, into Afghanistan through Pakistan's North West Frontier Province. There, assisted by the Pakistani Inter Services Intelligence (ISI), the ULFA representatives met Gulbuddin Hekmatyar, a top Afghan *mujahideen* leader of that time. No wonder ULFA rebels who surrendered in the wake of a Bhutanese military assault on them in December 2003 talked of the presence of an Afghan-trained artillery expert at one of their Bhutan bases.[51]

As to the origin of these bases, which were set up mainly in the district of Samdrup Jhongkar, bordering western Assam's Nalbari district, the major catalyst was a counter-insurgency operation launched by the Indian Army against ULFA elements in Assam on the night of 27–28 November 1990 codenamed 'Operation Bajrang'. The army's offensive was in retaliation for a ULFA reign of terror in the state. For months ULFA cadres had been killing, kidnapping and extorting money from tea companies' representatives and others. New Delhi dismissed the Assam

---

[48] Wasbir Hussain, 'We Picked Up our AKs and Fled', *The Sentinel* (24 Dec. 2003).
[49] Shelby Tucker, *Among Insurgents: Walking Through Burma* (New Delhi: Penguin Books, 2000), pp.82–3.
[50] This information was disclosed by a top ULFA leader who had surrendered during an interview with the author on 23 October 2002 at Guwahati.
[51] Hussain, 'We Picked Up our AKs and Fled'. Surrendered ULFA lieutenant Domeshwar Rabha stated that Afghanistan-trained rebel Satabda Kumar was the chief instructor of the ULFA's artillery squad inside Bhutan. Kumar, he said, was also the commander of the group's General Headquarters in Bhutan that was smashed during the Bhutanese military assault in December 2003.

government headed by Prafulla Kumar Mahanta for its failure to maintain law and order and sent in its troops. The Himalayan kingdom of Bhutan was selected as a refuge by the ULFA (and later by the National Democratic Front of Bodoland and the Kamatapur Liberation Organisation or KLO),[52] because its southern frontier was not properly policed, was densely-wooded and was located just across from Assam. Besides, Bhutan had very limited military capabilities and certainly none, in the beginning, sufficient to take on a band of heavily-armed rebels. These factors made Bhutan an excellent staging area for separatists bent on carrying out violent strikes in Indian territory. But unlike Thimphu, which has admitted the presence of these foreign militants from the beginning, Dhaka has always tried to deny the fact that Indian insurgents operate from within Bangladesh.

Strategic Alliances as Force Multipliers
Events in the insurgency front in India's Northeast have shown that rebel groups have often succeeded in neutralising reverses suffered by them by entering into deals with other insurgent groups that act as force multipliers. Insurgent politics in the region registered a very important development in the year 2000—the signing of a deal for joint operations by the Assamese ULFA and the United National Liberation Front (UNLF), a Manipuri insurgent group whose primary area of operation has been Manipur's Jiribam valley and neighbouring Assam's Cachar district. A UNLF statement of 29 July 2000 disclosed for the first time the agreement between the two groups. Significantly, that statement came less than a fortnight after the UNLF claimed responsibility for the 16 July 2000 killing of three Jat Regiment soldiers of the Indian Army in Cachar district in Southern Assam. Given its admission about the agreement, the ULFA could well have provided logistical support for that ambush.

Formed on 24 November 1964 by Areambam Samarendra Singh to fight for an independent socialist Manipur, the UNLF has had a rather impressive record in attracting allies. During the 1960s, the outfit had a close 'political relationship' with the government of East Pakistan, and in 1969 underwent military training in that country. It is also said to have supported the Pakistan Army during the Bangladesh liberation war in 1971. But the UNLF has not just depended on Pakistan. In 1975 it sent a team headed by N. Bisheswar Singh to Lhasa to ask for assistance from Beijing. Now headed by Rajkumar Meghen alias Sana Yaima, the UNLF is also close to the NSCN-K and has training camps in Myanmar and Bangladesh.[53]

---

[52] For profiles of the ULFA, NDFB and KLO, see South Asia Terrorism Portal [http// www.satp.org, accessed 27 Jan. 2004].
[53] Wasbir Hussain, 'Northeast Rebels: Strategic Alliances and Open Borders', paper presented at seminar on Dynamics of Border Management, Past, Present and Future, organised by the Border Security Force at the Police Officers' Mess, Shillong, 7–8 October 2002.

It is linkages such as these and the potential for immense trans-border movement by these groups that has made the ULFA–UNLF pact so significant. The ULFA would like to describe the agreement as a 'fraternal bond sealed to fulfil certain tactical goals'.[54] It may not have been an exclusive bilateral pact, but both the ULFA and the UNLF were part of the loose pan-Mongoloid coalition forged in May 1990 called the Indo–Burma Revolutionary Front (IBRF). Formed to wage a 'united struggle for the independence of Indo–Burma',[55] the IBRF was a failure. It failed primarily because it was too much of a problem for its leaders to hold on to a group of rebel outfits that claimed to represent diverse tribes and communities seeking to protect distinct ethnic identities and interests.

What then was the need for the ULFA to tie up with the UNLF and vice-versa? Until 2003 the ULFA's main fighting machine was located in Bhutan. But several years before that the ULFA had come under pressure from the Bhutanese government to vacate the kingdom. According to then-Bhutanese Home Minister Lyonpo Thinley Gyamtsho, by 31 December 2001 the ULFA had indeed closed down its four camps as per an agreement reached in June 2001.[56]

Forced to leave Bhutan, the ULFA would have been eyeing the UNLF's bases and training facilities in Myanmar and Bangladesh. Denials from Dhaka notwithstanding, it is a fact that Bangladesh has long been a favourite 'hiding' place for ULFA leaders. A pact with the UNLF was, of course, a prerequisite for the ULFA to gain access to these bases.

Meanwhile, the ULFA had been receiving arms consignments from the Khmer Rouge in Cambodia under a deal brokered in 1993 by General Bo Mya's Karen National Union (KNU), another long-standing anti-Burma government guerrilla group.[57] That deal was apparently clinched by the ULFA's self-styled foreign secretary Shasha Choudhury, who visited the KNU base at Manerplaw on the Thailand–Myanmar border. As surveillance increased, making the importation of weaponry more difficult, the ULFA might have pinned its hopes on the UNLF to serve as a conduit for shipments of military hardware.

---

[54] See Wasbir Hussain, 'Ominous Signs in the Northeast', *The Hindu* (9 Sept. 2002) [http://www.hinduonnet.com/2002/09/09/stories/2002090900041000.htm].
[55] *Ibid.*
[56] 'Bhutan to ask ULFA to Close Down HQ', *Assam Tribune* (internet edition) (8 July 2002) [http://www.assamtribune.com/jul0802/at02.html, accessed 15 Feb. 2004].
[57] Wasbir Hussain, 'ULFA gets New Weapons from Khmer Rouge', *The Asian Age* (14 Aug. 1995). Bo Mya, vice chairman and elder statesman of the KNU, has been engaged in successive rounds of talks with the Myanmarese authorities since January 2004. 'Karen Rebels Wrap Up Peace Talks with Junta, Describe It as "Successful"', Associated Press (25 Feb. 2004) [www.burmanet.org, accessed 26 Feb. 2004].

The UNLF has also had dealings with the military junta in Myanmar—but the relationship seems to have been a chequered one. In December 2001 as many as 192 UNLF cadres, including some top leaders, were 'arrested' by the Myanmarese Army. Interestingly, all of them were set free by 14 February 2002 in four phases. The entire episode is still shrouded in mystery, particularly because Yangon has been simultaneously promising New Delhi of its help in checking cross-border insurgency. Does this mean that the UNLF has some sort of an understanding with the junta in Myanmar, or a section of it? Answers are difficult to find, but theories abound, particularly because New Delhi, from the mid 1990s onwards, is supposed to have improved its relations with Yangon considerably.

Even groups (such as the NSCN-IM) engaged in peace negotiations with New Delhi supported the 48-hour general strike called in Assam and other parts of the region on 20 and 21 December 2003 by the ULFA, NDFB and the KLO in protest against what they termed the 'brutal operations' and 'human rights violations' of the Indian military inside Bhutan.[58] The conflict dynamics as well as the complex rebel equations have contributed to keeping India's Northeast on the boil.

Response of the Indian State

The response of the Union government towards resolving the ethnic conflicts in the country's Northeast has to be seen in the context of its stance towards the region as a whole, which has swung from apathy and negligence to generosity. According to Prime Minister Vajpayee, between 1998–99 and 2002–03 New Delhi pumped in more than Rs44,000 crore to the north-eastern states.[59] Not surprisingly, the Indian states that have been steadfast in their loyalty to the centre are bemused to see disaffected states in the Northeast receiving bigger per capita handouts than the rest of the country.[60]

But even the Union's dealings with the Northeast region are muddied by its appeasement of extremism. It tends to reward the more violent separatist outfits, while closing its eyes to the more subtle clamourings of groups pushing for autonomy within the country's legal framework. For instance, the more violent of the two

---

[58] See Nava Thakuria, 'Expectation Rose from Burma and Bangladesh to Drive Out Indian Insurgents', *BNI Weekly News* (29 Dec. 2003) [http://www.ibiblio.org/obl/docs/BNI2003-12-29.htm].

[59] Wasbir Hussain, 'NE should be Bridgehead to SE Asia, Centre ready to Meet NE Ultra Threat: PM', *The Sentinel* (Guwahati) (21 Jan. 2004).

[60] Between December 2003 and January 2004 the federal government advanced grants for the development of small towns in the Northeast. States like Arunachal Pradesh, where the BJP government was in power, received the sum of Rs192 crore while Assam, which was under Congress rule, received a paltry Rs40 crore. 'Arunachal Scores over Assam', *The Telegraph* (Guwahati) (22 Feb. 2004).

Naga outfits, the NSCN-IM, was preferred over the less militant NSCN-K during peace negotiations, even after ceasefire agreements had been signed with both. Likewise, the hard-line Bodo outfit, the Bodo Liberation Tigers, has been rewarded with a territorial Council. In these circumstances, there is little hope for the smaller outfits or more moderate tribal groupings to get their grievances redressed. Ironically, this has led to a rise in the number of ethnic organisations demanding autonomy and willing to take militant tactics to achieve it.

Thus New Delhi's strategy of giving precedence to its more strident opponents has turned out to be counter-productive. A change of policy is sorely needed if the nationalist aspirations of north-eastern India's diverse ethnic groups are to be diverted from the path of armed struggle into democratic and peaceful channels. Only recognition by the Union of their distinctive identities, and legal safeguards to preserve them, will achieve that transformation.

Identity Politics and Minorities in Pakistan*

Rasul Bakhsh Rais

In the past, as well as in our times, religion in multi-religious and -ethnic societies has polarised more than unified societies. Even within a single religious denomination one may find numerous strands that never tie up. Doctrinal differences, political contestation for power, material gains and territorial space can make the religion itself—and the question of authenticity—quite explosive. The political question of majority versus minority becomes salient and troublesome even in a society with one dominant religion. This question is a greater divisive force in states where religion is the source of political legitimacy or the basis of a state's identity. Religion turns out to be a dangerous political weapon when majority religious communities attempt to shape culture, social institutions and the state itself according to a specific belief system. It was not without some learning from history of bitter religious feuds that the neutrality of the state became the central element of theorising about the modern nation-state. The Western community of nations has accepted secular liberalism as the defining ideology of state, and this concept has found a considerable following even in the post-colonial states. But in some states, such as Pakistan, the role of religion is not a settled issue, which greatly impacts the statecraft, the status and rights of minorities, and the larger question of internal peace and security. In recent years, some of the Pakistani religious groups have become greatly involved in transnational terror networks, causing sectarian and communal violence within the country.

Complex historical and social factors have shaped the interaction between religion and politics in Pakistan. Islam was at the heart of the political struggle for the creation of Pakistan and has remained at the centre of post-Independence political discourse. Controversy about the role of Islam in politics continues to trouble the political landscape of the country. Even after half a century, the relationship

---

* An earlier version of this paper was published as 'Religious Radicalism and Minorities in Pakistan', in Satu P. Limaye, Robert G. Wirsing and Mohan Malik (eds), *Religious Radicalism and Security in South Asia* (Honolulu: Asia-Pacific Center for Security Studies, 2004), pp.447–65.

between religion and state is still as unclear as the nature and direction of the democratic enterprise. The question of what type of polity Pakistan should be—liberal democratic or Islamic—evokes different responses from different social sectors and political interests. Military leaders, mainstream political parties, and Islamists have all attempted to define this relationship according to their vision of democratic development and the role of religion in society and state affairs.[1]

Among the three main forces in the country, the quest for shaping the Pakistani state has added yet another dimension to religious and political polarisation in Pakistan. As a consequence of this unending conflict of interests and expedient coalitions, the autonomy of the civil political sphere and the general question of civil liberties and minority rights have suffered a severe setback. The central argument of this paper is that the common political strands of identity politics, state formation processes, and Islamic radicalism have caused the marginalisation of religious minorities, sectarian tendencies among Muslims sects and contributed to a wider problem of structured intolerance at the social level.

True representative democracy and constitutional politics are the best institutional tools to protect and advance the interests of religious minorities in any set of social conditions. For various reasons, Pakistan has never applied any of these tools during most of its history. The problem lies in the state formation process, in which the balance of power shifted toward the statist elites, the army and the civil bureaucracy.[2] Historical and geopolitical factors have determined this shift. At the moment, the army is once again restructuring the political system; the indications are that this will further institutionalise the army's power. The disjointed nature of democratic practice and its structural problems, which is a result of the army dominated state formation process, has not produced a social change capable of empowering minorities and other disadvantaged groups in society. Their marginalization is as much a result of the failure of democracy as it is due to deep-seated social and religious attitudes against them. Another important aspect of the state formation process in Pakistan is the contested issue of its identity—whether the state would be neutral among different religious communities or be Islamic.[3] Answers to this fundamental question continue to generate religious conflict and political confrontations in Pakistan.

To explain this dilemma, it is necessary to touch upon the Pakistani theory of the state. The movement for the creation of Pakistan, among other things, was aided

---
[1] Anwar Syed, *Pakistan: Islam and National Solidarity* (Lahore: Vanguard Books, 1984), pp.74–100.
[2] Hasan-Askari Rizvi, *Military, State and Society in Pakistan* (London: Macmillan Press, 2000), pp.1–16.
[3] Ayesha Jalal, 'Ideology and the Struggle for Democratic Institutions', in Victoria Schofield (ed.), *Old Roads New Highways: Fifty Years of Pakistan* (Karachi: Oxford University Press, 1997), pp.121–38.

by the acceptance of the demand of the Muslims as a religious minority. Since Muslims were a substantial minority—about 25 percent of the population in undivided India—the objective was to have proportionate representation in the elected assemblies under the British rule. For this, they demanded and achieved a system of separate electorates under which Muslim electorates voted only for Muslim candidates. Among other social and economic forces that influenced the growth of Muslim nationalism in British India, separate electorates further distanced Muslims from integration with the majority community on the basis of secular Indian nationalism. While separate electorates worked in some ways to the advantage of Muslims in undivided India—for example by getting larger numbers of their representatives in the elected assemblies than their population share warranted—it was politically divisive and created a bigger wedge between Congress and the Muslim League. After the creation of Pakistan, the issue of separate electorates became enshrined in the character of the Pakistani state. Even though Muslims became a majority, the state had the formidable task of reassuring religious minorities and integrating them into mainstream national politics.

In the 1956 Constitution, and later in the amended 1973 Constitution under the Zia ul-Haq regime, Pakistan practised separate electorates against the will of the minorities. The following sections explore minority discrimination and marginalization by examining the legal regimes that sustain discrimination, as well as informal social structures, values, and culture. The rise of Islamic radicalism during the past two decades has equally put religious minorities under tremendous social and political stress, in some cases provoking violence and terrorist attacks against their members and places of worship.

Identity Politics and the Marginalisation of Minorities

Until the recent changes in election laws, Pakistan had a system of separate electorates that was introduced by the military government of Zia ul-Haq in 1979. But the political roots of separate electorates go back to the pre-Partition Muslim politics in the subcontinent and also to the early debates after the creation of the country about how to best protect minority rights. One of the most important planks of Muslim politics under British rule was to ensure that Muslims scattered around the length and width of India have representation in the elected councils proportionate to their numbers. For this, Muslims demanded separate electorates, meaning they would be allocated seats in the local, provincial, and central legislative bodies according to their percentage in the population, and that only Muslims would vote for Muslim candidates. Although vehemently opposed by the Indian National Congress, this demand was accepted by the British government as both fair and expedient, and separate electorates were incorporated into the Minto-Morley

Reforms of 1909.[4] By this Act Muslims were in effect accorded dual voting rights: allowed to elect their own representatives and also to cast votes in the general constituencies. All elections thereafter adhered to this system. Some historians have argued—rightly I believe—that the establishment of separate electorates significantly strengthened the sentiment of Muslim separatism that led to the creation of Pakistan.[5]

Not surprisingly, the question of separate electorates was one of the focal points of debate and controversy in the Constituent Assembly of Pakistan when the post-Independence constitution was under discussion. On the issue of separate electorates, the views of the leaders of East Pakistan, where there was a sizeable Hindu minority, were different from those of the leaders of West Pakistan. While the West Pakistanis stressed the need for separate electorates, the East Pakistanis insisted on joint electorates. Members of the minority communities were also of the view that separate electorates would cast them off mainstream national politics. They demanded equal political, civic and legal rights that could be guaranteed only under the joint electorate system.

It is important to probe the reasons for support of the separate electorates. Why did post-Independence Muslim leaders support separate electorates for minorities? Was the move to protect the latter's democratic interests? A look at the arguments presented reveals that most Muslim leaders thought separate electorates were consistent with the two-nation ideology that Quaid-i-Azam Muhammed Ali Jinnah had expounded in 1940.[6]

Yet conservative religious leaders—and even some members of the Muslim League (the dominant political party at that time)—did not favour the idea of granting equal rights and status to non-Muslims in the Islamic polity they wished to establish.[7] Some of these leaders even questioned the loyalty of the Hindu minority to Pakistan and expressed their distrust of them openly. The religious parties and their supporters in the assembly refused to accept minorities as equal citizens with equal constitutional rights.

One wonders how separate electorates would have strengthened the foundation of Pakistan's ideology, promoted national integration and made Pakistan the

---

[4] Khalid bin Sayeed, *Pakistan: The Formative Phase 1857–1948* (Karachi: Oxford University Press, 2nd ed., 1998), pp.28–33.
[5] See for instance Ishtiaq Husain Qureshi, *A Short History of Pakistan* (Karachi: University of Karachi, 1988).
[6] See the views of the *ulema* (scholars of Islamic religion) in Sharif Al Mujahid, *Ideological Orientation of Pakistan* (Karachi: National Book Foundation, 1976).
[7] Government of Punjab, 'Report of the Court of Inquiry Constituted under Punjab Act II of 1954 to Inquire into the Punjab Disturbances of 1953' (Lahore: Superintendent of Government Publications, 1954).

progressive, moderate and liberal Islamic nation that its founder had wanted. Addressing the Pakistan Constituent Assembly Jinnah declared:

> You may belong to any religion or caste or creed—that has nothing to do with the business of the state. We are starting in the days when there is no discrimination between one caste or creed and another. We are starting with this fundamental principle that we are all citizens and equal citizens of one state. You will find that in the course of time, Hindus would cease to be Hindus and Muslims would cease to be Muslims, not in the religious sense, because that is the personal faith of each individual, but in the political sense as citizens of the state.[8]

There cannot be a more lucid and forceful expression of the founder's political ideology than this address to the Constituent Assembly. The occasion of entrusting the assembly with framing a constitution—and the forum itself—makes Jinnah's intent very clear about the direction and nature of Pakistan's polity. The liberals and minorities in Pakistan have taken this statement as the fundamental principle of the country's political structure. Likewise those who believe in liberal, secular and democratic values cite this historic address to support their vision of Pakistan.

Others have taken a long U-turn in reading the history of the Pakistan Movement and have reached opposite conclusions about the political character of the post-Independence Pakistani nation and state. In the formative phase of the country, some members of Jinnah's own party began to present a distorted, illiberal and retrogressive political map for the country. The argument that minorities could not be treated as equal citizens in the Islamic republic found a lot of support among the lawmakers from West Pakistan, many of whom hid their ideological bias in pleading that in a system of joint electorates minorities might not get representation in the national parliament and provincial assemblies. The members of the Constituent Assembly from East Pakistan vociferously contested this view.[9] They were right in arguing that separate electorates would leave minorities in both wings of the country disenfranchised, and that the system would work against national integration.

The Constituent Assembly, in the very contentious atmosphere of framing the 1956 Constitution, failed to reach any agreement on whether to have separate or joint electorates. After ascertaining the views of the provincial assemblies, the assembly left the matter for the future parliament to settle. The issue kicked up lot of public debate

---
[8] Quaid-i-Azam Muhammed Ali Jinnah, *Speeches as Governor-General of Pakistan 1947–1948* (Karachi: Pakistan Publications, n.d.), pp.8–9.
[9] The members of the Constituent Assembly from East Pakistan had vehemently argued in support of joint electorates, a political battle they later won.

and controversy, and the lines were drawn between liberal politicians and regional parties on one side and religious parties on the other. The Jamaat-e-Islami (Islamic Party) and its founder and prominent leader, Maulana Abul Ala Mauddudi, were at the forefront of opposition to the joint electorates.

Other religious political parties and, as mentioned above, some sections of the Muslim League, also supported separate electorates. Their reasons were as diverse as the leaders and groups themselves. They argued that, with the support of the Hindu minority, in a system of single member electoral constituencies, some pro-Indian parties and groups, especially in East Pakistan, might capture power. In their judgment, more Hindus would get elected to the provincial assembly in East Pakistan and to the national assembly than would be justified under joint electorates. They also argued that with the influence of Hindu lawmakers and their prominence in the political arena, Bengali nationalism would gain strength, undermine Pakistan's position on Kashmir and gradually erode the country's ideological foundations.[10] These arguments were flimsy, unconvincing and evasive of the real issues. The central principle of democracy is equality among all citizens with equal rights and duties. But a true democracy based on such principles was the last thing on the minds of many of these politicians, who were more interested in how to prevent religious minorities from becoming equal citizens and how to exclude them from electoral politics.

Why the religious and political parties wanted to build a political system in Pakistan where minorities would be marginalised and alienated is a question that has bothered true democrats from the beginning of the controversy to its end in 2002. All the major political parties in then East Pakistan supported joint electorates, except for the Muslim League, which had lost its influence there since the 1954 provincial election. After the adoption of the 1956 Constitution, when the issue was referred to the two provincial assemblies (East and West), a different resolution was passed: East Pakistan opted for joint electorates and West Pakistan for separate electorates. The national assembly, feeling the political pulse and sensible of the opposition from the East Pakistani parties, decided to approve two different methods: joint electorates for East Pakistan and separate electorates for West Pakistan.

When elections were about to be held under the 1956 Constitution, the military imposed martial law for the first time in the country, abrogated the constitution and set out to make a new one that would be 'appropriate to the genius' of the people of Pakistan. The issue of separate or joint electorates lingered on in political

---

[10] For details see M. Rafique Afzal, *Political Parties in Pakistan, 1947–58, Vol.1* (Islamabad: National Institute of Historical and Cultural Research, 1986), pp.185–9.

debates. The commission that was set up to frame the 1962 Constitution recommended separate electorates for minorities. General Muhammed Ayub Khan, the military ruler, did not accept the recommendation and decided for joint electorates. Pakistan held all subsequent elections under joint electorates, and the formal marginalisation of minorities in elections ended.

After the break-up of Pakistan in 1971, the parliament framed a new constitution more or less along the same lines as the 1956 Constitution, putting an end to the presidential system that Ayub Khan had earlier introduced. Pakistan was back to a parliamentary system. But this time around, even in the face of opposition from the religious parties, procedures for joint electorates were adopted.

Now the proportion of religious minorities in the population was just five percent. Perhaps because they were no longer a significant threat, the new government of Zulfikar Ali Bhutto introduced additional safeguards into the 1973 Constitution for representation of the minorities in national and provincial assemblies. Six seats were reserved for minorities in the national assembly. At the provincial level, five seats were reserved for them in the Punjab assembly, two in the Sindh assembly, two in the Baluchistan assembly, and one in the North West Frontier Province (NWFP) assembly. However, minority legislators at the Centre were not elected directly, but by the electoral colleges of their provincial assemblies. To further prove to the world that minorities were well represented in the power structure of Pakistan, the Bhutto administration—and almost all subsequent governments—recruited from the minority community at least one federal minister for some unimportant ministry. With this system, minorities had a better sense of participation but were far from being treated with equality as discrimination continued in many other forms.

A New Religious Minority

Ahmadiyyas who claim to be Muslims are a relatively new religious minority. Mainstream Muslims—both Shia and Sunni—do not accept Ahmadiyyas within the fold of Islam. The controversy over the Ahmadiyya sect is about one hundred years old. At the turn of the twentieth century, Muslim cleric Mirza Ghulam Ahmad from Qadian in Punjab declared himself a new prophet of Islam. He made many other controversial assertions, such as the claim that he was Jesus Christ re-sent to reform the world. People generally regarded Ahmad as an insane person and ignored him. When the ranks of his followers began to swell in numbers, mainly after his death, the leaders of Jamiat-i-Ulema-i-Hind (Association of Islamic Religious Scholars of India) took serious notice of the new prophet from Punjab. Maulana Shabbir Ahmad Usmani, a noted religious scholar, wrote one of the first comprehensive theses against the Ahmadiyya sect in 1935. He declared Mirza Ghulam Ahmad a false prophet and an apostate and said any person who accepted him as a prophet, or even as a religious scholar, was a heretic liable to be stoned to death. After his decree a number of Ahmadiyyas were stoned to death in the NWFP. The Deobandi *ulema* (religious forefathers of the Taliban) launched a nationwide movement against the Ahmadiyyas by declaring them non-Muslims and barring them from using Islamic symbols.

After the creation of Pakistan, the anti-Ahmadiyya push led by the Deobandi *ulema* built up a considerable head of steam, particularly in Punjab which had begun to emerge as the centre of Ahmadiyya preaching. The Majlis-i-Ahrar (Council for Liberation) and the Majlis e Khatme Nabuwat (Council for the Finality of Prophethood) were at the forefront of this movement.

They put forward three demands to the government in 1951 when the constitution of the country was being debated: (1) that Ahmadiyyas be declared as non-Muslims in Pakistan's constitution; (2) that Sir Zafarullah Khan, the first foreign minister of Pakistan, be removed from his position because he was an Ahmadiyya; and (3) that no Ahmadiyya be allowed to retain any key position in the country because Pakistan is an Islamic state. So strong was the movement by this time that Mumtaz Daultana, a Muslim League leader and chief minister of Punjab, lent his patronage. Nevertheless the central government remained unwilling to accede to its demands. Accordingly the anti-Ahmadiyya groups began to agitate in the streets of Lahore. The state of lawlessness and violence in 1953 provoked the first post-Independence imposition of martial law in the city, which curbed the movement's program for a time.

However a more violent form of the controversy revisited the country in the early 1970s. Among the many controversies created by the Bhutto government, one of the most crippling was the move to declare the Ahmadiyya sect 'non-Muslims' via constitutional amendment, which sparked pogroms in cities, towns, and villages across the country. Prominent Ahmadiyya families were pounced on, their houses and places of business attacked. Suspected Ahmadiyyas were harassed and physically beaten; eventually some thousands were killed. Far from impeding this terror campaign, the government condoned it, and afterwards legitimated it by the aforementioned Constitutional amendment by ordering the Ahmadiyyas' mosques to be closed down, and by debarring them from holding congregational prayers and from worshipping in the Sunni manner.[11] Last but not least, the government

---

[11] They are not allowed to make prayer calls or to display Islamic symbols or put up Islamic religious inscriptions in their places of worship.

added the Ahmadiyyas to the list of official minorities—along with Buddhists, Hindus, and Sikhs. This change required them henceforth to declare their status as 'Ahmadiyyas' in all official and legal documents.

These measures marked the beginning of official religious intolerance. Persecution of religious minorities—particularly against Ahmadiyyas—increased with the late General Zia ul-Haq's Islamisation project. A pervading sense of Islamic revival in the country fuelled another anti-Ahmadiyya wave around 1984. To placate the religious Right of the country and keep them on his side of the country's political divide, Zia further amended the Pakistan Penal Code by adding sections 298-B and 298-C, which made it a criminal offence for Ahmadiyyas to pose as Muslims, to preach or propagate by words (either spoken or written) and to use Islamic terminology or Muslim practices of worship. Once again, the state took the lead in implementing the political agenda of the religious political parties. In doing so, Pakistan has ignored its commitments to the Universal Declaration of Human Rights and violated its social contact with the minorities that supported the Pakistan movement.[12]

The wave of religious bigotry and extremism began with Zia courting the religious constituency for political support and legitimacy.[13] The Soviet military intervention in Afghanistan and the *mujahideen* resistance based in Pakistan were also factors that influenced the growth of religious militancy. The flow of arms and money from the oil-rich Middle Eastern countries to the Islamic *madrassa* (religious school) network further contributed to the power and influence of religious organisations.

Separate Electorates

After hanging an elected prime minister, Zulfikar Ali Bhutto, Zia appeared desperate to cultivate a support base among the religious groups to end his political isolation. He took two drastic measures at that time to bring himself closer to the religious groups: reintroducing separate electorates; and enacting blasphemy laws. Zia's actions are partly explained by his political need to have religious allies with 'street power' on his side. Equally important is the fact that his vision of Pakistan was not much different from that of most of the religious political parties. Zia had plans to remain in power; his only potential support base besides the military was the religious establishment. Zia adopted therefore the personal image of a pious, God-fearing, patriotic Pakistani, and vigorously pursued an Islamisation agenda in consonance with the long-standing demands of the religious Right, which rapidly gave a quite foreign

---
[12] Tayyab Mahmud, 'Protecting Religious Minorities: The Courts' Abdication', in Charles H. Kennedy and Rasul Bakhsh Rais (eds), *Pakistan: 1995* (Boulder: Westview Press, 1995), p.84.
[13] Mumtaz Ahmad, 'Revivalism, Islamization, Sectarianism and Violence in Pakistan', in Craig Baxter and Charles H. Kennedy (eds), *Pakistan: 1997* (Boulder: Westview Press, 1998), p.118.

Table 1
Population and Minorities in Pakistan

Minorities	Number	Percentage
Muslims	127,433,409	96.28
Christians	2,002,902	1.58
Hindus	2,111,271	1.60
Ahmadiyyas	289,212	0.22
Scheduled Castes	332,343	0.25
Others	96,142	0.07
Total Population	**132,352,279**	**100**

Source: Government of Pakistan, Statistics Division, No. SD. PER.E (53)/99–449 (Islamabad: Government of Pakistan, 2001).

orientation to Pakistan's political system—one not only Islamic, but Islamic in the most conservative tradition. His ordinances, laws, actions, and acts of omission and commission were passed into the Constitution through the Eighth Amendment, when the national assembly convened after the 1985 non-party elections. In this way the separate electorates became part of the 1973 Constitution.

The Zia regime increased the number of seats for minorities in the national assembly from five to ten, but maintained the same numbers in the provincial assemblies. There was also a change in how seats in the legislatures would be filled. The entire country was divided into ten constituencies for minorities, which made it utterly impossible for them to effectively contest or cast their votes. Since religious minorities are dispersed throughout the length of the country, drawing long territorial constituencies reduced the exercise of separate electorates to a mockery. Only a few influential, wealthy and well-connected minority figures could win in such a rough and unlevel electoral field.

With the death of Zia in 1988 there was a restoration of democracy and fresh elections. However, back in power, leaders from the mainstream political parties did not bother to address the issue of the marginalisation of minorities in electoral politics. Even with the unanimous removal of some parts of the Eighth Amendment through to the Thirteenth Amendment in 1997, the issue of joint electorates was not touched. Most politicians have not been keyed in to the issue or have never felt the need to understand the plight of religious minorities. Another reason could be the hesitation to offend the clamorous religious groups or to kick up a fresh controversy over an issue that to them seemed politically insignificant.

Blasphemy Laws

No other law has had as grave social and psychological implications for religious minorities as have the blasphemy laws. These laws have wide blanket coverage of acts that may fall within the offences of blasphemy, the violation of which carries long prison sentences and death by hanging. Offences include injuring or defiling places of worship with the intent to insult the religion of any class; deliberate and malicious acts intended to outrage religious feelings of any class by insulting its religion or religious beliefs; defiling a copy of the Holy Quran; the use of derogatory remarks with respect to the Holy Prophet of Islam; uttering words with deliberate intent to wound religious feelings; the use of derogatory remarks with respect to holy personages; the misuse of epithets, descriptions and titles reserved for certain holy personages and places; and a person of the Quadiani group or Ahmadiyya calling himself a Muslim or preaching or propagating his faith. In almost all cases, the law does not require any solid written proof, just the offensive remarks and few witnesses to get a conviction. More draconian is the procedure to file a complaint against an accused person. In addition to state functionaries, any private person can file a case in a police station against any person under these laws. For this reason, blasphemy laws have been repeatedly misused against religious minorities and Muslims. In almost all cases the complainants have been private individuals with a personal grudge or religious zeal.

The Human Rights Commission of Pakistan (HRCP) monitored the blasphemy cases registered from January to October 2000. The commission's newsletter listed fifteen cases against the Ahmadiyyas, five against Christians and eighteen against Muslims.[14] Common accusations against Ahmadiyyas included posing as Muslims, preaching, possessing Ahmadiyya literature, and building a minaret in the place of worship. Christians and Muslims were booked for making derogatory remarks about the Prophet of Islam, writing provocative slogans on walls, desecrating the Holy Quran or—like M. Yusuf Ali from Lahore—claiming to be prophets. Ali was sentenced to death in March 1997. While his appeal to higher courts was still pending in May 2002, a man convicted of sectarian terrorism and himself on death row shot Yusuf Ali dead with a gun that had been smuggled into the jail, presumably with the complicity of the authorities. This is not the first time a person accused of blasphemy has been murdered. The blasphemy laws have not only increased religious intolerance but have failed to provide any legal or institutional safety net for religious minorities.[15]

---

[14] Human Rights Commission of Pakistan (HRCP) Newsletter 11, no.4 (Oct. 2000), pp.13–14.
[15] See for instance, I.A. Rehman, 'A Critique of Pakistan's Blasphemy Laws', in Tarik Jan *et al.*, *Pakistan Between Secularism and Islam: Ideology, Issues and Conflict* (Islamabad: Institute of Policy Studies, 1998), pp.196–204.

Religious Intolerance and Terrorism

The rise of Islamic radicalism in Pakistan has greatly contributed to the growth of religious terrorism, especially against Ahmadiyyas and Christians, and in recent years also against the Ismaelis or Agha Khanis who are still officially classed in Pakistan as Muslims. The Deobandi faction has been the most active within the Sunni majority, supporting militant outfits such as Lashkar-i-Jhangvi and Sipah-i- Sahaba Pakistan (SSP). The Shia sect responded to this sectarian challenge by organising Sipah-i-Muhammad (SP). Both the SSP and SP have carried out brutal murders of religious scholars, political activists and young professionals. Thousands of Pakistanis have perished in the sectarian violence.[16]

Themajority of themembers of the Shia and Sunni communities have watched the sectarian killings with awe and disgust. But the sectarian violence of the last fifteen years could not have flourished as it has without the sympathy and support of influential people from the major communities. The fact that Pakistani Muslims can justify murdering fellow Muslims in the act of worshipping in mosques or assembled in religious congregations speaks volumes about the depth of religious hatred and intolerance in the country. In gross terms,moreMuslims have fallen victimto the religious intolerance of rival Islamic sects in Pakistan than have members of religious minorities.[17]

Beyond that, the rise in Islamic radicalism has produced a widespread sense of exclusion, inferiority, discrimination and above all, insecurity and fear. Although, as noted above, Ahmadiyyas have faced hostility and exclusion for a long time, never were they subjected to mass killings until their declaration as non-Muslims in the early 1970s. And even after that brief but troublesome period, most Ahmadiyyas continued to live in harmony with their neighbours. Only in recent years has the plight of the Ahmadiyya community become extreme.[18]

No other non-Muslim religious community has contributed more to the social sector development of Pakistan than the Christians have. Both missionaries and local members of the Christian community have built splendid educational institutions, hospitals and health facilities throughout the country. And they have remained peaceful even in the face of severe provocation, and have endured social discrimination and humiliation with grace and patience. But this stance has not brought

---

[16] The SSP and SP share an exclusivist religious outlook but conflicting interpretations of the history of Islam and its doctrines. Each questions the authenticity of the other and each proclaims the other is outside the pale of Islam. See Qasim Zaman, 'Sectarianism in Pakistan: The Radicalization of Shia and Sunni Identities', in *Modern Asian Studies*, Vol.32, no.3 (July 1998), pp.689–716.

[17] However this comparison may be misleading because the minorities are far fewer in number.

[18] Amnesty International, *Pakistan: Use and Abuse of Blasphemy Laws* (New York: Amnesty International, 1994), pp.6–7.

them respite. Christians are the new target of terrorism in Pakistan. Lashkari- Jhangvi terrorists attacked a Sunday Mass service in the Dominican Church in Bahawalpur on 28 October 2001 and massacred twenty-nine worshippers. In February 2002 terrorists attacked a church mostly attended by foreigners in the diplomatic enclave in Islamabad. On 5 August 2002 militants attacked a Christian school in the Murree Hills, killing six teachers and students.

How can one explain the rise of violence against the minority Shia sect of Islam, the Ahmadiyyas and the Christians? Is it due to the declining capacity of the state?

The state's declining capacity is part of the problem; while religious bigots have been preaching hatred and violence against minorities, the state has remained silent. Participatory politics and civic culture with a focus on citizenship rights have suffered gravely due to the repeated failure of the democratic process in Pakistan. In this democratic vacuum, religious extremism—riding on the wave of *jihad* in Afghanistan and with trans-national connections with similar groups—has taken strong root in society. The war against the Taliban and al-Qaeda, along with President Pervez Musharraf's policies to root out religious extremism, have produced a new wave of anti-Western feelings. This sentiment, however, is not new. Thinkers such as Maulana Mauddudi and Sayyid Qutb of Egypt, the two most powerful Muslim ideologues of the late twentieth century, linked the cause of Islamic revival to the historical grievances of Muslims against Western colonialism and and the need to cleanse the world of Western 'degeneracy' and 'barbarism'.[19] This ugly and quixotic mission, most infamously manifested in the killings of thousands of innocent people in New York and Washington DC on 11 September 2001 has, in Pakistan, underpinned attacks against foreigners and local Christians who are regarded by the extremists as an extension of Western religious influence.

Conclusion
Pakistan needs to create conditions for a true democratic polity and society to defeat terrorism internally and be able to help Afghanistan and other states to stabilise. As we know from the experience of other countries, democratic governance helps form social capital, build networks of trust and generate a sense of community that transcends sectarian, religious and ethnic differences. Nation- and state-building in any country, including Pakistan, is not about establishing a majority rule or simply holding elections (which in Pakistan have been few and mostly controversial), but about laying a solid foundation of representative legitimacy. For any student of democratic thought, nation- and state-building includes fundamental principles

---

[19] Amir Taheri, 'The Death of bin Ladenism', *The New York Times* (11 July 2002).

such as institutions and systems, citizenship, equality, inalienable fundamental rights, and the empowerment of all individuals without any discrimination. In most post-colonial states, ethnic, linguistic and religious minorities have found themselves at the receiving end of political distribution. Some saw their decline as a privileged group, while others found themselves reduced in number or branded as a new minority in the redrawing of boundaries. The example of Muslims in India and Hindus and Sikhs in Pakistan fits this description.

In Pakistan, the voice of the minorities has never touched the hearts or minds of the politicians. The tormenting experience of communal violence, transmigration of religious populations and the young and strident Muslim nationalism further muted it. In the bouts of political struggle for power, even liberal politicians remained silent on the issue of separate electorates. What could be more discriminatory than the classification of the citizen along religious lines? Most of the political parties decided to push the issue, while the religious groups feared a reversal of separate electorates would create a backlash. But the vision of democracy for such politicians was getting to the assemblies and obtaining ministerial positions and good salaries, not strengthening civic culture and participatory democracy.

Formal and informal discrimination against minorities has gone hand in hand; one has encouraged and deepened the other. Separate electorates have been more than separate electoral constituencies for religious minorities; they have contributed to the marginalisation of the minorities and a deepening sense among the groups that they are second-class Pakistanis. Mainstream political parties showed no interest in courting minorities and embracing prominent members and leaders of these groups because they could not vote for them.

Minorities were left to form their own parties, if they so wished. Only the Christians set up some loosely-organised parties. Other minorities have notable figures but no political organisations. Reversal of the separate electorates is very recent; it came with the political reforms introduced by the military regime. But decades of political alienation of the minorities has already done a great social and political harm to them.

In a traditional Islamic society such as Pakistan, non-Muslims hardly enjoy equality of social or religious status. Officially, placing non-Muslims in another category in electoral politics further deepened their alienation. Minority groups never supported separate electorates and have, for decades, struggled with whatever meagre political capital they possessed to have the joint electorates restored. In the urban constituencies where mainstream political parties have fought traditionally close contests, the balance held by minorities would make a major difference in joint electorates.

This paper shows how the practice of separate electorates effectively disenfranchised religious minorities in the name of giving them representation in the parliament and in the provincial assemblies. Recently the Musharraf government reversed the practice of separate electorates,[20] and enacted constitutional amendments giving reserved seats to the religious minorities in the parliament as well as in the provincial assemblies. This is a welcome and important step toward empowering minorities and bringing them back into mainstream national politics.

But discrimination against minorities remains embedded in the political mindset of the Pakistani elite. Although the 1970 and 1977 elections were held on the basis of joint electorates, not a single member from the minority communities won a seat. Fearing a repeat perhaps, none of the parties contesting the October 2002 elections saw fit to offer a ticket to a single member of any minority community to contest a general seat. Social prejudice is so strong among electors that no party wants to appear to be supporting a non-Muslim candidate against a Muslim candidate of a rival party.

The remedy for this sad state of affairs lies in affirmative action (as well as maintaining reserved seats for minorities in the provincial and national assemblies). Minorities do their best to change opinion via the press, seminars and publications. As well, civil society organisations in Pakistan and the foreign press and human rights organisations maintain a gentle pressure by questioning the authenticity of Pakistan's electoral democracy. But the Pakistan government has to take the main responsibility. It has to stem the tide of Islamic extremism and terrorism by reforming the *madrassa* network, cultivating civic culture, promoting democracy, and reorienting the political discourse on Islam, the state, and national identity. This is a tall order, but these issues must be faced if Pakistan is to protect its civil society against indiscriminate violence, instability and chaos.

---

[20] 'Electoral Changes: Bold and Innovative', *Dawn* (18 Jan. 2002).

The Evolution of Sectarian Conflicts in Pakistan and the Ever-Changing Face of Islamic Violence

Frédéric Grare

On 4 July 2003 three gunmen opened fire on a Shia congregation offering prayers in Quetta, Pakistan, killing 52 people and injuring at least 60. A few weeks later, 13 people died in a similar attack in Karachi. On 6 October Azam Tariq, leader of the banned Sipah-e-Sahaba, a sectarian Sunni militant group, was murdered on his way to the National Assembly in Islamabad. Between 1989 and 2003, 1468 Pakistanis were killed, and 3370 injured, in some separate 1813 incidents of (mainly) Shia–Sunni violence.[1] This violence is fuelled and exacerbated by highly inflammatory speeches by extremist *ulemas,* who constantly incite their followers to eliminate members of the other sect, invariably categorised as enemies of Islam.

Sectarian violence is not a monocausal phenomenon; it has deep social, political and geopolitical roots. However if sectarian conflict seems endemic in Pakistan, a closer look shows an evolution of the patterns of violence. For example, the link-up between sectarian and *jihadi* groups, as well as between local and internationalist organisations, first established during the Afghan conflict, has grown dramatically in recent years—even if the real nature of their relationships remains unclear. Social differences between internationalist and sectarian groups, the latter in general socially backward, certainly do play a role. And the change in the geopolitics of the region has also contributed. But some of the key factors in the *emergence* of sectarian violence in Pakistan, such as the regional impact of the Islamic revolution in Iran, are now of reduced importance; whereas others, such as the war against terrorism, have been more prominent to the extent that they are changing the relationship between the sectarian groups and the government, creating the conditions for new trends to emerge.

---

[1] Kanshan Lakshman, 'Deep Roots to Pakistan's Sectarian Terror', *Asia Times* (9 July 2003) [http://www.atimes.com/atimes/South_Asia/EG09Df09.html].

The present paper examines these evolutions from a prospective perspective. Starting from the emergence of sectarian violence in Pakistan, it tries to analyse systematically the enabling factors and to determine how their own evolution is likely to influence future sectarianism in Pakistan. The main argument is that, as the Shia–Sunni dimension loses its relevance due to the changing regional situation, sectarian and related organisations are likely to blend into the broader internationalist *jihadi* cause. This is not likely to lead towards less violence however; on the contrary, chances are it will pave the way for the emergence of more radical and professional extremists, making it as difficult for the government to eradicate violence.

Historical Background: The Islamic Revolution of Iran and the Emergence of Sectarianism in Pakistan

Shia–Sunni clashes were rare before the 1947 Partition of India in the areas which now constitute Pakistan. They started becoming commonplace in the 1980s as a result of Zia ul-Haq's Islamisation policies and the Iranian revolution. The Shias, representing about 20 percent of the population, have never been very enthusiastic about the Islamisation drive and in the 1970s they had generally supported the more secularly-oriented Pakistan's People's Party (PPP), fearing that the rising tide of militant orthodoxy might turn against them, as it had earlier against the Ahmadiyyas. Leaders of the Jamaat Ulema Islami (JUI) and Jamaat Ulema Pakistan had already taken an aggressive stance against the Shias, creating sectarian tensions in Karachi and Punjab.[2]

The Tehriq-e-Nifaz-e-Fiqah Jafria (TNJF), later renamed Tehrik-e-Jafria Pakistan (TJP), was established in 1979 two years after Zia's coup, at a convention of Shia Muslims in Bhakkar (Punjab). The move was a response to the new regime's Islamisation policy. Its explicit objectives were to assert separate Shia identity, protect their religious rights and prevent the Sunni majority from imposing its own interpretation of the Shariat. In 1979 when, encouraged by the Jamaat-e-Islami, Zia ul-Haq tried to impose *zakat* (a compulsory charity tax deducted by the government),[3] the TNJF violently opposed the measure[4] (which was later abandoned) and challenged both the Sunni hierarchy and the military regime.

In turn the military government found itself facing a wave of Shia activism openly sponsored by the newly-established Islamic Republic of Iran, which led to a number of violent incidents in those areas of Punjab with a recent history of Shia–Sunni

---

[2] Mumtaz Ahmad, 'Revivalism, Islamisation, Sectarianism and Violence in Pakistan', in Craig Baxter and Charles Kennedy (eds), *Pakistan 1997* (Boulder: Westview Press, 1998), p.108.
[3] Contrary to the Shia tradition where the payment of *zakat* is made on a voluntary basis.
[4] In the Shia tradition the payment of *zakat* is a free decision of each individual.

conflict.⁵ The rapid advance made by the organisation in rallying Pakistani Shias under its banner, as well as its alleged contacts with Iranian intelligence, set off alarm bells in Islamabad.⁶ The Zia regime started to wonder whether its western neighbour intended to export its revolution to Pakistan.

As a matter of fact, Iran's radicals *were* keen on promoting Islamic militancy; while the Iranian revolution gave a new sense of identity to Pakistan's Shia community which led it to enter the political arena in the early 1980s. Its political organisations have, since then, maintained close relations with Iranian authorities, and followed the Iranian line in all matters of foreign policy.⁷ Over the same period Iran provided funds to Pakistani Shias and opened cultural centres in every major Pakistani city, and paid for many young clerics, mostly from the Pushtun tribal areas of Gilgit and Baltistan, to undertake further study in the cities of Qom and Najaf, where they created contacts with Shias from the Middle East, and in particular from Lebanon.⁸

The development of Sunni sectarian organisation was partly a reaction to the new Shia assertiveness. Sunni Islamists considered Zia's capitulation over the *zakat* issue a threat to the entire Islamisation process.⁹ The first Sunni sectarian organisation to launch an anti-Shia movement in Punjab after the Islamic revolution in Iran was the Wahhabi Jamaat Ulema-e-Ahl-e-Hadith (Society of the Ulema of 'the People of the Hadith'). Not only did it denounce Shiism as heresy but also questioned the loyalty of the Shias *vis-à-vis* Pakistan. The Jamaat Ulema-e-Ahl-e-Hadith was closely associated with the Saudi government from which it received large amounts of money not only for its *madrassas,* but also for Afghan *jihad*-related activities. Being unable, however, to conduct operations on a large scale, it soon handed over the leadership of the violent anti-Shia campaign to the activists of JUI and the Sipah-e-Sahaba Pakistan.¹⁰

The Anjuman Sipah-e-Sahaba Pakistan was created on 6 June 1984 by a member of the Jamiat-e-Ulema Islam (Fazl-ur-Rehman Group) from the Jhang District,

---

⁵ On the roots of these conflicts see the section on 'Historical Roots and Social Factors' later in this paper.
⁶ B. Rahman, *Sipah-e-Sahaba Pakistan, Lashkar-e-Jhangvi, Bin Laden & Ramzi Yousef,* Paper No. 484, South Asia Analysis Group, 1 July 2002 [http: //www. saag.org/papers5/paper 484.html]. As noted by the author, the Zia regime may also have been alarmed by the sympathy of the Shias toward the Bhutto family.
⁷ Ahmad, 'Revivalism, Islamisation, Sectarianism and Violence in Pakistan', p.112.
⁸ Mariam Abou Zahab, 'The Regional Dimension of Sectarian Conflicts', in Christophe Jaffrelot, *Pakistan: Nationalism without a Nation* (Delhi: Manohar, 2002), p. 116.
⁹ Some Sunni started to pretend that they were Shia in order to be exempted from the compulsory payment of *zakat*. See Christophe Jaffrelot, *Le Pakistan* (Paris: Fayard, 2000), p.393.
¹⁰ The reasons behind the anti-Shia character of JUI are essentially theological and will not be dealt with here.

Maulana Haq Nawaz Jhangvi. Jhangvi was the first Pakistani to demand publicly that Shias be declared a non-Muslim minority.[11] With the tacit help of the Zia administration he persuaded poor people to send their sons for education to his *madrassa*, free of cost, and convinced the Saudi government to support his teaching of Deobandi school theology against the Iranian-sponsored educational initiatives of the Shias. Later he recruited hundreds of *madrassa* students for training in terrorist tactics with a view to unleashing them against Shia institutions and parties. In September 1985 the Anjuman Sipah-e-Sahaba was renamed the Sipah-e-Sahaba Pakistan (SSP).[12] Apart from its violent activism[13] and numerous links to terrorist organisations,[14] the SSP has always maintained an explicit political profile—contesting elections, and even serving in a Punjab coalition government.[15]

During and after the 1980s Iran–Iraq war, Pakistani sectarian groups fought a proxy war with Shia organisation supporting Iran and Sunni groups Iraq and Saudi Arabia. Funds also came from other Arab states as well as from private donors. However, specialists date the present state of organised sectarian conflict either to 1987, when Sunni Ahl-e-Hadith leaders Allama Ehsan Elahi Zaheer and Maulana Habib ur Rehman Yazdani were killed at a meeting near the Minar-e-Pakistan in Lahore, or to 1988, after the murder of the leader of TNFJ's Arif Hussain Al-Hussaini.[16]

The subsequent radicalisation of sectarian groups was the result of both internal dissent over religious and political issues, and of the escalation of violence between Sunni and Shia movements. While TNJF operated as a politico-religious organisation, in 1994 the Sipah-e-Mohammad (SMP) emerged as the militant wing of Shia political activism and the mirror image of the SSP. Although its declared objective was to eliminate sectarianism from Pakistan, its members dedicated themselves to the assassination of their political opponents.[17] The SMP distanced itself from the Tehriq-e-Nifaz-e-Fiqah Jafria when the latter decided to oppose the PPP in the 1988 elections. SMP leaders thought the decision was opposed to Shia community interests and felt that the shift from the TNJF to the

---

[11] Ahmad, 'Revivalism, Islamisation, Sectarianism and Violence in Pakistan', p. 109.

[12] The SSP also benefited from a large network of other Deobandi institutions (Sawad-i-Azam Ahle Sunnat, Sunni Tehrik, Sunni Council, Sunni Jamiyyat-i-Talaba, Pakistan Sunni Irtteghad, Tahafuzz-i-Khatam-i-Nabuwat) which serve as political arms of the SSP. See Ahmad, 'Revivalism, Islamisation, Sectarianism and Violence in Pakistan', p.110.

[13] The Iranian consul general, Sadeq Ganji, was killed by the SSP in 1990 in retribution for the 1990 killing of the SSP co-founder Maulana Haq Nawaz Jhanvi.

[14] Many SSP cadres have received arms training from the Harakat-ul Mujahideen and the Taliban. It is also reported to be closely linked to the Jaish-e-Mohammad [http://www.ict.org.il/organizations/orgdet.cfm?orgid=57].

[15] In 1995, two SSP leaders became provincial ministers in a PPP-led Punjab government.

[16] Musa Khan Jalalzai, *Sectarian Violence in Pakistan and Afghanistan* (Lahore: System Books, 2000), p.6.

[17] Sohail Mahmood, *Islamic Fundamentalism in Pakistan, Egypt and Iran* (Lahore: Vanguard, 1995), p.260.

TJP indicated a shift from religion to politics. More importantly however, they considered the party was doing nothing to combat SSP violence.[18]

The creation in 1996 of the Lashkar-e-Jhangvi (L-e-J), a Sunni sectarian and terrorist group, was the result of a similar process—a walkout by more radical and extremist elements of the SSP in protest against what they considered as a deviation from Jhangvi's ideals.[19] Throughout the latter part of 1990, L-e-J claimed responsibility for the assassinations of religious leaders, diplomats, priests and worshippers.[20] It also carried out, in 1999, an assassination attempt on then-Pakistani Prime Minister Nawaz Sharif who was trying actively to combat it.[21]

Historical Roots and Social Factors

Although relations between Sunnis and Shias remained generally calm, except for occasional disturbances, until the beginning of the 1980s, sectarian violence cannot be explained by the then-prevailing international situation alone. As observed by Mariam Abou Zahab, 'the external element has sometimes been no more than the enabling factor'.[22] Sectarian militancy has deeper historical roots and needs also to be understood 'as a reaction to a growing sense of insecurity and hopelessness resulting from the uneven distribution of resources, and as a revolt of the uprooted and marginalised periphery deprived of access to the political arena'.[23]

Sectarianism is, to a degree, an avatar of the 1947 Partition of colonial India. The migrants who went to what is now Pakistan's Punjab province mostly came from the eastern portion of the then-united Indian Punjab.[24] The vast majority were Sunnis with very few Shias. Their level of education was very low and most were either serving in the armed forces or working as farm labourers.

These migrants found little difficulty in integrating themselves into Pakistani Punjab since they spoke the same Punjabi or Seraiki languages as are spoken in Indian Punjab. Many landless labourers started working in the farms of Shia landlords in districts such as Multan and Jhang.[25] However the economic system kept them

---

[18] Jalalzai, *Sectarian Violence in Pakistan and Afghanistan*, p.47.
[19] Jhangvi had been assassinated in 1990.
[20] It also killed four American oil workers in 1997.
[21] See http://www.cdi.org/terrorism/lij.cfm.
[22] Mariam Abou Zahab, 'Sectarianism as Substitute Identity: Sunnis and Shias in Central and South Punjab', in Soofia Mumtaz, Jean-Luc Racine, and Imran Anwar Ali (eds), *Pakistan: The Contours of State and Society* (Karachi: Oxford University Press, 2005, p.79.
[23] *Ibid.*, pp.79-80.
[24] It has subsequently been bifurcated between Punjab and Haryana.
[25] Jhang, where the SSP and its offshoot the Lashkar-e-Jhangvi were created, has a very large population of poor settlers from East Punjab.

poor—and deprivation bred resentment. This was especially the case in South Punjab, an area which had remained socially and economically neglected and backward,[26] even as much of the rest of Punjab had benefited from the introduction of irrigation.[27] It is therefore no coincidence that sectarianism is to a large extent (although not exclusively)[28] a Punjabi phenomenon.

Indeed the subsequent economic and social evolution of the province only increased the class tensions there. The decline of permanent farm labour and rural migration due to the progressive rationalisation and mechanisation of Punjabi farming was not a new phenomenon. But the social evolution of the late 1970s was characterised by rapid urbanisation without industrialisation; while political power remained in the hands of the large landlords and urban elites.[29] Those of the rural poor who were able to take advantage of the burgeoning demand for labour in the Persian Gulf often returned with big money in their pockets, and hopes of bettering their status, but found the power structure closed off to them.

The SSP provided these discontented people with a political platform and access to the political arena. In its effort to counter the new Shia assertiveness the SSP, with the acceptance (and later support) of the regime, transformed what were essentially economic and social grievances into sectarian hatred. Religion thus became the new political currency—in part because of the strength of sectarian feelings among the politicians, and also because it was a handy way to mobilise people and gain a constituency. Those political aspirants who lacked other assets such as wealth, modern education or family connections could always fall back on religious rhetoric as their ticket to political power. It is no coincidence that Jhang, where Shia landowners had long held political power, became the first city to fall prey to sectarian violence in the mid 1980s. The SSP and its offshoot, L-e-J, were also created as instruments to fulfil this objective.[30]

Sectarian violence, therefore, rapidly acquired a dynamic of its own; and soon a large number of people became financially linked to the enterprise of violence. Moreover, allegiance to violence was locally empowering. The clergy in particular found that their sermons had a much greater impact if they were backed by real threats and

---

[26] According to the 1981 census, the literacy rate of South Punjab was the lowest of the country.
[27] Zahab, 'Sectarianism as Substitute Identity', p.91.
[28] Karachi also experienced some of the bloodiest sectarian violence. Sectarianism there revolved around ethnic conflicts and criminal rivalries within the city. In general, it was the the presence of a substantial Shia minority and local conflicts which led to the explosion of sectarian violence in the 1990s.
[29] The two major attacks of 2003 took place in Quetta, Baluchistan. On 8 June, 13 trainee police personnel belonging to the local Hazara community of Shia were killed and 8 others injured. On 4 July, 53 people were killed and more than 60 others injured. See Massoud Ansari, 'Valley of Death', *Newsline* (August 2003), pp.18–32.
[30] See also Eqbal Ahmed, 'The Conflict Within', *Dawn* (15 February

violence—hence their constant 'rage' posture.[31] And disillusioned youth lapped it up, convinced that the traditional religious parties had failed to defend the Islamic faith. The *mullahs,* however, became increasingly trapped in their own rhetoric. They had either to become more radical or risk losing their followers. The escalation of violence was a logical consequence. In turn this trend was reinforced by the moral degeneration of the movement when some militants started exploiting sectarian differences in pursuit of private interests.

Madrassas and Sectarianism

The *madrassas* were the main breeding grounds for sectarianism although they did not attract such great international attention until after 9/11. Of course *madrassas* are not a new phenomenon in Pakistan. But from the 1960s their numbers expanded exponentially. Between 1960 and 1971, 482 new schools were created. The number doubled under Zulfikhar Ali Bhutto. By 1979, another 852 had been established. Under Zia ul-Haq, 1151 new institutions were registered between 1979 and 1988. Seven years later, another 860 had been set up. The exact number of these establishments remains unclear even to the present day, but according to some estimates there are around 10,000 *madrassas* catering for approximately 1.7 million students.[32] In 2001 250,000 students attended 2715 *madrassas* in the Punjab.[33] The number of registered *madrassas* in the North West Frontier Province in 2003 was 1525.[34]

The exponential growth of *madrassas* was due partly to the Pakistan state's failure to provide basic educational facilities. The *madrassas* do not charge any fees and provide basic literacy for about one third of Pakistani school-age children. This helps explain, for example, their strength in South Punjab, where the landlords opposed establishing government schools for the rural poor.

Equally, however, their growth is related to the regional conflicts in the 1980s and to their impact on Pakistan's domestic politics. The violently anti-Shia characteristic of Deobandi and Ahl-e-Hadith *madrassas* brought them not only the largesse of the Zia regime, but also funds from Saudi Arabia and Iraq. Similarly, Shia *madrassas* were provided with Iranian literature, funds and networking. Regional conflicts thus exacerbated initial theological differences: later violence was fuelled by the Afghan *jihad.* It is no coincidence that all sectarian parties banned

---

[31] Khaled Ahmed, 'It's Mostly Muslim Kill Muslim Here', *The Friday Times* (22-28 August 2003), p.9.
[32] International Crisis Group (ICG), *Pakistan: Madrassas, Extremism and the Military,* ICG Asia Report, No. 36 (29 July 2002), p.9.
[33] Azmat Abbas, 'The Real Battlefront', *The Herald* (Karachi) (November 2001), p.50.
[34] *The News* (24 October 2003).

by the Musharraf government in January 2002, including Sipah-e-Sahaba Pakistan (SSP), Jaish-e-Muhammad, Lashkar-e-Jhangvi (L-e-J), Tehrik Nifaz-e-Shariah Muhammadi, and Sipah-e-Muhammad, originated in *jihadi madrassas*.[35]

In fact *madrassas* have served a dual purpose for the regime: as a tool in domestic politics (it was during the Zia era that splinter Deobandi groups such as SSP emerged); and as a support for its regional policy, in particular towards Afghanistan and Kashmir. *Madrassas* contributed to the process by mobilising public opinion, producing propaganda literature, recruiting and training the *jihadis*. The training in the same schools of both sectarian and *jihadi* extremists created the basis for the subsequent evolution of sectarian violence.

This is clearly evident in a party such as JUI, which played a distinctive role in the process. Belonging to the Deobandi school and strongly anti-Shia,[36] it is divided between two main factions, one led by Maulana Fazl-ur-Rehman and the other by Maulana Sami-ul-Haq. Both factions have strong Arab connections. Both welcomed many Arab *jihadis* to their ranks and participated in the creation of the Taliban—all the while continuing to spread an anti-Shia message.

Still, the link between sectarian violence, international terrorism and *madrassas* should not be overestimated. According to the International Crisis Group, only 10 to 15 percent of *madrassas* are actually involved in terrorist activities. The vast majority of them neither conduct military training nor provide arms to students— they are simply traditional religious schools. Yet if not all sectarian extremists have a *madrassa* background, the *madrassas have* contributed enormously to the sectarian phenomenon, using their influence over vulnerable minds to create an atmosphere of hatred conducive to the polarisation and radicalisation of some of the most fragile segments of the society.

Pakistan's Domestic Politics and Sectarian Violence: Between Ambivalence and Complicity

It is common knowledge that the Zia regime systematically promoted sectarianism in order to counter what it saw as a growing Iranian influence in the country. However, sectarianism also brought a considerable amount of domestic political benefit for Zia. The Shia–Sunni conflict was a convenient diversion from the PPP-led political

---

[35] ICG, *Pakistan: Madrassas, Extremism and the Military,* p. 12.
[36] The Sami-ul-Haq faction in particular keeps publishing anti-Shia pamphlets despite it being a member of the Mutahida Majlis-e-Amal (MMA), an alliance of six Islamic parties in which Shias are also represented.

agitation against the martial law regime; and it was a convenient way of sowing discord amongst the regime's opponents in the regions.[37]

Unfortunately, post-Zia governments did not do any better. Political parties continue to routinely compromise with sectarian groups and cynically manipulate sectarian conflicts for short-term political gains. Both the SSP and TJP were allowed to engage in electoral politics. Both entered into alliances with mainstream parties, the PPP, or the Pakistan Muslim League. Even Benazir Bhutto, whose party and family have suffered greatly from the policies of Zia, was happy to turn a blind eye to sectarian extremism when it suited her political agenda. On 22 January 1995, federal Interior Minister Naseerullah Babar announced that the government intended to ban direct funding of all *madrassas* as well as tracking down those institutions which were fanning sectarianism. He also promised that an anti-sectarian bill would be passed in the National Assembly.[38] But the bill was never even submitted to the Assembly. Instead, an eminent SSP leader, Sheikh Hakim Ali, was jobbed in as minister of fisheries in the Punjab government because the PPP needed the SSP's support to achieve a majority in the legislature.[39] It is also reported that SSP leader and member of the National Assembly, Azam Tariq (recently assassinated), enjoyed complete immunity from law enforcement agencies during the entire Bhutto tenure (despite his active role in anti-Shia violence) because he was an arch enemy of Syeda Abida Hussain, a veteran Shia leader from Jhang at political odds with Benazir Bhutto.[40]

Nawaz Sharif was the only prime minister who tried to address the issue seriously. In 1997, he enacted an Anti-Terrorism Act which gave added powers to the army and police to combat sectarian violence. On 3 January 1999 Nawaz narrowly escaped an assassination attempt. The government responded with the Anti-Terrorism Ordinance of July 1999.

Even though different governments did not necessarily approve of sectarian violence, they were not prepared to actively disband groups. Indeed they opted for half-hearted measures—encouraging dialogue between different groups and eventually giving police protection to threatened religious congregations.[41] After the military take over of 1999 General Musharraf adopted a similar strategy. He banned two groups—one Sunni (Lashar-e-Jhangvi) and one Shia (Sipah-e-Muhammad

---

[37] Ahmad, 'Revivalism, Islamisation, Sectarianism, and Violence in Pakistan', p.117.
[38] Jalalzai, *Sectarian Violence in Pakistan and Afghanistan,* p.74.
[39] Zahab, 'The Regional Dimension of Sectarian Conflicts in Pakistan', p. 119
[40] Ahmad, 'Revivalism, Islamisation, Sectarianism, and Violence in Pakistan', p.117.
[41] Yunas Samad, 'Pakistan, Pro-Taliban Elements and Sectarian Strife', *Middle East Report Online* (16 November 2001) [http://www.merip.org/mero/mero 111601 .html].

Pakistan)—and warned that other groups (SSP and TJP) were being watched. But he failed to take any decisive action against these hardliners.[42] On the contrary Azam Tariq, although in prison, was permitted to run for the 2002 general elections. Having won a seat in the National Assembly, he was released from prison and thereafter supported the government until his assassination on 6 October 2003. To retain Tariq's support the government ignored the non-bailable warrants out against him including those issued under anti-terrorism laws in July 2000.[43]

Even after the U-turn of the Pakistani government on Afghanistan, which contributed to the fall of the Taliban regime in Kabul, the authorities felt unconfortable with the idea of actively fighting sectarian organisations because of their role in sustaining the government's strategy in Kashmir. This role, however, has to be spelled out more precisely. The distinction between *jihadi* and sectarian organisations is not always clear. Jaish-e-Muhammad, for example, though essentially a *jihadi* movement, occasionally participated (or at least some of its members did) in sectarian violence. On the contrary, groups such as SSP, which are clearly sectarian organisations, cooperated with the Pakistani intelligence agencies in order to be accepted domestically. SSP has fought alongside the Taliban in Afghanistan and L-e-J has allegedly sent men to Kashmir. This strategy has made it difficult for successive Pakistani governments to effectively combat them in spite of the strong consensus against the *domestic violence* they have wreaked around the country.

General Musharraf's policy reflected this ambivalence. On 15 and 17 November 2003, he issued orders against six organisations which had been to all intents and purposes banned before, but were now operating under new names: Tehrik-e-Islami Pakistan (formerly Tehrik-e-Jafria); Millat-e-Islami (formerly Sipah-e-Sahaba Pakistan); Khuddam-e-Islam (formerly Jaish-e-Muhammad); Jamaat-ul-Furqan (a breakaway group of Jaish-e-Muhammad); Hizbut Tahrir; and Jamaat-ul-Ansar (formerly Harakat-ul Mujahideen). All these groups (with the exception of Hizbut Tahrir) had been previously involved in sectarian violence.[44] On the other hand Jamaat-ul-Dawa (formerly Lashkar-e-Taiba), which was not involved in sectarian violence but was active in Kashmir, was simply put on the watch list. Not surprisingly, the renewed ban on sectarian groups operating under new names has been described by many as mere 'window dressing'. No specific charges have been laid against the some 600 militants arrested in raids on the offices of these organisations, which suggests that the government does not intend to keep them in jail

---

[44] The ban hardly changed the reality on the ground because the police were already after the members of the two outfits.
[43] International Crisis Group (ICG), *Unfulfilled Promises: Pakistan's Failure to Tackle Extremism*, International Crisis Group, 16 January 2004, p. 12.
[44] Zaffar Abbas, 'Inaction Replay', *The Herald* (December 2003), p.56.

for a long time. Accordingly, the Islamists are confident that it will soon again be business as usual.[45] Thus, while there is no reason to doubt General Musharraf's desire to eradicate sectarian violence (especially since he himself has become a target of some of the banned organisations), the Pakistani government seems to be hesitating between the needs of the moment and its traditional strategy over Kashmir. This in turn raises a number of questions about Pakistan's actual determination to fight the problem.

Sectarian Violence and the Afghan *Jihad*

The Afghan war was not a cause of sectarian violence in Pakistan. However its contribution was significant in terms of the supply of manpower, military training, weapons, networking and funds to the sectarian militants. This became particularly obvious after 1989, with the Soviet withdrawal from Afghanistan, and even more after 1996 after the Taliban took over Kabul[46]—at which point Pakistan became the destination for thousands of motivated young *jihadis* with plenty of weapons at their disposal. The level of violence witnessed a qualitative change.

After the Soviet withdrawal, as the battlefield shifted from Afghanistan to Kashmir, a number of young Pakistanis continued to receive military training in Afghanistan and in the tribal areas. The training camps welcomed militants from all the *mujahideen* parties supported by Pakistan, essentially Hezb-e-Islami, Lashkar-e-Taiba and Jamaat-e-Islami. With the emergence of the Taliban, these camps were initially closed and many militants headed back to Pakistan.

Jamaat-e-Islami, which has always opposed sectarianism, sent a significant number of recruits to Afghanistan. It was quick to realise the gravity of the situation and mobilised the party's youth wing to form the Pasban[47] in order to save their soldiers from falling into the sectarian trap. Other religious parties such as Jamiat-e-Ulema Islam (Fazl-ur-Rehman faction) however, did not realise, or were not willing to accept, the seriousness of the situation—and left their young cadres to fend for themselves.[48] The number of sectarian incidents had been on the rise since the end of the 1980s. However it more than doubled in 1997 (see table below), although the number declined slightly over the following two years.

---

[45] *Ibid.*
[46] The Taliban initially closed all *jihadi* camps in Afghanistan in the provinces they controlled. Some of these camps were later re-opened at the request of the Pakistanis.
[47] The Pasban were a youth organisation created by the Jamaat-e -Islami in the mid 1990s in order to control the flow of young militants coming back from Afghanistan.
[48] Jalalzai, *Sectarian Violence in Pakistan and Afghanistan*, pp.23–4.

After the Taliban took over Kabul, some of the camps were reopened under Inter-Service Intelligence (ISI) pressure, and handed over to Harakat-ul Mujahideen and other outfits involved in Kashmir. Nevertheless, the inability of the Taliban to achieve a quick victory led them to look for additional manpower which SSP and related organisations were only too keen to provide given their anti-Shia and anti-Iranian stance.

The links between SSP, L-e-J and the Taliban have since then been well documented. SSP and L-e-J activists were trained in Afghanistan and fought against the Northern Alliance alongside the Taliban. In 1996, together with other *mujahideen* groups such as Harakat-ul-Hansar, SSP and L-e-J militants entered Afghanistan and helped capture Jalalabad and Kabul.[49] It was also reported that they massacred Shias living in the Hazara belt.[50] Similarly, when relations between Iran and Pakistan soured due to the killing of Iranian diplomats in Mazar-i-Sharif in Afghanistan, Azam Tariq, the then-leader of SSP, announced that his party was 'ready to send 20000 militants to fight alongside the Taliban if Iran tried to impose a war on Afghanistan'.[51] It was also in Afghanistan that links with internationalist militant groups were established. The sectarian militants trained in the same camps as al-Qaida, Lashkar-e-Taiba, Jaish-e-Muhammad, Harakat-ul Mujahideen, Hizbut Tahrir, and Jamaat-ul-Furqan, paving the way for alliances which would materialise in Pakistan after the end of the Taliban regime.

Similarly, the Hazarajat area in Afghanistan whose population is mainly Shia became a training ground for Shia militants. As a consequence, Shia militancy in Pakistan suffered a major setback when the Taliban overran the region. Afghanistan became a safe haven and training ground for Sunni extremist organisations only.[52]

With the ousting of the Taliban regime, Afghanistan ceased in the short term to be a sanctuary for militants; hence many returned to Pakistan. Both sectarians and internationalists were now on the run. This phenomenon was similar to the one observed in 1997, when the then-new Taliban government closed the *mujahideen* camps. The number of sectarian incidents picked up again. 2001 was the worst year ever in Pakistan's twenty-year-long history of sectarian violence.[53]

---

[49] Rahman, *Sipah-e-Sahaba Pakistan, Lashkar-e-Jhangvi, Bin Laden & Ramzi Yousef.*
[50] *Ibid.*
[51] Quoted in Zahab, 'The Regional Dimension of Sectarian Conflicts', p. 123.
[52] Zaffar Abbas, 'Root Causes: A Brief History of Sectarian Violence in Pakistan', *The Herald* (December 2003), p.59.
[53] See Table 1.

Table 1
Sectarian Violence in Pakistan

Year	Number of Incidents	Number Injured	Number Killed	Percentage Killed per Incident
1989	67	102	18	0.26
1990	274	328	32	0.11
1991	180	263	47	0.26
1992	135	261	58	0.43
1993	90	247	39	0.43
1994	162	326	73	0.45
1995	88	189	59	0.67
1996	80	168	86	1.08
1997	103	219	193	1.87
1998	188	231	157	0.84
1999	103	189	86	0.84
2000	109	NA	149	1.37
2001	154	495	261	1.70
2002	63	257	121	1.92
2003	21	103	100	4.76
Total	**1817**	**3378**	**1479**	–

Source: South Asia Intelligence Review, 'Sectarian Violence in Pakistan' (online version) [www.satp.org/satporgtp/countries/pakistan/database/sect-killing.htm].

However, increasing American pressure followed by the intensification of the war against terrorism meant that Pakistan was no longer a safe sanctuary either. After Musharraf chose to ally with the US, he banned a number of *jihadi* and militant outfits in 2002.[54] In Afghanistan internationalists and sectarians had kept separate identities and had had a different focus. Now they had a common enemy: the United States and its ally, the Musharraf government. This led to the creation of a number of new umbrella associations such as Lashkar-e-Omar, a group formed from the conglomeration of Harakat-ul-Jihad-al-Islami (HUJI), L-e-J and Jaish-e-Muhammad.[55] These associations were created to serve the needs of the

---

[54] In his 12 January 2002 speech, Pervez Musharraf announced the banning of 5 organisation: Jaish-e-Mohammad, Lashkar-e-Taiba, Sipah-e-Sahaba, Tehrik-e-Jafria and Harakat-ul Mujahideen.
[55] Rahman, *Sipah-e-Sahaba Pakistan, Lashkar-e-Jhangvi, Bin Laden & Ramzi Yousef.*

moment. They helped internationalist militants on the run and conducted joint operations, but lacked real unity of command or long-term objectives.

Changing Patterns of Terrorism: Sectarian Violence and International Islamic Terrorism

In recent times, each major event in Afghanistan has had an impact on sectarian violence in Pakistan. As noted above, the closing down of the *mujahideen* training camps shortly after the Taliban took over Kabul and Jalalabad was followed in 1997 by an increase in the number of sectarian incidents. Similarly in 2001, the fall of the Taliban regime led a number of Taliban and their Pakistani allies to seek refuge in Pakistan. The sectarian frenzy again reached unprecedented levels (see Table 1).

The link between the Afghan war and sectarian violence in Pakistan has been long established. However, not only did the number of incidents jump after 1996,[56] but one observes a qualitative change over time in the pattern of sectarian violence.

The first significant evolution was in respect of its geographical extension. Initially the fighting was contained to specific areas, Central and Southern Punjab and Karachi essentially. After 1995 it jumped these boundaries and soon infected the entire country. Even Baluchistan, previously unaffected by religious sectarianism despite the presence there of a strong Hazara Shia community, has not escaped the pandemic. The second change was that sectarian terrorism became much more lethal, a sign of the growing professionalism of the terrorists. The number of deaths per sectarian incident has continued to increase since the end of the 1980s. In the early 1990s, bombs were detonated after dark to cause damage but minimise possible casualties; targets identified for assassination were usually attacked when alone; and most killings were of sect leaders. In 1997 there was a dramatic change, as the terrorists began indiscriminate bombings of ordinary citizens designed to ensure maximum casualties. They are prepared to kill not only their putative targets, but also anyone unfortunate enough to be nearby.[57]

Finally, the distinction between sectarian and *jihadi* groups, although never, as we have seen, totally clear-cut, is now tenuous. Investigations into the two-pronged suicide attacks launched against General Musharraf on 25 December 2003 pointed to the involvement of Brigade 313, a loose alliance of five militant organisations incorporating both *jihadi* and sectarian elements: Jaish-e-Muhammad;

---

[56] According to Musa Khan Jalalzai, the hard core cadre of the sectarian parties comprises youngsters who took part in the Afghan war. Jalalzai, *Sectarian Violence in Pakistan and Afghanistan*, p.23.
[57] *Ibid.*, p.26.

Harakat-ul-Jihad-al-Islami; Lashkar-e-Taiba; Lashkar-e-Jhangvi; and Harakat-ul Mujahideen al-Alami.[58]

The evolution of Lashkar-e-Jhangvi, perhaps the most lethal of the sectarian groups, is particularly significant in this regard. In September 2001 three small chemical laboratories were found in L-e-J safe houses in Karachi. On 8 May 2002 an explosive-filled car killed 14 people including 11 French technicians. On 14 June 2002 another car bomb was driven into the American consulate, killing 12 Pakistanis. L-e-J was considered responsible for both attacks.[59] Yet though L-e-J was said to be more than knowledgeable about basic explosives, it was thought it lacked the expertise required to develop poison gas.[60] Similarly, it was not considered capable of manufacturing car bombs such as those used against Western targets in the spring of 2002. Evidently L-e-J has got help from al-Qaida.[61]

Thus Lashkar-e-Jhangvi seems to have emerged as a provider of logistical support and personnel to the remnants of al-Qaida and the Taliban still present in Pakistan (targeting foreigners was new for L-e-J). But it is not the only group to have done so. Post-9/11 developments have led to a growing rapprochement in Pakistan between sectarian and internationalist organisations. True, the relationship is not an entirely new one.[62] Still, the banned organisations SSP, Lashkar-e-Jhangvi, Jaish-e-Muhammad, Harakat-ul Mujahideen and various other groups of minor importance seem now closely linked with the Taliban and al-Qaida.[63] One obvious reason is Pakistan's participation in the war against terrorism: both al-Qaida and the banned organisations are under pressure from the government. But the ban has also had some secondary consequences which contributed significantly to the rapprochement. Lack of money, for example, made L-e-J a particularly vulnerable target for internationalist militant groups, in particular al-Qaida. In exchange for funds, the organisation is provided with manpower.[64]

Money does not explain everything, though. Many activists do not fight for financial reasons, but because they are disillusioned, 'bitter and indignant at the hypocrisy and

---

[58] Amir Mir, 'Friends Turned Foes', *The Herald Annual* (January 2004), p.40.
[59] 'Lashkar-e-Jhangvi', CDI, Terrorism Project, March 2003 [http://www.cdi.org/terrorism/lij.cfm].
[50] Azmat Abbas, 'Trail of Terror', *The Herald* (Karachi) (August 2002), pp.46–8.
[51] Lakshman, 'Deep Roots to Pakistan's Sectarian Terror'.
[52] In 1998, just before the US bombing of the camps in Afghanistan, the Pakistani weekly *The Friday Times* had reviewed a report from intelligence agencies implicating activists from the Harakat-ul Mujahideen in the massacre in Lahore of over 20 Shiite mourners.
[63] See Hasan Mansoor, 'Karachi Killings Reveal Sectarian-Jihadi Nexus', *The Friday Times* (10–16 October 2003).
[64] Abbas, 'Trail of Terror', pp.46–8.

injustice found in society'.⁶⁵ Not only has *jihad* become associated with the cult of violence, the only way to cleanse the *ummah,* but it has become an end in itself. Men who believe they are assured of entry to Paradise are likely to be willing to kill and die for the cause.⁶⁶ Many *jihadis* who have lost the support of the Pakistani government evidently think this way.

Conclusion

The elements considered in this paper may augur a somewhat different future for sectarian violence than one would have predicted a few years ago. As stated in the introduction, we believe that sectarianism as it has been experienced by Pakistan since the beginning of the 1980s will decline, and be replaced by other forms of Islamic violence. According to statistics, the ban of several sectarian groups since January 2002 has already led to a sharp decline in the number of casualties even as the ferocity of terrorist incidents has increased.

To be sure, the social factors which led to the emergence of sectarianism in Pakistan have not disappeared, and violence continues to be fuelled by the propaganda and activism of both Shia and Sunni groups. However, the Shia–Sunni dimension, although still important, is no longer the main focus. It is quite clear, for example, that the 4 July 2003 attack against a Shia mosque in Quetta was essentially aimed at destabilising the Musharraf government. For many groups, the top priority is no longer the targeting of the Shia community, but the destruction of non-Muslims and foreigners.⁶⁷

This has been caused essentially by the changing geopolitics of the region. Over the years, the Iranian revolution has lost its charismatic character. Along with the fall of the Taliban regime, this has contributed to a rapprochement between the governments of Iran and Pakistan that makes the use of sectarianism as an instrument of state policy increasingly irrelevant. For instance, it is reported that Iran ceased financing Pakistani Shias in 1996 because it found this tactic had become counterproductive.⁶⁸ Similarly the regime change in Baghdad brought a halt to the financing by Iraq of anti-Shia elements in Pakistan.⁶⁹ Again, caution is warranted; the present trend of normalisation between India and Pakistan could well make both sectarian and *jihadi* groups less useful for the latter regime.

---

⁶⁵ Zahab, 'Sectarianism as Substitute Identity', p.87.
⁶⁶ *Ibid.*
⁶⁷ See Abbas, 'Trail of Terror', pp.46–8.
⁶⁸ *Zahab,* 'The Regional Dimension of Sectarian Conflicts', p. 116.
⁶⁹ The funding of Sunni extremist groups or even the MQM by Iraq declined after the end of the Iran–Iraq war in 1989 but did continue on a smaller scale.

Finally, despite the hesitation of the present Musharraf government, American pressure could gradually alter the balance of power within Pakistan itself. The war against al-Qaida and its regional allies, whether *jihadi* or sectarian, and their subsequent banning by Islamabad, have made the regime one of their priority targets. Once an ally of the army, sectarian groups have now turned against their former patrons; General Musharraf has become 'Enemy No. 1'. Should, however, the military as an institution ever feel threatened by the sectarian groups and their new al-Qaida allies, it might consider lending its support to a crackdown on the extremists.

This is not to say that all form of Islamic political violence will disappear from Pakistan any time soon. New sponsors may imply new targets and perhaps, new forms of organisation. The emerging groups may well become even more radical than their predecessors—as is suggested by the recent emergence of the technique of suicide bombing (a form of terrorism unknown previously in Pakistan). But no matter how spectacular the terrorist actions that might ensue in the future, the current trend towards the regrouping of disparate militant elements could also be an indicator of the impending decline of the movement. Its ultimate disappearance would then be a matter of time and determination on the part of the Pakistani authorities.

Islamic Militancy in Bangladesh: The Threat from Within

Sreeradha Datta

Religious extremism is on the rise in Bangladesh and the groups identified with or espousing the cause of radical Islamic trends have brought havoc to the country. Far from being a marginal and sporadic element, these militant groups have grown in strength and reach to the extent where they are able to conduct organised terror campaigns all over the country. The nationwide bomb blasts that rocked Bangladesh on 17 August 2005 highlighted the organisational capability of these groups, and the onset of suicide bombings a couple of months later brought into focus the existence of a section of people within Bangladesh with a deep-rooted dislike of the prevailing system and motivated enough to try and bring about change through extra-constitutional means. While the bomb blasts and the suicide bombings point towards a supportive role being played by external extremist groups, terrorism in Bangladesh is essentially a home-grown war militants are waging against their own people.[1]

The conventional wisdom has been to place the growing level of violence and intolerance at the doorstep of the ruling Bangladesh Nationalist Party (BNP) and its four-party coalition government. The massive victory of Khaleda Zia in the October 2001 Jatiya Sangsad (Bangladesh parliament) elections was often seen as the beginning of the current wave of militancy.[2] While militant acts have increased since then, it is argued here that the problem has deeper roots and that all political forces in the country, including the Awami League, have been responsible for the present situation. Specifically our claim is that religious militancy rather than terrorism is the primary problem facing Bangladesh.

---

[1] 'Poverty, Misinterpretation of Islam behind Rise of Militancy', *The Daily Star* (13 Dec. 2005).
[2] Haroon Habib, 'The Menace of Militancy', *Frontline* (11–24 Oct. 2003).

Contributing Factors
Islamisation

Islamisation has been a principal factor contributing to the growth and sustenance of militancy in Bangladesh. This Rightward religious shift has not only contributed to the weakening of the country's secular moorings but also strengthened perceptions of its religious identity. Since the early nineteenth century, the Bengal region has witnessed a strong contest between secular and religious culture. Even as part of Pakistan, the eastern wing retained its distinct cultural pre-eminence, which came to the fore during the Language Movement. This secular orientation formed the basis of the Bengali nationalism that eventually led to the division of Pakistan and the formation of Bangladesh.

Within a short period, the secular orientation of the infant state came under pressure. At one level, foreign policy compulsions—especially the need for economic aid from oil-rich Islamic countries—compelled the founding leader Mujibur Rahman to adopt a benign view of conservative forces.[3] Despite the official ban on religious political parties, Mujibur's secular socialist policies led, as several critics have pointed out, to the introduction of 'multi-theocracy in the name of secularism'. Mujibur not only failed to separate religion from the affairs of state,[4] but bestowed legitimacy on religious influences in the public domain by yielding to Islamic symbolism.[5]

Nevertheless the failure of Mujibur Rahman's socialist experiment and his untimely assassination in August 1975 fundamentally shifted the balance against secular identity. Political expediency on the part of the military, which was at the helm of affairs for over a decade, compelled Bangladesh to rediscover and reinforce its Islamic identity. The new constitution introduced in 1977 eliminated secularism and reiterated 'absolute trust and faith in the almighty Allah'. Indeed the preamble began with a salutation to Allah. Needing allies and political legitimacy, the military rulers revoked the erstwhile ban on religious parties.[6] Even those conservative groups that had opposed the liberation of the country from Pakistani rule were allowed to take part in the political process.

---

[3] On the role of Saudi financial aid, see Zayadul Hasan, 'Inside the Militant Groups-2. Foreign Funding, Local Business Keep Them Going', *The Daily Star* (22 Aug. 2005).
[4] Nurul Kabir, 'De-Secularising Bangladesh: Will the Whimper of the Minority Sink into the Thunder of the Majority?', *Holiday* (11 Nov. 2004) [http://www.weeklyholiday.net/2004/anni40/s15.html].
[5] In March 1975 Mujibur Rahman upgraded the Islamic Academy which had been banned in 1972 to a foundation. See Saleem Samad, 'The State of Minorities in Bangladesh: From Secular to Islamic Hegemony' [www.sacw.net/DC/CommunalismCollection/ArticlesArchive/ssamad_Bangaldesh.html - 52k].
[6] While Pakistan also went through a similar process during the late 1970s, it did not have to face any secular cultural force similar to Bengali nationalism.

Thus during the 1980s, Bangladesh underwent a distinct political change. The immediate impact of this new trend was not severe, but it gave out signals of an impending religious intolerance and the growth of fundamentalist tendencies. Yet when democracy was re-introduced in 1991, religious extremism and intolerance still remained a marginal element. The Sufi tradition within Islam and the secularist Bengali culture still kept Bangladesh insulated from similar developments taking place in other countries.

Short-sighted polices introduced by post-1991 democratic governments, however, placed Bangladeshi society firmly on the path of militancy. The publication in 1993 of a novel by Taslima Nasreen generated uproar among conservative circles which took strong exception to her characterisation of Bangladesh as an intolerant and anti-Hindu society. Following a *fatwa* against her, in 1994 Nasreen fled Bangladesh. Driven by political calculations, political parties were unwilling to recognise the religious extremism that was brewing in the country. On the contrary, they began to adopt positions that were friendly to the increasingly-conservative segment of the society. Even the BNP that was formed by General Zia-ur-Rahman as a counter to the secular Awami League positioned itself as party in tune with religious beliefs. As we will see, both the Awami League and the BNP, the two principal political forces in the country, were equally willing to seek and benefit from the support of religious parties.

But the electoral victory of the BNP in October 2001 brought a significant shift in the political equation. For the first time in the history of Bangladesh, religious parties—namely Jamaat-e-Islami and Islami Oikya Jote (IOJ)—became part of the government. Having fought the election jointly, these parties began to wield significant influence in the direction of policy. While the BNP could have secured a simple majority on its own, its pre-election alliance with Jamaat-e-Islami was instrumental in the four-party coalition securing a two-thirds majority in the Jatiya Sangsad. The portfolios allotted to its two ministers, namely Social Welfare and Agriculture, endowed Jamaat-e-Islami with greater visibility and gave it access to the rural population, its natural constituency.

Even before the results of the October 2001 Jatiya Sangsad elections had been officially announced, supporters of the winning coalition turned on the minority Hindus (historically known as supporters of the Awami League). At the same time anti-Ahmadiyya sentiments that had flourished during the 1950s, when Bangladesh was still part of Pakistan, resurfaced. Constituting about 100,000, the Ahmadiyyas form a miniscule proportion of the population, yet they have always been the principal target of religious intolerance. Recently, a number of organisations have mushroomed dedicated to having them declared non-Muslims, headed by the Khatme Nabuwat Andolon

Samannay Committee (KNASC). Other groups such as Amra Dhakabashi (Citizens of Dhaka) and Hifazate Khatme Nabuwat Andolon Coordination Committee (Movement to Conserve the Right of the Last Prophet), are committed to similar objectives. Some of these groups have threatened to take punitive action against those MPs elected on an Islamic manifesto if they fail to support their cause.

Ahmadiyya congregations and places of worships have come under repeated attack, and their properties have been vandalised. As well, the government has come under pressure to introduce strict blasphemy laws that would declare the Ahmadiyya to be *kafirs*.[7] Some of these agitations were led by people and groups close to the religious members of the ruling coalition. Shaikhul Hadith Azizul Hoque, chief of a faction of IOJ, castigated the government for its lack of 'courage' on the issue,[8] while factions of the IOJ threatened to launch a 'vigorous agitation' across the country to force the government to adopt anti-Ahmadiyya measures.[9] Partly yielding to such pressures, on 8 January 2004 the Khaleda government imposed a ban on Ahmadiyya publications.

There were also other incidents that would underscore what many would describe as a 'shrinking of liberal space' in Bangladesh.[10] They include:

- Attempts to ban foreign television channels because of their 'un-Islamic' content;
- Banning of the feature film *Matir Moina* because of its negative portrayal of a *madrassa* student;
- Periodic attacks against secular authors, poets, leaders and media personalities because of their criticism of religious extremism;
- *Fatwas* against various leaders and target groups that often led to individual or mob violence;
- The mushroom growth of militant groups committed to the establishment of an Islamic state in Bangladesh;
- The cancellation of women's sports events in response to demands from religious groups such as Islamic Shashantantra Andolon (Islamic Constitution Movement or ICM) and the Anti-Islamic Activities Prevention Committee (AIAPC). (For example, the first-ever women's wrestling competition scheduled for 4 July 2004 was cancelled because of threats from the ICM).

---

[7] There were suggestions that American pressures prevented Bangladesh from introducing such measures against the Ahmadiyyas. See US State Department, 'Annual Report on International Religious Freedom 2004' [http:// www.state.gov/drl/rls/irf/2004/, accessed 18 May 2004].

[8] 'Declare Them Non-Muslims to Get Electoral Support. Bigots at Dhaka Meet', *The Daily Star* (3 Dec. 2005) [http: //www.thedailystar.net/2005/03 /12/].

[9] Shamim Ashraf, 'Fanatic Tempers Run High Against Ahmadiyas, Attack on Sect's HQ on Aug 27 Planned', *The Daily Star* (18 Aug. 2004).

[10] Many Bangladeshi authors like Haroon Habib, Shariar Kabir and Saleem Samad, as well as Samina Ahmed, South Asia Director for the International Crisis Group, and Abbas Faiz, South Asia Region Researcher for Amnesty International, have referred to this phenomenon occurring over the last few years in Bangladesh.

Religious intolerance particularly manifests itself through the *fatwas* issued by various religious leaders. Significantly, since the controversial *fatwa* against Taslima in 1994, the incidence of these edicts has greatly increased. Sitting in judgement on a test case brought by liberals, in January 2001 the Bangladesh High Court ruled against *fatwas* and declared them to be illegal. Jubilant NGO cadres at once organised a rally in Dhaka in support of the ruling. Orthodox Islamic groups, however, countered that *fatwas* were an integral part of Islamic life and the High Court ruling tantamount to an attack on religious freedom. The confrontation between the two sides resulted in violence and the killing of a police officer inside a mosque. A senior IOJ member was charged with the murder, but the High Court subsequently dismissed all charges.[11]

Growth of Madrassas
A powerful incentive for religious extremist terrorism in Bangladesh could be located in the accelerated growth of *madrassas*. Recognised and often funded by the state, these religious schools complement the state-run non-religious education system. Even at the height of Mujibur's popularity, the secular–religious distinction remained blurred in the education system. For Mujibur, secular meant separation of religion from politics, not education from religion. Today, both religious as well as secular parties, including the Awami League, run *madrassas*. During Awami rule (1996–2001), an education commission headed by Shamsul Haque recognised 'madrassa education as an integral part of the national education system'.

Since the foundation of Bangladesh, therefore, various governments have contributed to the growth of *madrassa* education. It is estimated that Bangladesh has about 15,000 primary school *madrassas* with over 2.6 million children enrolled. By the end of 2002 it had in total over 64,000 religious schools—as against 1,830 during 1975–76. While the advent of military rule spurred their steady growth, their numbers really accelerated in the 1990s, which suggests that the democratic governments played a key role in the process.[12]

---

[11] Bureau of Democracy, Human Rights, and Labor, US Department of State, 'International Religious Freedom Report for 2004' [http://www.state.gov/g/drl/rls/irf/2004/, accessed 18 May 2004]. In 2003, 36 *fatwa* cases occurred in which 5 persons were lashed, and others faced punishments ranging from physical assault to shunning of families by their communities. One human rights organisation recorded 32 *fatwa* cases in 2002 in which 19 persons were lashed, and others faced similar punishments as were meted out in 2003.

[12] For example the number stood at 2,386 in 1978 and just over 2,700 in 1988. See testimony of Samina Ahmed to US Senate Foreign Relations Committee Hearing on Combating Terrorism Through Education—the Near East and South Asia, 'U.S. Should Condition Education Aid to Pakistan, Bangladesh', International Crisis Group [http://www.iacfpa.org/p_news/nit/iacpa-archieve/2005/04/29/cap-icg1-29042005.html, accessed 10 April 2005]. For more details see Government of Bangladesh, *1980 Statistical Yearbook of Bangladesh* (Dhaka: Government of Bangladesh, 1981), p.421.

This unbridled growth symbolises two distinct but inter-related developments. At one level, it indicates a gradually-declining role for the state in education[13]—one that is being filled by the *madrassas*. The inability of the state to provide basic primary and secondary education in rural areas works in favour of the *madrassas* which have a better network in these areas. With just over 2 percent of GDP being spent on education, the state education system has become insufficient to meet the growing demands upon it. During the past two decades the number of students registered in junior and higher grade *madrassas* increased by 818 percent—as against a 317 percent growth of pupils in ordinary secondary schools.[14]

Secondly, in contrast to the state-run schools, *madrassas* offer a very narrow religious curriculum that focuses on Quranic teachings. Though important in the development of moral values, such exclusivism not only limits the scope of the students' knowledge but impedes their job opportunities. Employment avenues for graduates trained solely in Islamic studies are limited to the *madrassa* system or its affiliated activities. The limited educational basis of this system precludes them from most government jobs. Since the late 1980s, efforts have been made to modernise *madrassa* education by including secular subjects in the curriculum of *madrassas* under the Bangladesh Madrassa Education Board. But the impact has been marginal.

These two impediments—namely non-imparting of secular subjects and non-availability of jobs outside the religious education system—ironically work against *madrassa* education. Easily available, *madrassa* education has not proved to be easily absorbable in the job market. The unemployment rate among *madrassa-edu*cated graduates is higher than that of products of the ordinary educational stream.[15] As a result, *madrassa* education has had a direct impact upon the growth of religious extremism in Bangladesh. Driven by a radical world view and saddled with more or less permanent unemployment, many youth find militancy an attractive alternative. The traditional argument about poverty breeding terrorism is valid for Bangladesh.[16] If the rise

---

[13] Pushkar Maitra, 'Schooling and Educational Attainment: Evidence from Bangladesh' [www.ingentaconnect.com/content/routledg/cede/2003 /].
[14] Harun ur Rashid, 'The Rise of Islamic Extremism in Bangladesh', *The Daily Star* (2 March 2005). For a detailed study on *madrassa* education in Bangladesh, see Uzma Anzar, 'World Bank Report on Islamic Education: A Brief History of Madrassas with Comments on Curricula and Current Pedagogical Practices', Draft Report (World Bank, March 2003) [siteresources.worldbank.org/EDUCATION/Resources/278200-1 1217032742].
[15] Taj I. Hashmi, 'Islamic Resurgence in Bangladesh: Genesis, Dynamics and Implications' [http://www.apcss.org/Publications/Edited%20Volumes/ReligiousRadicalism/Pages%20from%20Religious%20Radicalism].
[16] M. Abdul Latif Mondal, 'Educated but Unemployed', *The Daily Star* (12 Dec. 2005); and Md. Asadullah Khan, 'Suicide Bombing: The Madrassah Angle', *The Daily Star* (7 Dec. 2005) [http://www.thedailystar.net/2005/12/07/d512071501100.htm].

of Osama bin-Laden destroyed the symmetry of the poverty–terrorism linkage, the growth of *madrassas* in Bangladesh shows that when poverty–stricken youth have no hope of a decent living, they can as easily be drawn into criminal and terrorist activities for material as for doctrinal reasons.

As will be discussed shortly, a number of terrorist attacks in the country can be directly attributed to the extremist beliefs that have infiltrated the Bangladesh education system. Moving away from a secular or at least non-religious Bengali culture, the society has embraced religious intolerance and extremist attitudes towards secular individuals, events and state symbols. For instance, some militant groups even consider the national anthem and the state flag as anti-Islamic symbols that need to be rectified.[17]

The linkage between *madrassas* and religious indoctrination and unemployment should not be over-stretched, however. These problems existed long before *madrassas* flourished in Bangladesh. Hence, *madrassas* cannot be the sole cause. Moreover, if *madrassas* were responsible for the growth of religious extremism, why did they escape public attention for so long?

The rapid growth of militancy, however, has compelled Bangladesh to take a closer look at the *madrassas* and their negative influences. In this post-factor analysis, they are seen as a principal contributing factor. While political compulsions prevent political parties from adopting a stronger position *vis-à-vis madrassa* education, there have been growing calls for the 'streamlining' of religions schools from scholars and commentators.[18]

Upsurge of Religious Parties
The most striking development in Bangladesh following the return of democracy in 1991 was the growth of religious parties.[19] In tune with his secular politics, shortly after the formation of the state Prime Minister Mujibur banned religious parties and proscribed them from participating in elections. His assassination in August 1975 and the subsequent advent of military rule brought about a definite shift. Desperately needing a constituency that would accept and legitimise their role in politics, General Zia and his successors sought to placate conservative religious leaders: the ban was

---
[17] 'How Dare!', Editorial, *The Daily Star* (19 Dec. 2005).
[18] For example see Bertil Lintner, 'Is Religious Extremism on the Rise in Bangladesh?', *Jane's Intelligence Review* (May 2002).
[19] The different religious parties (Jamaat-e-Islami, Muslim League, Islami Oikya Jote and Islamic Jatiya Oikaya Front) won 14 seats in the 3rd Jatiya Sangsad elections in 1986, 18 in the 5th Jatiya Sangsad elections in 1991, 4 in 7th Jatiya Sangsad elections in 1996, and as many as 33 seats in 8th Jatiya Sangsad elections in 2001.

slowly relaxed; political participation allowed; and the clergy was gradually recognised as a player in national politics.

Therefore by the time the first multi-party elections were held in February 1991, Jamaat-e-Islami was legal, erstwhile religious leaders who had supported Pakistan during the liberation war of 1971 had been accommodated politically, and religion was no longer a taboo in Bangladeshi politics. Since then, religious parties have flourished in the country—although, conscious of their limitations, they have often joined hands with the larger parties to consolidate their support base. Conversely, political compulsions compelled the two large parties, the Awami League and the BNP, to forge closer ties with the religious parties.

A recent study suggests that the diminishing role of the state in overall welfare and developmental programs has accorded a space to religious groups and religious political parties to endear themselves especially to the rural populace hitherto largely untouched by progress.

> The result of such preparation was capturing the village by using deep tube-well-centric society, peasant society, Mosque and Madras [sa]— whatever is the medium, establishing [an] undisputed stronghold in religious institutions, capturing the state institutions, capturing the economic-activity-based institutions, and in the name of private institutions taking [a] position among the low-income groups of people of the villages and towns and strengthened their presence. To execute this strategy, [the] economic institutions of fundamentalists played [a] definite role. Likewise due to adopting this strategy those institutions were also strengthened. And these generated synergistic effects. In this respect, religious fundamentalists were not idealistic in the least in giving political leadership; in fact, they were realistic manifold *[sic]*. Following this process, during half a century, they have now reached a position where they can get an average vote of 15,000 people in each of the seats of the parliament. At the same time, they have now acquired the capacity to spend millions of black money and use...muscle power in national parliamentary elections. On the other hand, as displayed on 17th August 2005, they are well capable of organizing nation-wide serial bomb blasts, and that with 100% military accuracy. By no means is this a weak opponent.[20]

---

[20] Abdul Barkat, 'Economics of Fundamentalism in Bangladesh: Roots, Strengths, and Limits to Growth', paper presented at a conference on Religious and Social Fragmentation and Economic Development in South Asia, Cornell University, 15–16 Oct. 2005.

The verdict of the October 2001 elections vindicated the growing power of the religious parties. On the eve of the elections the popular perception gained strength that international disapproval of religious extremism in the wake of the 9/11 attacks in the US would tell against the religious parties. The results, however, exploded this theory. The religious parties were a prime beneficiary in the polls, making their largest gains since the founding of the state. Together the four religious parties secured 33 out of 300 seats in the Jatiya Sangsad.[21]

Jamaat-e-Islami has emerged as the primary beneficiary of this trend. Committed to the formation of an Islamic state in Bangladesh, the party has been aware of its limitations. The largely-secular Bangladesh polity was not conducive to any rapid radical transformation. At the same time, the multi-party parliamentary election provided an opportunity for Jamaat-e-Islami to reach its objectives through the ballot. Therefore, since 1991 it has been expanding its base by shrewdly aligning with the BNP as well as with the Awami League.[22] Capitalising on the intense rivalry between the two main parties and their leaders, Jamaat-e-Islami has managed to use the available political space to its advantage. Without diluting its Islamic credentials, Jamaat-e-Islami was able to forge issue-based partnerships with diverse political groups.

The backing of Jamaat-e-Islami was critical for the success and survival of both the Khaleda Zia (1991–96) and Sheikh Hasina (1996–2001) governments. When Jamaat-e-Islami switched its support in 2001, the ruling party lost the elections; while its pre-election alliance with the BNP helped it secure 17 seats in parliament. Moreover following the election, Jamaat-e-Islami became a part of the government when two of its members became cabinet ministers.

With its large welfare network activities, Jamaat-e-Islami enjoys considerable support in rural areas. It has organisational bases (accompanied by affiliated *madrassas*) in all 64 districts of Bangladesh. Responding to political reality, it has toned down its conservatism and encourages rural women to play an active role in the party. In the words of one Western commentator: 'Jamaat is using its swing position effectively to acquire more influence in government than its numbers suggest'. Indeed its attractive qualities on moral grounds are not missed either: 'Jamaat has not pressed an Islamic agenda too overtly, but its ministers have acquired a reputation for being competent and incorrupt, which could serve it well if disillusion with the major parties spreads'.[23] The growth of

---

[21] Jamaat-e-Islami won 17 seats, IJOF 14 seats, and IOJ 2. Jamaat also secured 2 seats from the 30 seats reserved for women in the Jatiya Sangsad.
[22] Sreeradha Datta, 'Ascendance of Jamaat-e-Islami in Bangladesh', in *ISIM Review*, No. 13 (Dec. 2003), pp.44–5.
[23] Philip Bowring, 'Not Doing Badly, Thank You', *International Herald Tribune* (16 April 2005) [http://www.iht.com/articles/2005/04/15/news/edbo wring.html].

religious parties is also reflected in the subtle shifts that are taking place in the agendas of the other parties. Adopting a conservative stance in order to commend himself to the religious Right, General Ershad attributed the problems of Bangladesh to the country being led by two women. Ironically, this anti-women line runs contrary to Islamic teachings.[24]

Thus religion has firmly entrenched itself in Bangladeshi politics. But the process of 'Islamisation' has been complicated and erratic. The *mullahs* and other conservative religious groups who have legitimised the importation of Islam in politics have been trying to outmanoeuvre the more moderate Jamaat-e-Islami. This in turn has forced mass-based parties like the BNP and Awami League to 'use the Islamic card firstly to neutralize the Jamaat and secondly to appease the vast majority of God-fearing and anti-Indian Bengali Muslims for the sake of political legitimacy and leverage'.[25] Arguably the Bengali 'fatalist' psyche is another factor that compels Bangladeshis to fall back on religion in the face of abounding corruption and lack of opportunity from which they yearn to escape.[26]

The growth of Jamaat-e-Islami has impacted on the polity in two ways. With its large base and organisational skills and welfare programs, it has lent credibility to the religious style in political life and second, its participation in the democratic political process has provided a congenial atmosphere for the growth of militancy. A number of conservative, strident and militant religious groups have found ways to voice their opinions without much opposition from within the system.

There are media suggestions that Jamaatul-Mujahideen Bangladesh (JMB), the most active militant group in Bangladesh, started out as a splinter group from Jamaat-e-Islami. Certainly it has close links with senior Jamaat-e-Islami functionaries. At any rate, Jamaat-e-Islami has also given rise to a large constituency that is impatient with current shaping of Bangladesh society and wants the country to imbibe more fundamental Islamic ways of doing things. This constituency—most of which has some past or present linkages with Jamaat-e-Islami—has shown its strength through various acts of violence and terror.

---

[24] 'Oli Ahmed Sees Govt Link With Terrorism. The BNP Lawmaker Says Godfathers of Terrors Remain Untouched', *Independent* (26 Nov. 2005).
[25] Hashmi, 'Islamic Resurgence in Bangladesh: Genesis, Dynamics and Implications'.
[26] *Ibid.*

Nevertheless most of the religious groups and political parties are experiencing severe tensions within their ranks over the different ways to implement their ideology. In fact, even within the BNP there is significant opposition to the prevailing official line *vis-à-vis* militancy. Indeed Abu Hena, a BNP MP for Rajshahi-3, was expelled for talking to the press about alleged links between the Islamist militants and some ministers of the ruling coalition.[27] According to a petition filed in the High Court, Abu Hena had specifically named the Post and Telecommunications Minister Aminul Haque for harbouring militants in Rajshahi. The petition also referred to a statement by Oli Ahmed—a BNP standing committee member and former minister—that elements within the ruling four-party alliance were responsible for the rise in militancy. The whip of the BNP parliamentary party, Ashraf Hossain, has made similar allegations, naming Jamaat-e-Islami.[28]

Perceived Official Patronage
Even if direct corroborative evidence has not been forthcoming, there are enough indications to suggest that the BNP and its allies, especially Jamaat-e-Islami, have contributed to the growth of militancy in Bangladesh. At one level, the government has been lenient toward the growth of extremist violence and the presence of various militant groups operating with impunity. Even while claiming that such attacks were aimed at 'tarnishing' the good image of Bangladesh, it has been unable to evolve an effective counter-militancy strategy. Spiralling militancy has not brought about a sense of urgency in official policy.

On the contrary, the opposition and unknown 'foreign' elements are increasingly blamed officially for the militancy. Between the first terrorist bombing in Jessore in March 1999 and the Netrokona bombing in December 2005, Bangladesh witnessed as many as 33 major bomb blasts, most of them attributed to militant groups or individuals.[29] Yet official investigations into these blasts were either inefficient or partisan. For example, within days of coming to power, Prime Minister Khaleda appointed a commission headed by retired judge Abdul Bari Sarkar to inquire into the Baniarchar (Gopalganj) church bomb blast that occurred in June 2001. The commission blamed Sheikh Hasina and other Awami leaders not only for this blast, but also for six of the seven other blasts which had taken place during 1999 and 2001.[30]

---

[27] 'Abu Hena Expelled: What Next?', *Bangladesh Observer* (26 Nov. 2005).
[28] 'HC Asks Govt to Explain Action Against Bombers', *The Independent* (1 Dec. 2005).
[29] 'Udichi Again. 33 Major Blasts since 1999', *The Daily Star* (9 December 2005).
[30] *Internationa Religious Freedom Report 2003 (Bangladesh)* [http://www.state.gov/g/drl/rls/irf/2003/ 24468.htm, accessed 20 April 2005]. Such a partisan conclusion resulted in two other members publicly distancing themselves from the Commission's report.

Instead of acting on reports in the media concerning the presence and growth of religious extremism, the government opted for intimidatory tactics:

- In April 2002 the Hong Kong-based *Far Eastern Economic Review* carried a story by Bertil Lintner that highlighted religious extremism in Bangladesh. The government retaliated by ordering the confiscation of the offending issue.
- In November 2001 noted journalist Shariar Kabir was arrested for visiting India to document the plight of Hindu refugees who had fled Bangladesh following the October violence.
- In November 2001 journalist Saleem Samad was charged with sedition and conspiracy for helping Britain's Channel 4 make a documentary on Bangladesh.
- An exposé of militant activities in Chittagong resulted in a mob attack against the Bengali-language daily *Prothom Alo* in August 2004.
- There was growing incitement against journalists critical of the militancy, Jamaat-e-Islami MP Maulana Delwar Houssain Sayeedi warning in March 2002: 'The blood of journalists who cannot tell the difference between Muslims and Islamists should be analyzed to see if they are true Muslims'.[31]

It is obvious that the participation of Jamaat-e-Islami in government has also impeded Bangladesh from decisively acting against known militant groups. The organisation has been at the forefront in denouncing media reports about Islamic militancy. Its leaders dismissed the presence of well-known militant leader Siddiqul Islam (alias Azizur Rahman, popularly known as Bangla Bhai), as a figment of imagination and a media creation.[32] Likewise the reluctance of the Khaleda government to act decisively, even against known militants, can be attributed to Jamaat-e-Islami's presence in the government. It was only under intense international pressure that the government eventually banned two groups in February 2005 and proscribed Harakat-ul-Jihad-al-Islami (HUJI)[33] in August 2005.[34] Meanwhile, Jagrata Muslim Janata Bangladesh (JMJB) continues to issue threats to the judiciary administration, educational institutes, and secular Bangladeshis.

A spin-off from the law and order problem has been the proliferation of small arms. The nation-wide Operation Clean Heart (2002) resulted in the confiscation of 2,028 weapons and 29,754 rounds of ammunition. Subsequently in April 2004, the largest arms cache in Bangladeshi history was confiscated from the Chittagong port area.

---

[31] Reporters Without Borders, 'Bangladesh Annual Report 2003' [http://www.rsf.fr/article.php3?id_article=989, accessed 10 Nov. 2004].

[32] Industry Minister Nizami asserted this in July 2004; as did State Minister for Home Babar in an interview with the BBC on 26 January 2005. See Alex Perry, 'Reining in the Radicals', *Time Asia* (online) (7 Mar. 2005).

[33] HUJI is also known as HUJI-B, denoting it as the Bangladeshi branch of HUJI.

[34] By contrast the US government banned HUJI in 2002.

Previously quantities of small arms had been found in Bogra (north-western Bangladesh) and in Dhaka.

According to recent estimates there are at least 250,000 illegal firearms in the country. Recently the Chittagong Hill Tracts has become the principal conduit for trafficking small arms into Bangladesh. But the flow of these clandestine goods is outward as well as inward. Some say that Bangladesh is on the verge of becoming the 'biggest clandestine arms supplier' in South Asia.[35] Besides the large number of firearms entering through the borders, small arms are also manufactured locally in illegal factories within the country. Studies indicate that there are about 1,000 such illegal arms factories, run mainly with foreign spare parts.[36] With the huge financial backing that the militant groups enjoy, easy access to arms and ammunition has made it possible for them to spread havoc and terror without much difficulty.

Taliban/al-Qaida Presence
Any meaningful discussion on militancy in Bangladesh would be incomplete without the al-Qaida dimension. Indeed, until the recent spate of terrorist attacks, much of the debate about extremism in Bangladesh revolved around the presence of, or support from, external militant groups such as al-Qaida and their allies in Afghanistan.

Formally, Bangladesh's assimilation into the al-Qaida network was occasioned by Osama bin-Laden's *fatwa* of 23 February 1999 that called for *a jihad* against 'the Jews and Crusaders'.[37] Without preamble or justification, the *fatwa* was endorsed by Fazlul Rahman, a local religious leader commonly identified as 'the Amir of Jihadi movement in Bangladesh', in his capacity as leader of HUJI. Yet the domestic and international reaction to this putative al-Qaida link was surprisingly belated. Even after 9/11, when attacks led the US to proscribe a number of Islamic militant groups suspected of committing terrorist offences, HUJI was left out. Only in April 2004 did the US Department of State notify HUJI-B as a terrorist organisation. And Bangladesh took even longer to follow suit, because the Khaleda government maintained that HUJI was 'not present' in the country. However, in the wake of series of bomb blasts, Dhaka banned HUJI in August 2005.

As early as 1998, long before bin-Laden's controversial *fatwa* against the West, arguments for the Talibanisation of Bangladesh began to figure prominently in the

---

[35] Anand Kumar, 'Bangladesh Emerges as Biggest Clandestine Arms Supplier in South Asia', *South Asia Tribune* (11–17 April 2004).
[36] Imitiaz Ahmed, 'Contemporary Terrorism and Limits of the State', *The Independent* (11 Dec. 2005).
[37] For the complete text of the declaration, see Yonah Alexander and Michael S. Swetnam, *'Usama bin-Laden's al-Qaida: Profile of a Terrorist Network* (New Delhi: Aditya Books, 2001), Appendix 1B, 1–3.

country's political discourse. Alarmed, Prime Minister Sheikh Hasina warned the country that Bangladesh risked becoming another Afghanistan, and ordered the cancellation of some official engagements outside Dhaka during US President Bill Clinton's visit in March 2000 as a precautionary measure.

Then in 2001 the issue cropped up again during the campaign for the Jatiya Sangsad elections. There were fears that some of the Taliban activists who had fled Afghanistan following the US offensive had taken refuge in the country.[38] During the campaign, *'Aamra hobo Taliban, Bangla hobe Afghan'* ('We will be the Taliban, Bangladesh will become Afghanistan') became a popular slogan among religious voters, and it was not uncommon to find rickshaws in Dhaka plying their trade with bin-Laden posters prominently displayed.

Ever since her electoral defeat in 2001, Sheikh Hasina has been using the prospect of Bangladesh becoming another Afghanistan as a stick to belabour the Khaleda Zia government. For their part, Prime Minister Khaleda and her allies have vehemently denied that the government contains any Taliban elements.[39]

The controversy received further impetus in April 2002 when Bertil Lintner warned in the *Far East Economic Review* that:

> A revolution is taking place in Bangladesh that threatens trouble for the region and beyond if left unchallenged. Islamic fundamentalism, religious intolerance, militant Muslim groups with links to international terrorist groups, powerful military with ties to the militants, the mushrooming of Islamic schools churning out radical students, middle-class apathy, poverty and lawlessness—all are combining to transform the nation.[40]

This led to uproar in the country, and the government banned the issue that contained Lintner's article. The whole episode, however, led to increasing debate inside the country over growing Islamic extremism and its adverse consequences for society.[41]

---

[38] Sultan Shahin, 'India Looks at Bangladesh in Alarm', *Asia Times* (1 Feb. 2005).
[39] Haroon Habib, 'No Taliban in my Govt.: Begum Zia', *The Hindu* (11 Jan. 2002).
[40] Bertil Lintner, 'A Cocoon of Terror', *Far Eastern Economic Review* (4 April 2002), p. 14.
[41] For example, the pro-Awami *Daily Star* periodically carries long write-ups on religious extremism and in the process often gets into difficulties with religious parties such as Jamaat. On the role of religious extremism, see also Bertil Lintner, 'Is Religious Extremism on the Rise in Bangladesh?', in *Jane's Intelligence Review* (May 2002); Alex Perry, 'Deadly Cargo', *Time Magazine* (15 Oct. 2002); Eliza Griswold, 'For a New Taliban: The Next Islamist Revolution?', *New York Times* (23 Jan. 2005); and Haroon Habib, 'Report and Reality,' *Frontline* (9 Nov. 2002).

In fact the prospect of the Talibanisation of Bangladesh looks remote. Yet there are persistent indications that pro-Taliban and pro-al-Qaida elements are present and active in the country:

- On 7 January 1999 Bangladeshi national Syed Abu Nasir, a top Lashkar-e-Taiba activist alleged to have supervised an operation to bomb the US consulates in Chennai and Kolkata, was arrested. It appears that Nasir had been instructed to arrange safe passage across the Bangladesh border into India for six agents of the Kashmiri militant group Lashkar-e-Taiba.[42] In the past he had worked for the International Islamic Relief Organisation, a Saudi-based NGO linked to Osama bin-Laden.[43]
- In June 2001 25 al-Qaida members arrived in Bangladesh to train members of HUJI.[44]
- In February 2002, circumventing American search operations, another batch of 100 al-Qaida operatives arrived in Chittagong by sea.[45]
- On 18 May 2002 Bangladeshi police arrested five al-Qaida members in the northeast of the country carrying a large quantity of Saudi rials.
- On 25 June 2002 a Sudanese student, Karrar Kakki Karrar, was arrested at Dhaka University for having suspected links to al-Qaida.
- On 15 August 2002 during a Saudi crackdown against a suspected al-Qaida terrorist in Jizan in southwestern Saudi Arabia, eleven Bangladeshis were arrested.
- In early October 2002 the government of India expressed its concern over signs of the growing presence of al-Qaida in Bangladesh.[46]
- In October 2002 *Time Magazine* carried a story by Alex Perry documenting various al-Qaida activities in Bangladesh included the smuggling of small arms and arms training. Perry further asserted that Osama bin-Laden's Egyptian deputy, Ayman al-Zawahiri (who was tried for and acquitted of the assassination of Anwar Sadat), came to 'Dhaka in early March and stayed briefly in the compound of a local fundamentalist leader'.[47]
- In October 2002, speaking to the BBC, Awami League spokesman Saber Hossain Chowdhury declared that 'there are Members of Parliament and even some ministers in the ruling coalition...sympathetic towards the Taliban'.[48]

---

[42] Praveen Swami, 'A Terrorist Plot Unearthed', *Frontline* (27 Feb.-12 Mar. 1999) [http://www.flonnet.com/fl1605/16050340.htm].
[43] *Ibid.*
[44] Pramit Pal Chaudhuri, 'Osama's Deputy is in Your Country, Delhi tells Dhaka', *The Times of India* (28 Nov. 2002).
[45] *Ibid.*
[46] 'Sinha blames Pak. mission in Dhaka', *The Hindu* (28 Nov. 2002); Chaudhuri, 'Osama's Deputy is in Your Country, Delhi Tells Dhaka'; and 'ISI, Al-Qaida Present in Bangladesh. We Have Proof: Fernandes', *The Hindu* (13 Nov. 2002).
[47] Perry, 'Deadly Cargo'.
[48] 'Bangladesh's al-Qaida links', *BBC News*, 24 October 2002.

- In October 2002 police in Kolkata arrested a HUJI member, Fazle Karim, who claimed that al-Zawahiri had returned to Bangladesh in September 2002.[49]
- In November 2002 the Indian government announced in parliament that it had prepared a detailed report on al-Qaida operations in Bangladesh to be sent to Dhaka for further action.[50]
- On 7 December 2002 a series of bomb blasts in four movie halls in the Mymensing district resulted in the deaths of 17 people. Within hours, Home Minister Altaf Hossain Chowdhury had blamed al-Qaida for the bomb blasts. But afterwards the government retracted the charge. The Reuters correspondent who filed the story, and his family, were briefly placed under house arrest.[51]
- On 25 October 2002 the United Nations included three international organizations operating in Bangladesh—al-Haramain Islamic Foundation, Benevolence International Foundation and Global Relief Foundation—on its list of organizations whose assets are blocked for suspected links with al-Qaida or the Taliban.
- In December 2003 the Canadian Security Intelligence Service published a report that highlighted al-Qaida's links with Bangladesh.
- On 9 February 2004 the Indian Deputy High Commissioner Rajshahi received a ransom letter claiming to be from al-Qaida that threatened to blow up the office unless he paid 50 million taka.
- In May 2004 two Bangladeshi nationals were indicted by the Tokyo Prosecutor's Office for suspected links to al-Qaida.[52]
- In October 2004 media reports suggested that the Saudi charity, al-Haramain Islamic Foundation, was still operating in Bangladesh despite having been dissolved by Riyadh for its involvement in al-Qaida.[53]

Seen against this backdrop, the repeated accusations by Sheikh Hasina of the imminent Talibanisation of Bangladesh should not be dismissed as petty politics. In the wake of the series of bomb blasts that rocked the country in 2005, it has become difficult to ignore the warning issued by Awami leader Saber Hossain Chowdhury in December 2002 when he said:

> There are certain elements in Bangladeshi society—it may be very small but there are elements—sympathetic towards the Taliban. There are members of parliament in the current ruling coalition who are sympathetic towards the Taliban, and there are perhaps even

---

[49] Earlier, American journalist Alex Perry reported that in March 2002 Zawahiri came to Bangladesh through Chittagong and temporarily located himself in Dhaka before moving out. Perry, 'Deadly Cargo'.
[50] Chaudhuri, 'Osama's Deputy is in Your Country, Delhi tells Dhaka'.
[51] 'Bangladesh Probes Cinema Blasts', *BBC News* (14 Dec. 2002) [http://news.bbc.co.uk/2/hi/south_asia/2576079.stm, accessed 13 Jan. 2003]; and Haroon Habib, 'Terror Struck', *Frontline* (21 Dec. 2002–3 Jan. 2003).
[52] 'Japan Indicts 2 Bangladeshis for al-Qaeda "Ties"', *The Daily Star* (16 June 2004).
[53] 'BB finds Suspicious Transactions by Al-Haramin', *The Daily Star* (23 Oct. 2004).

ministers in the current government who are sympathetic towards the Taliban.[54]
Even those Bangladeshis who were not prepared to go that far admitted that there were groups inside the country 'which may be formenting [sic] religious intolerance'.[55]

Manifestations of Militancy
Militant Groups
In 2002 Bertil Lintner warned that Bangladesh was becoming a hotbed of religious extremism and a potential trouble-spot in South Asia. Since then the problem has grown in magnitude and intensity. Not only has militancy gathered momentum, it has also gained in sophistication—a tendency which reached its climax on 17 August 2005 when terror blasts rocked 63 out of 64 Bangladesh districts. Such nationwide action could only have been carried by a well-organised network and a highly-motivated cadre. The same goes for the other new and dangerous phenomenon, suicide bombing. In the light of these developments it is no longer possible for anyone in Bangladesh to maintain that the multiplying political violence is the handwork of some disgruntled elements keen to discredit the image of the country.

How many such groups are active in the country? Estimates vary. Some sources claim that dozens of such groups are active.[56] Indeed the opposition Awami League has identified 33 such Islamic groups, namely:[57]

- Jamaatul-Mujahideen Bangladesh (JMB);
- Shahdat-e-al Hikma;
- Jamaat-e-Yeaheya-al-Turat;
- Hizbut Touhid;
- Al-Harat-al-Islamia;
- Al-Markajul-al-Islami;
- Jamaatul Faliaya;
- Touhidi Janata;
- the International Islamic Front;
- Jummatul-al-Sadat;
- Shahadat-e-Naboyed;

---
[54] Sakil Faizullah, 'Bangladesh's Split Personality' (13 Dec. 2002) [http://www.rnw.nl/hotspots/html/ ban021213.html, accessed 20 Jan. 2004].
[55] *Ibid.*
[56] Zayadul Ahsan, 'Trained in Foreign Lands, They Spread Inland', *The Daily Star* (21 Aug. 2005).
[57] Awami League, 'Growing Fanaticism & Extremism in Bangladesh: Shades of the Taliban' (15 June 2005) [http://www.albd.org/aldoc/growing/growing.fanaticism.pdf].

- Harakat-ul-Jihad-al-Islami (HUJI);
- Allahar Dal;
- Joisea Mustafa Bangladesh;
- al-Jihad Bangladesh;
- the World Islamic Front for Jihad;
- Joisea Mohammed;
- Jamaat-ul-Muzahidul Bangladesh;
- Warot Islamic Front;
- Jamaat-us-Sadat;
- al-Khidmat;
- Jagrata Muslim Janata Bangladesh (JMJB);
- Harakat-e-Islam-al-Jihad;
- Hizbullah Islami Shomaj;
- Muslim Millat Sharia Council;
- Ahl-e-Hadith;
- Hizbul Mahadi;
- Basbid;
- Hizbut Tahrir;
- al-Qaida;
- al-Islam Martyrs Brigade;
- the International Khatme Nabuwat Movement;[58]
- Amra Dhakabashi.

As in other countries, most of these groups operate periodically under different names or reinvent themselves when faced with political pressures. Most of them are committed to bringing about an Islamic revolution in Bangladesh. Opposition figures and secular personalities have been the main targets of their violence.

Of the abovementioned organisations, HUJI, JMJB and JMB are probably the most prominent. HUJI achieved prominence, as noted earlier, when Rahman joined Osama bin-Laden's 1999 *fatwa* against the West. At the time of the official ban imposed in February 2005, JMB was seen as a minor player. But the rapid increase in attacks since then indicates that it was much more. Indeed, the group is thought to be responsible for many of the 2005 attacks, including the nationwide blasts on 17 August. The group has expressed its displeasure with the prevailing political system in Bangladesh, which it considers not 'Islamic enough', and claims to be working towards building 'a society based on the Islamic model laid out in Holy Quran-Hadith'.[59]

---

[58] On the Awami League website *(ibid)* this organisation is spelt International Khotme Noboyet Movement.
[59] For a brief background on JMJB, see 'Jagrata Muslim Janata Bangladesh (JMJB)' [http://www.satp.org/satporgtp/countries/bangladesh/terroristoutfits/JMJB.htm].

Other groups, too, have periodically indulged in violence when their interests and beliefs came under threat. The student wing of Jamaat-e-Islami, Islami Chatra Shibir, and anti-Ahmadiyya groups like KNASC, Amra Dhakabashi, and Hifazate Khatme Nabuwat Andolon Coordination Committee (HKNA) all come within this category. Similarly, the student wing of the BNP, Jatiyatabadi Chhatra Dal, is frequently accused of terrorist activities.[60] In short the political climate in Bangladesh has become conducive to organised and unorganised extremist violence.

Another aspect of rising militancy in Bangladesh has been the ease with which some militant groups have managed to forge close ties with external militant groups. In the wake of the 17 August blasts, financial connections between JMB and some local and international NGOs have come into the limelight.[61] It has been revealed that the Kuwait-based Revival of Islamic Heritage Society has provided financial support to some of the militant campaigns taking place in Bangladesh.

Besides these indigenous groups, Bangladesh also houses a number of militant outfits from neighbouring countries such as India and Myanmar, most of them tribal-based groups fighting for separation from the Indian Union. Various formations of Muslim Rohingyas in neighbouring Myanmar, for example, have begun operating in the Chittagong Hill Tracts area of southern Bangladesh. Other Rohingya refugees have organised front organisations, the Rohingya Solidarity Organisation (RSO) being the most prominent. Subsequently the RSO split into several factions, some of whom are said to have established links with militant Islamic groups including Jamaat-e-Islami and HUJI, Gulbuddin Hekmatyar's Hizb-e-Islami in Afghanistan, Hizb-ul-Mujahideen of Jammu and Kashmir, and Angkatan Belia Islam sa-Malaysia (ABIM), the Islamic Youth Organisation of Malaysia.

Attacks Against Moderate and Secular Targets
Religious extremism in Bangladesh also manifests itself through physical and verbal attacks on moderate and secular individuals and institutions. Some examples are:

- In March 1999 a bomb blast disrupted the New Year's celebrations in Udichi.
- On 19 January 1999 prominent poet Shamsur Rahman, well-known for his secularism and criticism of growing communal intolerance, was attacked by religious extremists inside his house.

---

[60] CPJ (Committee to Protect Journalists), 'Asia Cases 2005: Country List Bangladesh' [www.cpj.org/cases05/asia_cases05 /bangla.html].
[61] Sudha Ramchandran, 'Mixing Aid with Terror', *Asia Times* (22 Sept. 2005).

- On 14 April 2001 eight people were killed in a bomb explosion set off by suspected Islamic militants at a Bengali New Year cultural function in Ramna, Dhaka.
- On 3 June 2001 ten persons were killed and 25 others injured in a bomb blast at a Catholic mission church at Baniachar, Gopalganj district.
- On 28 September 2002 a bomb went off inside a movie theatre in Satkhira in south-western Bangladesh. Minutes later another bomb exploded at a nearby site that was hosting an outdoor exhibition.
- On 7 December 2002 Id-ul-Fitr, a national holiday, was disrupted by bombs exploding in four cinema halls in Mymensing.
- On 17 January 2003 seven persons were killed and 20 others injured in a bomb blast at a fair in Tangail.
- On 4 December 2003 the leader of an Islamist outfit, Jaise Mostafa, who is also the *khatib* (preacher) of Rahim Metal Mosque in Tejgaon, vowed to offer Juma (Friday) prayers in the Ahmadiyya Mosque of East Nakhalpara. He honoured his promise after 'grabbing' the mosque the following day.
- On 5 December 2003 KNASC issued an ultimatum calling on the government to declare Ahmadiyyas 'non-Muslims'.
- On 12 January 2004 two persons were killed and 37 others injured by a bomb explosion at the shrine of Sufi saint Hazrat Shahjalal in Sylhet during the annual *Urs* celebration (the anniversary of the saint's death).
- On 23 January 2004 Amra Dhakabashi and HKNA held a joint meeting in Dhaka at which the government was warned that it would pay a heavy price unless it declared the Ahmadiyyas 'non-Muslims'.
- On 27 February 2004 Humayun Azad, a professor at Dhaka University, was stabbed in front of the Bangla Academy in Dhaka. The attack was seen as a retaliation for his book *Pak Sar Zamin Saad Baad* (the first line of the Pakistani national anthem) which was critical of religious groups who had collaborated with the Pakistan Army during the 1971 liberation war.[62]
- On 1 March 2004 a bomb blast at an international trade fair in Khulna killed one person and injured over 50 others.
- In March 2004 the US government added Delwar Hosasain Sayeedi, a Jamaat-e-Islami member of the Jatiya Sangsad, to its 'no-fly' list of individuals whose entry into the US was declared undesirable.
- On 19 March 2004 Islamists belonging to International Majlishe Tahaffuze Khatme Nabuwat Bangladesh tried to capture Ahmadiyya mosques in Barguna District.
- On 20 May 2004 a grenade was thrown at a prayer meeting at the Hazrat Shahjalal Shrine in Sylhet again, injuring Anwar Hussain Choudhury, the

---

[62] 'The Book that Got Him Marked for Death', *The Daily Star* (29 Feb. 2004).

British high commissioner to Bangladesh. Scotland Yard attributed this attack on the envoy (incidentally a man of Bangladeshi origin) to Islamic extremist groups.[63]
- On 11 July 2004 a number of politicians, journalists and intellectuals received death threats from an Islamic outfit calling itself Mujahideen-al-Islam.[64] Since then a number of Awami leaders, especially Sheikh Hasina, have received death threats from militant groups.[65]
- On 13 August 2004 Khulna police thwarted attempts by activists of the International Khatme Nabuwat Movement Bangladesh (IKNMB) to destroy the Nirala Ahmadiyya Mosque complex.
- On 18 August 2004 a group of Chittagong men, incensed by a newspaper story about alleged Islamic militant activities in the town, attacked the premises and journalists of the Bengali-language national daily *Prothom Alo*.[66]
- On 21 August 2004 Awami leader Sheikh Hasina was attacked at a party rally. Twenty people including senior Awami leader Ivy Rahman died in the mayhem. According to the US State Department, HUJI was behind the attack.[67]
- In September 2004 Christine Wallich, World Bank Director for Bangladesh, was forced to leave the country following a death threat believed to be from HUJI.
- On 4 October 2004 Islamists demanded the cancellation of a women's football tournament being held in the capital. Women playing such a game in public, they argued, was against Islamic tradition.
- In November 2004 Ziaul Huq Zia, a leader of the Bangladesh Chatra, the student wing of the Awami League, was killed by members of JMJB.
- In December 2004 threats from a little-known HUJI splinter group almost jeopardised the India-Bangladesh cricket series.
- On 24 December 2004 Professor Muhammmad Yunus, a teacher at Rajshahi University, was stabbed by suspected members of Jamaat-e-Islami.
- On 13 and 16 February 2005 Bangladesh Rural Advancement Committee (BRAC) offices in Joypurhat and Naogoan were attacked by members of JMJB. A member of the group boasted to a magistrate after his arrest that the group's bomb squad would continue its attacks on NGOs like BRAC and Karitas and on cultural activities deemed un-Islamic.

---

[53] 'Bangladesh Timeline Year 2004' [http://www.satp.org/satporgtp/countries/bangladesh/timeline/Year2004.htm].
[54] Media Watch, 'Bangladesh Monitoring Report July 2004' [http://www.ifex.org/en/content/view/full/60885/].
[65] 'Sheikh Hasina gets New Death Threat', *The Independent* (29 Dec. 2004).
[66] CPJ (Committee to Protect Journalists) Asia, 'Bangladesh Attacks on Press 2004' [http://www.cpj.org/attacks04/asia04/bangla.html].
[67] 'Morshed Denies Presence of Int'l Terrorist Group', *The Independent* [http://www.independent-bangladesh.com/news/may /03/03052005pl.htm].

- On 14 February 2005 a bomb blast disrupted a Valentine's Day function at Dhaka University.
- On 14 February 2005 a bomb detonated near the Ekushey Book Fair being held at the Bangla Academy.[68]
- On 14 May 2005 a bomb blast occurred at a circus in Bagerhat.

The bomb blast at the New Year's celebrations in Udichi in March 1999 was the first major act of terrorism in Bangladesh and the indication of an upsurge of religious militancy. If one examines the chain of incidents since then, a pattern is discernible. The prime targets of the violence have been people with a secular worldview and lifestyle, places such as movie halls, cultural events such as *jatras* (village pageants) and circuses perceived as non-Islamic, and the offices of political parties that have been critical of rising extremist tendencies.

Secondarily attacks were directed against Ahmadiyya places of worship which, for the fundamentalists, are not proper mosques and hence not sacrosanct or inviolable; and against Sufi shrines which in orthodox interpretations are seen as centres of idolatry and superstition—practices unacceptable to Islam.

Counter-Militancy Strategy

Bangladesh appears to be lacking an effective counter-militancy strategy. Prolonged official denials, and the ruling political compulsions of party life, seem to have incapacitated the ability of the ruling coalition to adopt a strong stand against militancy. For months after the 11 September attacks in the US, the Western media was publicising the growing Islamic militancy in Bangladesh, but the Khaleda Zia government remained indifferent. Why? Because Islamisation and the Rightward shift of the electorate it produced were favourable to the BNP and its allies. The two-thirds majority secured by the BNP-led coalition in 2001 was only possible because of the party's pre-election alliance with Jamaat-e-Islami and IOJ. It was therefore not possible for Prime Minister Khaleda to act against Islamic militants without antagonising her key coalition partners.

On the contrary, the government dismissed militancy as merely part of the prevailing lawlessness in the country—a law and order problem. Even outside powers, who were otherwise critical of Islamic extremism, endorsed the government's position on this account. For example, while praising Bangladesh's support in its war on international terrorism, the US State Department admitted that the ability of Dhaka to combat terrorism was vitiated by 'weak institutions, porous borders,

---

[68] The Ekushey Book Fair is held annually to mark the 21 February anniversary of the Language Movement of 1952.

limited law enforcement capabilities, and debilitating infighting between the two major political parties'.[69]

Thus it became possible for the Bangladesh government to assert with some credibility that Islamic militancy in the country was 'a conspiracy and an orchestrated campaign by some vested quarters',[70] or even that it was the creation of 'some newspapers'.[71] Indeed, less than a month before the first decisive step against militancy, a junior minister claimed: 'We don't know officially about the existence of the JMJB. Only some so-called newspapers are publishing reports on it. We don't have their constitution in our record'.[72] Citing police sources, a Bangladeshi report suggested that since 1998 as many as 435 Islamic militants have been arrested on charges of terrorism but that none have been convicted because of a lack of political will and a lack of co-ordination between different investigating agencies.[73] Prime Minister Khaleda aptly summed up the prevailing view when she observed: 'Awami League is the al-Qaida. They are the Taliban.... [Otherwise] Bangladesh has no al-Qaida or Taliban'.[74]

However, in a sudden shift of strategy on 23 February 2005, the government banned two, till-then lesser-known militant groups, JMB and JMJB, and thereby formally acknowledged the presence of Islamic militancy in Bangladesh. Initial reports attributed the ban to intelligence that the two groups were planning to provoke an armed Islamic rebellion.[75]

Yet even this belated action—which came hours before a crucial meeting of aid donors—did not dilute, let alone modify, the official denial posture. The government went out of its way to maintain that the ban on the two organisations was not connected to Islamic fundamentalism but was aimed at improving law and order. Even the naming of HUJI as a terrorist outfit by the US did not materially alter this stance. In the words of Foreign Minister Morshed Khan: 'I don't see any activity of such organization in Bangladesh. [Hence] the question of accepting or rejecting [the US decision] does not arise'.[76]

---

[69] Office of the Coordinator for Counterterrorism, Dept. of State, *Country Reports on Terrorism, 2004* (Washington DC; Department of State, 2005), p.72.
[70] 'Morshed Refutes US Claim of Terror Link', *The Daily Star* (9 May 2005).
[71] 'Islamist Militancy is a Propaganda by Media: Saifur', *The Daily Star* (24 Feb. 2005).
[72] Quoted in 'Eating Own Words', *The Daily Star* (24 Feb. 2005).
[73] '435 Militants Arrested in Last Six Years Most Have Been Freed, *Prothom Alo* (26 Feb. 2005).
[74] 'Bogra-haul Round-up', *Holiday* (4 July 2003) [http://www.weeklyholiday.net/040703/last.html].
[75] 'Govt Finally Cracks Down on Militants; Galib Arrested', *The Daily Star* (23 Feb. 2005) [http://www.thedailys-tar.net/2005/02/24/].
[76] 'Harkatul Jihad Banned at Last. Govt Terms it "A Terrorist Outfit"', *The Daily Star* (18 Oct. 2005).

The manner in which the Khaleda Zia government handled the ban not only reveals the choices facing Bangladesh but also the growing threat posed by extremist violence. At one level, Prime Minister Khaleda sought to placate Western donors and convey an impression that she was keen to take concrete measures against extremist groups that were targeting various secular leaders, personalities and motifs in Bangladesh. At the same time, in choosing two smaller groups, she also exhibited a firm grasp of political expediency; for diffidence toward the religious electorate was essential if Khaleda was to continue her co-habitation with the religious parties. Since 2001, the opposition has been gradually stepping up its efforts to criticise, de-legitimise and if possible even unseat her before her term ends in October 2006. To this end they have been harping on the rise of Islamic militancy. In the words of one senior Awami leader: 'Whatever is taking place in the country in the name of Islamist militancy is of the Jamaat, by the Jamaat, and for the Jamaat'.[77] In this context a portrayal of the ban and arrests as motivated by an anti-militancy clamp-down would have been suicidal for Khaleda. Were the religious parties to join hands with the opposition or even merely abandon the ruling coalition, it would be almost impossible for Khaleda to return to power in the next parliament election.

The timing of the move underscored the rationale behind the ban. The aid donors, especially the US, agreed to go along with the Khaleda government's fiction that Islamic militancy in the country was merely a law and order problem. Yet the continuing terrorist campaign, especially the assassination of former finance minister and senior Awami leader S.A.M.S. Kibria in January 2005, worried international onlookers and contributed to India pulling out of the South Asian Association for Regional Cooperation (SAARC) summit meeting planned for February. Hence, pressures began to mount on Bangladesh to act.

Citing deteriorating law and order problems, Bangladesh was excluded from the next donors' meeting in Washington in February 2005. Attended by representatives from the World Bank, the European Union and the US, the meeting over-ruled protests from Dhaka and dealt with the question of aid to Bangladesh without input from representatives of the Khaleda government. At the time Khaleda retorted to the snub with righteous anger, saying Bangladeshis knew how to run their country and could do so without any external aid and assistance, but afterwards the Bangladeshi government banned two Islamic militant groups and issued an

---

[77] 'Opposition Parties Think it is Eyewash', *The Daily Star* (25 Feb. 2005).

arrest warrant against Siddiqul Islam (Bangla Bhai), the notorious figure belonging to JMJB.[78]

The ban, however, proved not only ineffective but counter-productive. It sparked an accelerated campaign of agitation by militant groups and the incidence of violence and terrorism actually increased, nine major incidents occurring over the following five months.[79]

Moreover the ban appears to have led to numerous groups consolidating behind JMB, the prime suspect behind the new spate of bomb blasts. Defying the official ban, the organisation continued issuing periodic threats against secular institutions and state symbols, and for the first time, in December 2005, it called for sanctions against women, Muslim or non-Muslim, appearing in public without a veil. Last but not least, the involvement of a Hindu member of JMB in a suicide attack in Jessore on 8 December gave rise to speculation that the organisation was turning to mercenaries to carry out brutal attacks against civilians.[80]

Speaking at the third extra-ordinary summit meeting of the Organisation of the Islamic Conference in Mecca in December 2005, the Bangladesh prime minister warned against the spectre of terrorism facing Muslim countries.[81] It was a significant shift from a leader who not long before had been dismissing terrorism as a mere law and order problem for Bangladesh.

Conclusion

In contrast to similar developments in other countries of South Asia, and elsewhere, Islamic militancy in Bangladesh has been largely home-grown; has emanated from, and thrives on, domestic issues and agendas. As we have shown, it has taken advantage of a regional milieu that has become increasingly embracing of Islamic values, and of an export-fuelled economic boom which has left a great many people,

---

[78] In the past, Jamaat-e-Islami leaders have denied the very existence of Bangla Bhai. At the same time, however, a senior aide to the prime minister told the BBC on 23 May 2005 that the prime minister had ordered the arrest of Bangla Bhai. See *The Daily Star* (24 Feb. 2005). Despite these statements on the subsequent banning of JMJB, Bangla Bhai is still at large. There are reports that in March 2005 he escaped to India. *The Daily Star* (5 Mar. 2005).

[79] On 12 August 2005, one person was killed at an Akhura shrine; on 17 August 2005 three people died in countrywide serial blasts; on 3 October 2005 three died in bomb attacks on three district courts; on 18 October 2005 a failed suicide bomb attack was made on Sylhet judge Biplob Goshswami; on 14 November 2005 two judges were killed in Jhalakathi; on 29 November 2005 ten people were killed in suicide bomb attacks in the Gazipur and Chittagong courts; on 1 December 2005 one person was killed in a suicide attack on the Gazipur DC office; on 2 December 2005 there was a grenade attack on Sylhet mayor and AL leader Kamran; and on 8 December 2005, eight were injured in a suicide attack in Jessore.

[80] 'Hindu Bomber in JMB a New Dimension: Babar', *The Daily Star* (9 Dec. 2005).

[81] 'OIC Must Involve Itself First with the Cause of Muslim Anger', *The Nation* (10 Dec. 2005) [http://nation.itte-faq.com/artman/publish/article_23738.shtml].

especially in rural areas, marginalised, desperate and angry. In turn, the spread of violence in the society has given militancy a political profile. It is now something that governments have to reckon with. The hot-house economic transformation of the country and the interlocked nature of its political systems are both major impediments to any decisive move against religious militancy.

There remain conflicting views within the ruling party, however, regarding the best way to deal with the militancy. One section shares the view of the opposition and concedes that Jamaat-e-Islami's inclusion in the ruling coalition contributed to the growth of extremism within the country. This is echoed by a popular perception that the government has been held hostage by the religious party to adopt a lenient policy *vis-à-vis* militancy even after the number of bomb blasts had increased.

A majority within the BNP, however, are committed to maintaining the current alliance with the religious parties. In their assessment, the Rightist shift within Bangladeshi society and the growing strength and influence of 'religious' voters make any sudden divorce problematic. They argue that, having reaped the benefits of an alliance with Jamaat-e-Islami and IOJ, the BNP cannot suddenly drop them.

Frankly, given the deep-rooted nature of the militancy and the widespread nature of its networks as witnessed by the 17 August 2005 blasts, it will be extremely difficult for *any* government in Bangladesh to adopt an effective counter-militancy strategy. Instead of consolidating its democracy, Bangladesh appears to be drifting towards authoritarianism. The gap between the political parties is widening and neither seems prepared to enter into meaningful dialogue over the problem of militancy and ways to address it. But in the absence of any determined intervention by the government, the challenge of the extremists bent on establishing an Islamic state in Bangladesh through violence and terror attacks will only continue to grow.

Political Terrorism of the Liberation Tigers of Tamil Eelam (LTTE) in Sri Lanka

Gamini Samaranayake

Introduction

Terrorism is perhaps the major issue of the modern world. No country is free from its threat or challenge. The occurrence of terrorist attacks is unpredictable and pervasive, affecting weak and powerful states indiscriminately. Nor are its targets confined by political structures or ideologies. And it is not a new phenomenon. Terrorism is as old as the political history of human civilisation, and has been used at various times by both states and sub-state organisations for a whole variety of causes and purposes.[1] Recently, though, the development of telecommunications and increasing globalisation have provided new channels for global terrorism.

The literature on terrorism is understandably extensive. Yet most of it is concerned with international incidents, whereas 90 percent of terrorist acts are related to domestic situations.[2] This paper addresses the terrorist violence which has been unleashed in Sri Lanka by the Liberation Tigers of Tamil Eelam (LTTE) in support of their quest for an ethnic homeland in the north and northeast of the country.[3] It is a divided into six sections. The first part briefly examines the definition of political terrorism; the second examines the causes of the origin and development of the LTTE and its political terrorism; the third deals with the profile of the LTTE; the fourth examines the patterns of political terrorism of the LTTE in the context of

---

[1] Pau l Wilkinson, 'The Strategic Implications of Terrorism', in M.L. Sondhi (ed.), *Terrorism and Political Violence* (Har-Anand, 2000), p. 19.
[2] See US Department of State, *The Pattern of Global Terrorism* (Washington DC, 2000).
[3] Sri Lanka has been subject to insurrection and political terrorism since the early 1970s. The first wave occurred as part of a Left-wing insurrection by the People's Liberation Front or the Janatha Vimukthi Peramuna (JVP) composed of youth from the majority Sinhalese community. The JVP launched two insurrections, the first in April 1971 and the second from 1987 to 1989; during the latter it made increasing use of terrorism. The forces of government, by means of a vigorous counter-insurgency cum terrorism campaign, defeated the JVP. Now the JVP operates within the mainstream politics of the country.

ethnic insurgency; the fifth deals with the varying response of successive governments in Colombo to the terrorist threat; and the final offers some broader reflections by way of conclusion.

Definition

Prior to examining and analysing the causes, patterns and impact of political terrorism in Sri Lanka, it is vital to establish a clear definition of what it is we are studying. There is no commonly-agreed definition of 'terrorism' although, as Paul Wilkinson points out, more than a hundred have been published. Nevertheless Wikinson offers a good starting point by pointing to the things which distinguish terrorism from other forms of political violence. Terrorism, he says, is typically premeditated and aims to create a climate of extreme fear or terror; is directed at a wider audience than the immediate victims targeted; inherently involves attacks on random and symbolic targets, including civilians; uses means that are seen by the wider society as extra-normal, in the literal sense that they breach social norms, thus sparking outrage; and is generally employed to influence political behaviour in some way. On the basis of the above-mentioned characteristics terrorism can be defined as the deliberate creation and exploitation of fear through violence or the threat of violence in the pursuit of political change.[4] Hijacking, bombing, kidnapping, destruction of property, political murder and assassination all come within its purview.

Causes of Terrorism

The causes which have contributed to the political terrorism of the LTTE need to be viewed in the context of the ongoing ethnic conflict between the Sinhalese, who comprise 74.5 percent of the population, and the Sri Lankan or indigenous Tamils who comprise 12.5 percent. These two ethnicities are divided by differences of race, language and religion. The Sinhalese claim descent from the Aryans of north India, speak Sinhala, and are mainly Buddhist. They consider themselves to be the original settlers of the country. They are mainly concentrated in the south, west and central parts of the country. The Tamils are the majority in the north and east. They originate from Dravidian stock of South India, speak Tamil, and are mainly Hindu. They are mainly concentrated in the northern and eastern provinces of the country. Both communities however have been exposed to the influence of Christianity. The Muslims form the second largest minority group, making up 8 percent of the population. They are mainly concentrated in the eastern province. The Indian Tamils are the country's third minority. Brought as indentured labour in the tea plantations by the British, they are concentrated in the central highlands.[5]

---

[4] Paul Wilkinson, *Terrorism and the Liberal* State (London: Macmillan, 1986), pp.54–6.
[5] The Moors and the Indian Tamils comprises 7.4 and 5.5 percent of the population respectively. Both speak Tamil, but there are cultural differences among them.

The ethnic conflict is a political phenomenon of recent origin. Nevertheless, sporadic invasions from South India and ensuing power struggles as in the seizure of the Sinhala throne by South Indian adventurers, the contest for part of the Sinhala kingdom, and wars between the invading South Indian armies and defending Sinhala kings are evidenced throughout history. This historical antagonism was exacerbated by socio-economic and political transformations during the British colonial period from 1815 to 1948. In particular, the imperial constitutional reforms introduced between 1920 and 1948 paved the way for competition and conflict between the two ethnicities by bringing to the fore the issue of representation. The concept of 'balanced' representation, popularly known as the 50:50 formula, was the solution favoured by the Tamil Congress (TC). This arrangement held little appeal, however, for the majority Sinhalese.

After independence in 1948, a section of the Tamil political elite rolling itself into the Federal Party (FP) broke away from the Tamil Congress (TC) and put forward a demand for Ceylon (as it was then known) to be reconstituted as a federal state. This demand caught on, fuelled by post-independent Colombo government policies on land settlement in the northern and eastern provinces, the adoption of Sinhala (in place of English) as the official language, the introduction of ethnic quotas for public sector employment, and district-based quotas for university admission. The Tamils perceived these policies as a deliberate attempt to discriminate against them.

Although condemned as a claim for a separate state by the Sinhala majority, the federal state demand initially fell far short of that. But over time it became more and more a demand for autonomy. In the 1960s the Federal Party started talking about an 'Historical Homeland' based on the former Jaffna Kingdom, which was said to have prevailed from the thirteenth century until the arrival of the Portuguese in the early sixteenth century. Then in 1976, encouraged by the separation of East Pakistan from West Pakistan and the creation of the state of Bangladesh, the FP transformed itself into the Tamil United Liberation Front (TULF) and began to push for a separate Tamil or *Eelam* state. Campaigning on this platform at the elections of 1977, the TULF won a majority of seats in the northern province—but fewer in the eastern province.

Meanwhile, the ethnic riots in 1956, 1958, 1978 and 1983 strengthened support for the separatist cause; the viciousness of the riots of July 1983 particularly causing the Tamils to eschew politics for an armed insurgency. Another factor was youth unrest, caused by high levels of unemployment among Tamil school-leavers. Thirdly, the JVP insurrection of April 1971 highlighted the efficacy of violence as a means for achieving political goals while revealing weaknesses in the state security apparatus. Lastly, the example of Bangladesh, while also showing what could be achieved by armed struggle indicated, too, the possibility that the Indian government might be persuaded to take up the Tamil cause as it had that of the people of East Bengal.

Background of the Liberation Tigers of Tamil Eelam

The foundations of the Liberation Tigers of Tamil Eelam (LTTE) made a significant impact on the direction of the ethnic insurgency. The LTTE, popularly known as the Tamil Tigers, grew out of the Tamil youth guerrilla movement launched in the northern and eastern provinces in Sri Lanka by the Tamil Student Union (Tamil Manavar Peravai) and the Tamil Youth Federation (Tamil Illangnar Peravai). Initially it was only one of more than 35 competing groups, but gradually the number was whittled down, and by the 1990s five groups had achieved dominance over the others—the LTTE, the Tamil Eelam Liberation Organisation (TELO), the People's Liberation Organisation of Tamil Eelam (PLOTE), the Ealam People's Revolutionary Liberation Front (EPRLF), and the Eelam Revolutionary Organisation of Students (EROS). The latter four were, in turn, marginalised and then ruthlessly crushed by the LTTE to the point where today, it stands unchallenged as the voice of Sri Lanka's Tamil minority. The objective of the LTTE is to establish an independent socialist Tamil state, Tamil Eelam, by violence and terrorism.

Ethnically, all members of the LTTE are Sri Lankan Tamils. The participation of other minorities such as the Muslims and the Indian Tamils are either nominal or minimal. There is no evidence of the mobilisation of Muslim youth and not surprisingly, given the terrorist violence unleashed by the LTTE in the north and east against the local Muslim community. And thus far there is no substantial evidence either of the participation of Indian Tamils within the LTTE's rank and file. In terms of religion, a majority of the members of the LTTE are Hindus. However, there appears to have been some involvement of Tamil Christians in the movement.

The exact number of LTTE members is not known. But the LTTE is estimated to have 8,000 to 10,000 armed combatants with a core of trained guerrillas in the order of 3,000 to 6,000. It also has a significant overseas support structure for fundraising, weapons procurement, and propaganda activities. The current LTTE leadership, who started out in the 1980s as young men and women, are middle-aged now. But their main catchments for conscription remain adolescents and youths. The LTTE sees no moral problem with recruiting children as soldiers. However the organisation is most notorious for its seasoned cadre of suicide bombers, the 'Black Tigers'.

Ideologically, the LTTE is an action-oriented group with scant theoretical or ideological orientation.[6] Such limited ideology as the LTTE has is built around Tamil ethno-nationalism.

---

[6] 'Making of a Militant Leader: An Interview with V. Prabhakaran', *Lanka Guardian,* Vol.9, no. 10 (15 Sept. p. 10.

The top leadership of the LTTE has remained unchanged for years under the leadership of Velupillai Prabhakaran. Generally it embodies a two-tier structure: a military wing; and a subordinating wing. Overseeing both is a Central Governing Committee headed by the supreme leader Prabhakaran, which also directs and controls the organisation's specialist subdivisions such as the Sea Tigers, Air Tigers, a Charles Anthony Regiment, the Black Tigers, a secretive intelligence group, a political section, and an International Secretariat which monitors the outfit's global network. As well, the LTTE draws on the support of a number of mostly overseas-based front organisations, the most active being the World Tamil Association (WTA), the World Tamil Movement (WTM), the Federation of Association of Canadians Tamils (FACT), the Australian Federation of Tamil Associations, the Swiss Federation of Tamil Associations, the French Federation of Tamil Associations, the Illankai Tamil Sangam in the United States, the Tamil Coordinating Committee in Norway, and the International Federation of Tamils in the United Kingdom. These front bodies engage in publicity and propaganda, fundraising activities, and arms procurement.

According to Peter Chalk, by 1988 the LTTE had offices and cells in at least 54 countries.[7] But the bulk of LTTE funding comes from the Sri Lankan communities in Switzerland, Canada, Australia, the United Kingdom, the United States and the Scandinavian countries.[8] It is estimated that the total amount of refugee funding of the LTTE worldwide has averaged about $US2 million a month since December 1995.[9]

The strategy and tactics of the LTTE is a vital aspect of its insurgency. It has a definite strategy to achieve its political objectives. The basic objective of the organisation is to defeat the government forces in the north and east through a protracted armed struggle. According to the LTTE, guerrilla warfare is the hallmark of a true people's war, and the only effective means of winning a separate state. They have integrated a battlefield insurgent strategy with a terrorist programme, which targets civilians but also political leaders, activists and members of the police and army intelligence services. Political assassinations and bombings are part and parcel of the strategy and tactics of the LTTE.

Ethnic Insurgency

The terrorist activities of the LTTE should be examined and analysed in the context of the ethnic insurgency popularly known as the Ealam War, but this was actually

---

[7] Peter Chalk, 'The LTTE's International Organization and Operations—A Preliminary Analysis' (Canadian Security Intelligence Service (CSIS), Commentary No.77 (17 March 2000) [http://www.fas.org/irp/world/para/docs/com77e.htm].
[8] Anthony Davis, 'Tiger International', *Asiaweek* (26 July 1996), pp.30–8.
[9] G.H. Peiris, 'Secessionist War and Terrorism: Transactional Impulses', in *The Global Threat of Terror: Ideological, Material and Political Linkages* (New Delhi: Buwark Books, 2002), pp.85–126.

three distinct campaigns. The first phase of the Eelam War, which started in the mid 1970s, consisted of acts of sporadic violence in retaliation against the police, and the assassination of pro-government Tamil politicians residing in the north. As the movement expanded and gathered momentum, a distinct pattern of protracted rural guerrilla warfare laced with acts of terrorism emerged.

The Eelam War One lasted from the mid 1970s to March 1990. The ethnic riot of July 1983 marked the turning point of this phase. The riots broke out as a backlash against an ambush of government military troops by the LTTE at Thirunelveli in Jaffna on 23 July 1983, resulting in the deaths of 13 army personnel. After the men's funeral in Colombo, anti-Tamil riots spread throughout the city and the suburbs. About 400 Tamils died in the violence, and many more were injured or were victims of arson and looting. From 1987 to 1990 in the second phase of Eelam War One, the LTTE fought against the Indian Peace Keeping Force (IPKF) in the northern and eastern provinces.

The period from July 1991 to December 1994 marked Eelam War Two, which began with the killing by the LTTE of more than 600 security personnel. After a lull, the LTTE revived hostilities by blowing up two naval ships in Trincomalee harbour in April 1995. Although the LTTE signed a Memorandum of Understanding (MOU) with the government in February 2002, its programme of assassinations of political opponents and intelligence personnel has not ceased. This latter campaign constitutes Eelam War Three.

Political Assassinations

In the Eelam War One, the LTTE concentrated on assassinations of Tamil politicians and on executing police informers. The assassination of the mayor of Jaffna, the central town of the northern province, in 1975 was the first of these political murders. From 1977 to July 1983, the Tigers killed 11 Tamil politicians, 13 police informants and 16 civilians.[10]

These attacks were followed by a chain of assassinations of established and emerging Sinhalese political leaders both in Sri Lanka and in India. These included the assassination of Ranjan Wijeratne, the deputy defence minister of Sri Lanka in March 1991, Lalith Athulathmudali, the deputy minister of defence in April 1993, and Gamini Dissanayake, minister and the United National Party (UNP) candidate for the presidential election in 1994; and most infamously Ranasinghe Premadasa, the president of Sri Lanka in 1993 and Rajiv Gandhi, the prime minister of India in May 1991 in a bid to pre-empt a reintroduction of the Indian Peace Keeping

---

[10] See W.I. Siriweera, 'Recent Development in Sinhala–Tamil Relations', *Asian Survey* (1980), pp.903–13.

Force. Both of these latter assassinations utilised the suicide body suit. In December 1999 the LTTE attempted to assassinate another Sri Lankan president, Chandrika Kumaratunga; she survived but lost an eye in the blast.

Ironically the LTTE has killed more moderate Tamil politicians than it has Sinhala leaders. Of 37 prominent politicians assassinated by LTTE cadres, 24 were Tamils, 9 Sinhalese, 3 Muslims and one an Indian (Rajiv Gandhi). Among the prominent Tamil political leaders assassinated by the LTTE, 9 were members of parliament, and 3 mayors of Jaffna. They included, importantly, A. Amirthalingam, TULF general secretary and Neelan Thiruchelvam, TULF president.

The LTTE initiated its campaign of extermination against other militant groups in 1986. More than 300 members of TELO, PLOTE and EPRLF were murdered as a consequence, including Sri Sabarathnam, the leader of TELO, Uma Maheswaram, the leader of PLOTE, and K. Padmanabha, the leader of EPRLF. Later the campaign of assassination against members of rival militant groups was extended to India, France, Germany, Britain, and Canada. These internecine killings enabled the LTTE to become the main guerrilla organisation aiming at a separate Tamil state, and to promote itself as the sole legitimate representative of the Tamil-speaking people in the country. The politics of the Tamil areas are thus no longer decided by the ballot box but by the whims of the Tiger leadership.

Massacres of Civilians
In furtherance of its goals, the LTTE has not flinched from massacring civilians, particularly Sinhalese and Muslims residing in the north and east of the country. It murdered 49 Sinhalese civilians at Kent Farm in Vavuniya in November 1984; and shot dead 11 more in the same area in December 1984. In 1985 LTTE cadres invaded the ancient capital of Anuradhapura disguised in army uniform, and shot more than 200 townsfolk including pilgrims worshipping at the Sri Maha Bodhi temple; and later that year LTTE militants killed 65 Sinhalese in the Mullaitivu district. In 1987 the LTTE massacred 175 bus passengers in Trincomalee. In January 1987 its operatives shot dead 30 Buddhist priests and 4 Sinhalese laymen at Arantalawa in Ampara district.

After the Indo–Sri Lanka Accord in 1987, Muslims resident in the northern and eastern provinces became the main targets of the LTTE. The LTTE considered the Muslims to be informers and collaborators with the government. And they hoped, through terrorism, to deter them from joining the Sri Lankan armed forces and home guard units. During.1987–88, 34 incidents were reported. Of these, the massacres at Allinapothana in April 1992 and at Palliyagodalla in October 1992 (both in the Polonnaruwa district in the North Central Province) were the most serious.

Table 1 documents the killing of civilians by the LTTE from 1984 to 2004. It shows that in total over 3000 civilians including women and young children were brutally killed during the period.

Suicide Bombings

Among the LTTE's fighting cadres are squads of men and women called 'Black Tigers' who carry cyanide capsules to ensure that the secrets of the movement are

Table 1
Numbers of Civilians Killed or Injured due to LTTE Attacks

Year	Killed	Injured	Total
1984	60		60
1985	221		221
1986	168	135	303
1987	547	425	972
1988	275	23	298
1989	96	11	107
1990	485	117	602
1991	147	62	209
1992	390	302	692
1994	17	3	20
1995	161	71	232
1996	86	1338	1424
1998	97	668	765
1999	93	192	285
2000	143	329	472
2001	36	26	62
2002	9		9
2003	13	2	15
2004	1		1
Total	**3045**	**3704**	**6749**

Source: http/www.sinhaya.com/Massacres.htm.

safeguarded in the event of their capture. But that said, capture is rare because the Black Tigers' mission is to detonate bombs strapped to their bodies with the aim of wreaking mass destruction. Suicide bombing has been the main LTTE terrorist weapon since 1987 and has been used both on and off the battlefield.

The first suicide bombing by the LTTE was unleashed on an army camp at Nelliadi in the Jaffna Peninsula in 1987. That attack—which featured a truck packed with explosives—killed the bomber himself and 39 soldiers. Since then 19 suicide attacks have been directed against the Sri Lankan Navy alone. Other targets have included the twin-tower World Trade Centre building in October 1997 in Colombo, and the Temple of the Tooth in Kandy (the holiest Buddhist shrine in the country). Altogether since 1987 the LTTE has carried out 169 suicide operations. According to Rohan Gunaratna, the LTTE in 2000 led the global list of groups judged to be capable of carrying out suicide attacks,[11] a judgement confirmed by Table 2.

Indeed, of the countries which have experienced terrorism, Sri Lanka has lost more political leaders per capita of population during this period of time than any other.

The LTTE suicide bomber is motivated by his or her politico-social environment and by indoctrination carried out by the organisation. Interestingly, suicide operations were not used in the struggle against the IPKF. Another significant feature of the LTTE's suicide bombing campaign has been its use of females, in preference to males, to carry out missions. For example, a female suicide bomber of the LTTE assassinated Rajiv Gandhi in Tamil Nadu in 1991.

Economic Targets

Terrorist attacks on economic targets are a major aspect of the LTTE's political terrorism. In 1986 its guerrillas damaged the cement factory in Trincomalee jointly owned by Japan's Mitsui Cement Company and a group of Colombo investors. It has threatened to poison the Sri Lankan tea crop, the major export commodity of the country, and has issued warnings to multinational corporations operating in the north and east of the country. In January 1996 an LTTE suicide bomber rammed a truck full of high explosives and shrapnel into the Sri Lankan Central Bank in the heart of the commercial district of the capital Colombo. And in July 2001 the LTTE attacked the air force base at Katunayake and the Bandaranaike International Airport, destroying or damaging eight military aircraft and six passenger aircraft. These incidents resulted in the deaths of over 130 and injuries to more

---

[11] Rohan Gunaratna, 'The LTTE and Suicide Terrorism', in *Frontline*, Vol.17, no.3 (Feb. 2000).

Table 2
Number of Suicide Attacks between 1980 and 2000

Name of Organisation	Number of Incidents
The Liberation Tigers of Tamil Eelam	168
Hizbullah and Pro-Syrian Groups in Lebanon, Kuwait and Argentina	52
Hamas in Israel	22
The Kurdish Workers Party (PKK) in Turkey	15
The Palestinian Islamic Jihad (PIJ) in Israel	08
Al-Qaida in East Africa	02
The Egyptian Islamic Jihad (EIJ) in Croatia	01
The Islamic Group (IG) in Pakistan	01
Barbar Khalsa International (BKI) in India	01
The Armed Islamic Group (GIA) in Algeria	01

Source: 'Suicide Terrorism: A Global Threat', *Jane's Intelligence Review*, 20 October 2000 [http://cfrterrorism.org/terrorism/suicide.html].

than 1,600 civilians.[12] As well, the LTTE conducted bank robberies and targeted tourist hotels in the northern province.

Impact of Terrorism

The annual monetary cost of the civil war is reckoned at some 18 billion Sri Lankan rupees. By 1990, 18 percent of the national budget was being consumed by 'defence'—in effect, counter-insurgency—expenditure, leading to a curtailment of infrastructure expenditure.[13] By 1990 the figure was 21.6 percent. Much of this extra military expenditure was used to finance a massive increase in the strength of the Sri Lankan security forces, as summarised in Table 3.

The tourist industry has been the major economic casualty of terrorism. The expansion of terrorist incidents has affected the reputation of Sri Lanka as an attractive tourist destination. The tourist industry in Sri Lanka started growing in the 1970s

---

[12] Rohan Gunaratna, 'Tamil Tiger Terror in Sri Lanka', in *International Encyclopaedia of Terrorism* (New Delhi: S. Chand & Company, 1999), p.493.
[13] See John M. Richardson Jr. and S.W.R. de A. Samarasinghe, 'Economic Dimensions of Ethnic Conflict', in S.W.R. de A. Samarasinghe and Reed Coughlan (eds), *Economic Dimensions of Ethnic Conflict: International Perspectives* (London: Pinter Publishers, 1991), pp.194–223.

Table 3
The Manpower Strength of the Security Forces of Sri Lanka, 1986–1996

Security Forces	1986	1988	1993	1996
Army	30,000	40,000	90,000	129,000
Navy	3,960	5,500	10,100	21,000
Air Force	3,700	3,700	10,700	17,000
Police	21,000	21,000	40,000	68,000
Total	58,660	70,200	150,800	235,000

Source: Saman Kelegama, 'Economic Costs of Conflict in Sri Lanka', in Robert I. Rotberg (ed.), *Creating Peace in Sri Lanka: Civil War and Reconciliation* (Washington DC: Brookings Institution Press, 1999), p.75.

and peaked just before the ethnic riots of 1983. In 1982, 407,230 tourists came to Sri Lanka. By 1987, their numbers were down to 182,620.

But the economic cost pales before the human cost of the civil war. There are no reliable figures of the numbers killed or injured in the war because, under the emergency regulations, the government is authorised not to disclose any matters which it deems prejudicial to the national interest. However it is widely believed that from 1983 to mid-1997 more than 50,000 people were killed, including approximately 10,000 Sri Lankan military personnel. The number of LTTE deaths was 22,116 according to the government, although the LTTE put it at not more than 9,301. By 2002, the total death toll was probably in the order of 65,000.

Massive displacement of populations, emigration and refugee problems have added to the human tragedy of the conflict. According to the US Committee for Refugees, there were 604,730 internally displaced persons in Sri Lanka by August 1994.

Finally, the insurgency and terrorism gave rise to a dramatic increase in human rights violations such as torture, disappearances, extra-judicial killings, detention without trial, and reprisal killings of civilians. The violation of human rights by both government forces and Tamil guerrillas has been heavily criticised by human rights organisations.

---

[14] Ministry of Reconstruction, Rehabilitation and Social Welfare, US Committee for Refugees, Washington DC, 1994, cited in S.D. Muni and Lok Raj Baral (eds), *Refugees and Regional Security in South Asia* (New Delhi: Konark Publishers, 1996), p.13.

Counter-Terrorism

The counter-terrorism programme of the government of Sri Lanka can be divided into two distinct periods based on the strategy of the party in power. The first period, from 1977 to 1994, corresponds to the term of the United National Party (UNP) government; the second period 1994 to 2001, that of the People's Alliance (PA) government. The UNP government's initial response could be broadly divided into (1) military and (2) legal and political measures. In the initial stages of the ethnic insurgency, the existing criminal and civil law was enforced through the police to curb the trouble but as violence escalated the police were further empowered. As provided for in Article 155 of the 1978 Constitution, a Public Security Ordinance was enacted. Under this provision a state of emergency was declared in the northern province in 1978 and renewed throughout the 1980s whenever circumstances required. The emergency regulations permitted supervision, search and arrest, and indefinite detention of suspects. Under these regulations many persons have been held incommunicado for years without access to either lawyers or relatives. But the legal clampdown did not stop there.

In 1979 the Prevention of Terrorism Act (Temporary Provisions) was enacted. This Act empowered the police and members of the armed forces to arrest and search persons and places, and to impose internment. It also declared kidnapping and abduction punishable offences carrying life imprisonment.[15] Originally, as its title suggests, the Act was envisaged only as a temporary measure. However in July 1982 it was made a part of the permanent law of the country.

Apart from military and legal measures limited political steps were taken to address the grievances of the Tamils. The policy of standardisation applied to university admission was abolished and Tamil was given the status of a regional language under the Constitution of 1978. Under the District Development Councils (DDC) Act of August 1981 a measure of autonomy was accorded to the country's 25 districts including—importantly—the Tamil-majority districts of the north. Last but not least, under the Indo–Sri Lanka Accord of 1987, a 13th Amendment to the Constitution of 1978 was enacted which devolved limited power to eight provincial councils including one for the northeast (pending a referendum to determine its makeup).

However the Northeast Provincial Council was beset by internecine problems from its inception, while the assassinations of Rajiv Gandhi and Ranasinghe Premadasa

---

[15] See 'Prevention of Terrorism (Temporary Provisions) Act 1979, No.48'; and 'Prevention of Terrorism (Temporary Provisions) of 1982, No.10'.

further undercut the political initiatives, resulting in a policy shift to military options under the regime of Prime Minister D.B. Wijetunghe.

The second period was ushered in with the electoral defeat of the UNP government in 1994, which placed responsibility for the country's security in the hands of the People's Alliance Party led by President Chandrika Kumaratunge. The People's Alliance had campaigned vigorously for a negotiated settlement of the conflict and upon assuming office tried to secure a breakthrough in the conflict by opening peace negotiations with the LTTE. By focusing on the root causes of the ethnic conflict rather than the insurgency itself and the terrorism of the LTTE, the Kumaratunge government hoped to arrive at a long-term political settlement. But the intransigence of the LTTE thwarted the government's plan, which compelled it to revert to the military option when the LTTE unilaterally resumed hostilities after the talks broke down. This phase lasted until the electoral defeat of the PA in December 2001, when a new UNP government headed by Ranil Wickramasinghe again proffered the olive branch, which led to the signing of a ceasefire agreement and the resumption of peace talks, a move facilitated by third-party mediation from the government of Norway. But this, too, proved a false dawn. The LTTE withdrew from the peace talks in April 2003, and the UNP government was defeated in February 2004, by which time the LTTE had tabled its 'Interim Self Government Agreement' as a precondition for further negotiations. But even while the ceasefire held, the LTTE continued to kill its political opponents—a tendency accentuated by the schism created within the organisation by Karuna, the breakaway commander of the eastern province, in March 2003. On the above evidence, it is moot whether the LTTE is serious in wanting to negotiate for a peaceful settlement of the conflict within the framework of a united Sri Lanka.

Conclusion

The social, political and economic impact of terrorism is manifold. The terrorism experience of Sri Lanka is manifest in a weakened economy, a challenged state and a human toll of displacement, death, human rights violations, the criminalising of society, an upsurge in the numbers of widows and orphans, and socio-psychological trauma. Sri Lankan governments since the late 1970s have adopted various stances toward the insurgency in the light of changing circumstances and according to their ideological convictions, but all have sought to address the violence of the LTTE and arrive at a durable solution to the ethnic conflict. Nonetheless the process has been drawn out and convoluted. Arriving at a negotiated solution that has the consensus of the Sinhalese and Muslim communities appears to be distant. Therefore, the violence of the LTTE continues, taking different forms as the organisation hones its skills and tactics.

Notes on Contributors

Sreeradha Datta is Research Fellow at the Institute for Defence Studies and Analysis, New Delhi.

Frédéric Grare is Fellow, Carnegie Endowment for International Peace, Washington.

Wasbir Hussain is Director, Centre for Development and Peace Studies, Gawahati.

P. R. Kumaraswamy is Professor at the School of International Studies, Jawaharlal Nehru University, New Delhi.

Rasul Bakhsh Rais is Professor at the Lahore University of Management Studies.

Rajesh Rajagopalan is Professor at the School of International Studies, Jawaharlal Nehru University, New Delhi.

Gamini Samaranayake is Professor, University of Peradeniya, Sri Lanka and Chairman, University Grants Commission, Sri Lanka.

Marika Vicziany is Professor of Political Economy at Monash University, Australia and Director of Monash Asia Institute.

Robert G. Wirsing is Professor at Asia–Pacific Centre for Strategic Studies (APCSS), Honolulu, USA.

Index

abduction, daughter of Mufti Mohammed Sayyid 22; K. Doraiswamy, 13
Adivasi Cobra Militants of Assam 105
Afghan *jihad* 133, 137, *see also jihad(i)*
Afghanistan as training ground for Shia militants 142
Ahmad, Mirza Ghulam 121–2
Ahmad, Mumtaz on the study of Islamic law 72
Ahmadiyyas 121–2; anti-ahmadiyya groups 122–3, *see also* Bangladesh; Pakistan
Akshardham Temple in Gujarat, attack 19
Al-Hussaini, Arif Hussain 134
Ali, Saleem 74
Ali, Sheikh Hakim 139
All Assam Students' Union (AASU) 99
All-India Anna Dravida Munnetra Kazhagam (AIADMK) 16
al-Qaida camps, sectarian militants trained at 142
Aminul, Haque, harbouring militants 158
Anjuman Sipah-e-Sahaba Pakistan 133–4
Arab *jihadis* 138
Assam Accord 99
Assam, anti-foreigner violence in 13, 99, *see also* Bodo Accord
assassinations 12; A. Amirthalingam 181; A.S. Vidya 12; Beant Singh12; Gamini Dissanayake 12; Gamini Dissanayake 180; Harchand Singh Longowal 12; Indira Gandhi 12; K. Padmanabha, 181; Lalith Athulathmudali 180; Liaquat Ali Khan 12; Mahatma Gandhi 12; Mujibur Rahman 12; Mujibur Rahman 20; Neelan Thiruchelvam, 181; Rajiv Gandhi 12, 17, 22, 180, 183, 186; Ranasinghe Premadasa 12, 180, 186; Ranjan Wijeratne 12, 180; Sri Sabarathnam 181; Thiruchelvam 12; Zia ul-Haq 124; Zia ur-Rahman 12
Australian Federation of Tamil Associations 179
Autonomous State Demand Committee (ASDC) 108

Awami League and BNP ties 156
Azhar, Maulana Masood 60

Babar, Naseerullah 139
Babri Masjid controversy 1 9, 24
Bangladesh Nationalist Party (BNP) 23, 149, 151
Bangladesh Operation Clean Heart (2002) 160
Bangladesh, Ahmadiyyas 25–6, 151–2; ammunition seized from mosques and *madrassas* 27; anti-Hindu society 151; anti-Hindu violence in 25; attacks against secular targets 167–70; bomb blasts 149; communal riots in 25–6; counter-militancy strategy 170–3; domestic terrorism 21–3; *fatwa* against Nasreen 151, 153; growth of *madrassas* 153–5; *Islamisation* 150–3; manifestations of militancy 165–6; mosques for terror networks 27; *mullahs*158; official patronage 159–61; political asylum in Anup Chetia and Sanjib Debbarma 21; religious extremism in 149; role of religion 23–4; *Taliban/al-Qaida* presence 161–5; Talibanisation of 161–5; upsurge of religious parties 155–9
Bangla-ethnic Chakmas 17
Bengali nationalists 15
Bharatiya Janata Party (BJP) 22, 33
Bhutto, Zulfikar Ali 25,121; expansion *madrassas* 137
Bodo Accord 104–5
Bodo Liberation Tigers (BLT) 98–9
Bodo People's Progressive Front 99
Bodoland Autonomous Council (BAC) 104–5
Bodoland Territorial Council (BTC) 98
Boer War (1899–1902) 81, 85
Border Security Force (BSF) 90
British, counter-insurgency in Malaya 85, 91; 'ferret force' in Malaya 86
Bru Liberation Front of Mizoram (BLFM) 107
Bru National Liberation Front (BNLF) 107

China's 'oil-spot' strategy 85, 87
Chittagong Hill Tracts (CHT) 17
Chittagong Hill Tracts accord 17
counter-insurgency 80–4; warfare 84–95

Daultana, Mumtaz 122
Deobandi *ulema* 122
Dima Halam Daogah outfit 108
District Development Councils (DDC) Act of August 1981
Dixit, J.N. 16
Dosa, Mohammed 57
Dutt, Sanjay 52–5, 61–3

fatwas 152–3
Fazl-ur-Rehman, Maulana 138
Federal Party (FP) 177
Federation of Association of Canadians Tamils (FACT) 179
French Federation of Tamil Associations 179
French instituted a 'quadrillage' or grid system in Algeria 85
French military violence against Algeria's civilian 85

Gandhi, Indira 22, *see also under* assassinations
German Army Jagdkommando (commando hunters) 86
guerrilla warfare, Viet Minh manual on 83

Harakat-ul-Jihad-al-Islami (HUJI) 143; banning of 160; as terrorist organisation 161
Hasina, Sheikh (1996–2001) 157, 162
Hifazate Khatme Nabuwat Andolon Coordination Committee (Movement to Conserve the Right of the Last Prophet) 152
hijacking, Air France plane 14; of Indian Airlines IC 814 22
Hindu fundamentalism 62
Hindu militants 24
Hindu–Muslim communal violence 8, 24; Ashutosh Varshney on 40–1; Donald L. Horowitz on 39, 44–5; in India 38–42; Paul Brass on 39–40; Sudhir Kakar on 41–2
Hizbut Tahrir; and Jamaat-ul-Ansar (formerly Harakat-ul Mujahideen) 140
Hmar People's Convention (HPC) 108–9
Hoagland, Jim 'Pakistan Today Is the Most Dangerous Place on Earth' 31–2

Hoodbhoy, Pervez 72
Hoque, Shaikhul Hadith Azizul 152
HPC-Democracy (HPC-D) 109
Human Rights Commission of Pakistan (HRCP) 125
Hussain, Syeda Abida 139

Ibrahim, Anis (Dawood's brother) 57–9
Ibrahim, Dawood 57, 58, 76; Kaksar's 'D-company' 49–50
Illankai Tamil Sangam in United States 179
Indian Parliament attack on the 19
Indian Peace Keeping Force (IPKF) 16, 92–4, 180, *see also* Indo-Sri Lanka Accord
Indo-Bangladeshi relations 20
Indo-Burma Revolutionary Front (IBRF) 112
Indo-Pakistani talks 20
Indo-Sri Lanka Accord 1, 27, 181, 186
insurgency' and 'guerrilla' 81–4
Inter-Service Intelligence (ISI) 142
inter-ethnic feuds 104–6
Interim Self Government Agreement 187
International Federation of Tamils in United Kingdom 179
international Islamic terrorism 144–6
inter-tribal conflicts 90
Iran, financing Pakistani Shias 146; sponsored educational initiatives vs Zia's *madrassa* education 134, 137
Islam industry 45
Islami Oikya Jote (IOJ) 151
Islamic sects 73–4; terrorists 19

Jagrata Muslim Janata Bangladesh (JMJB) banning of 160
Jamaat Ulema Islami (JUI) 132
Jamaat Ulema Pakistan 132
Jamaat Ulema-e-Ahl-e-Hadith 133
Jamaat-e-Islami 23, 151, 156–8; opposed sectarianism 141
Jamaat-ul-Dawa (formerly Lashkar-e-Taiba) 69, 77, 140; and Lashkar-e-Taiba 64–9
Jamaat-ul-Furqan (a breakaway group of Jaish-e-Muhammad) 140
Jamaatul-Mujahideen Bangladesh (JMB) 158
Jamiat-e-Ulema Islam (Fazl-ur-Rehman Group) 133–4
Jamiat-i-Ulema-i-Hind (Association of Islamic Religious Scholars of India) 121

Janatha Vimukthi Peramuna (People's Liberation Front or JVP) 26, 177
Jhangvi, Maulana Haq Nawaz 134
jihad(i) 8, 19–20; and sectarian organizations, distinction between 140; curricula of Pakistan's state schools 71–2; groups 131; groups in Kashmir 15
Jinnah, Muhammad Ali 119

Kachin Independence Army (KIA) 110
Kamatapur Liberation Organisation (KLO) 113
Karen National Union (KNU), General Bo Mya's 112
Karuna 187
Kashmir 9, 25–7, 34–8; *jihadi* movement 27; *jihad*-inspired recruits 32; militants refuge in Hazratbal shrine 24; Muslim insurgency in 29; Pakistani involvement in 25; separatist violence in 34–8; anti-Pundit violence 13, 29
Khan, Morshed 171
Khan, Sir Zafarullah 122
Khaplang, S.S. 90
Khatme Nabuwat Andolon Samannay Committee (KNASC) 151–2
Khuddam-e-Islam (formerly Jaish-e-Muhammad) 140
Kibria, S.A.M.S. 172
Kukis 90; Naga riots 105–6
Kumaratunge, Chandrika 187

Laldenga 91
Larma, Santanu 17
Lashkar-e-Jhangvi (L-e-J) 135; evolution of 145; and Jaish-e-Muhammad 143
Lashkar-e-Taiba 60, 64
Lashkar-i-Jhangvi 126–7
Leo, K.S. Paul 103–4
Liberation Tigers of Tamil Eelam (LTTE) 16–17, 26, 92–5,175, 178–9; as guerrillas 79
Lintner, Bertil 162

madrassas 47; 123; are Deobandi, 73; as *'jihadi* factories' 47; of India 76; in Pakistan 76–7; Robert Pape on 48; and Terrorism 73–5; William Sleeman on 47
Majlis e Khatme Nabuwat (Council for the Finality of Prophethood) 122
Majlis-i-Ahrar (Council for Liberation) 122
Malayan Communist Party (MCP) 85

Malayan People's Anti-British Army (MPABA) 85
Maria, Rakesh's 58
Mauddudi, Maulana Abul Ala 120
Maulana Habib ur Rehman Yazdani 134
Meghen, Rajkumar alias Sana Yaima 111
Memon, Abdul Razzak 57
Memon, Mohammed Yusuf Shah (or 'Tiger' Memon) 50, 57–7, 63
Memon, Yaqub 50
Millat-e-Islami (formerly Sipah-e-Sahaba Pakistan) 140
Minto-Morley Reforms of 1909 118
Mizo Hills, famine in 91; insurgency 79
Mizo National Front (MNF) 91–2
Muivah, Thuingaleng 90
mujahideen 123
Mujibur's secular socialist experiment 150; banned religious parties 155
Mumbai bombings 49; characteristics of 52–6; terrorist attacks 9; trains 64; Swati Deshpande on 63
Musharraf, Pervez 20, 25; attacks against 144–5; policies of 127, 129; sectarian parties banned by 137–8, 139–40

Naga Federal Army (NFA) 90, 100
Naga Federal Government (NFG) 100–1
Naga Hills–Tuensang Area (NHTA) 88–9
Naga Hills, Indian Army into 88; Indian Air Force (IAF) in 91
Naga, Kuki ethnic groups 98; alliances as force multipliers 111–13; foreign links 109–11; homeland dream 100–4, 106–9; and Indian State 113–14; inhabited areas and NSCN-IM 106; insurgency 90; Mizo territories 88; rebels 89
National Democratic Front of Bodoland (NDFB) 113
National Socialist Council of Nagaland (NSCN-K) 90
National Socialist Council of Nagaland by Isak Chishi Swu and Thuingaleng Muivah (NSCN IM) 90, 98, 101–4; dream of a 'Greater Nagaland' 108
National Socialist Council of Nagaland (NSCN) 90, 101
Nawaz, assassination attempt on 139
Naxalite People's War Group (PWG) 23

Nehru, Jawaharlal, death of 95
Nepal, Maoist insurgency in 7–8, 17–18
Non-Aligned Movement (NAM) 14
North East India, 'Chicken's Neck' 97
North West Frontier Province (NWFP) 121
North-East Frontier Agency (NEFA) 88

Operation Bajrang 110
Operation Blue Star *see under* Punjab
Operation Jericho 91

Pakistan, accused India 16; against Ahmadiyyas and Christians 9, 126–7; against minority Shia sect 127; anti-blasphemy laws 75; anti-Christian violence 9; anti-Shia campaign 131, 33; anti-Shia characteristic of Deobandi and Ahl-e-Hadith *madrassas* 137; Anti-Terrorism Act 139; attack against Shia mosque 146; Baghdad financing anti-Shia elements in. 146; banned organisations 145; blasphemy laws 125; break-up in 1971 121; civilians killed 7; Deobandi faction 126; electorates 123–4; government of Zia ul-Haq 117; Hazara Shia community 144; ISI organised Islamic terrorist organizations 62; Islamic revolution of Iran and sectarianism in 132–7; Ismailis or Agha Khanis 126; *jihad* in 127, 69–71; *madrassa* training the *jihadis* 138; *madrassas* and sectarianism 137–8; minorities in 117–21, 124; military 1971 11; politics and sectarian violence 138–41; religious and political polarisation in 116; religious intolerance and terrorism 126; rise in Islamic radicalism 126; role of in Kashmir militancy 18–19; sectarian violence and Afghan *Jihad* 141–4; sectarian violence in 143; students for training in terrorist tactics 134; *zakat* imposition in 132; Zia's capitulation over 133
Pakistan's People's Party (PPP) 132
Palestinian movement 14
Parbattya Chattagram Jana Sanghati Samiti (United Peoples' Party of Chittagong Hill Tracts or PCJSS) 17
partition 11
Pawl, Mizo Zirlai 107
People's Liberation Organisation of Tamil Eelam (PLOTE) 178
Phanse, Dawood Mohammed 58–61

Phizo, Adinno 100
Phizo, Angami Zapu 88
political violence 12–13; forms of 12
Prevention of Terrorism Act (Temporary Provisions) 186
Punjab, Akali Dal 21–2; Bhindranwale took refuge in Golden Temple 24; insurgency in 24; Operation Blue Star 24; Sikh extremists in 15; Sikh homeland or Khalistan 18; Sikh militancy 18, 21; Sikh militancy in 8–9

Rajkhowa, Arabinda 110
Ramachandran, M.G. 16
Rashtriya Swayamsevak Sangh (RSS) headquarters, attack on the 19
religion-centric violence 9
riot 24

Sami-ul-Haq, Maulana 138
Shia–Sunni conflict 138–9; riots 75; sectarian violence 26–7, 131
Shillong Accord on 11 November 1975 101
Sindh, Mohajir violence in 8, 9
Singh, V.P. 22
Singh, Giani Zail 22
Sipah-e-Mohammad (SMP) 134
Sipah-i-Sahaba Pakistan (SSP) 126
Sleeman, Colonel William 47;
South Asia Terrorism Portal (SATP) 7
Sri Lanka, anti-Tamil riots 12, 180; assassinations in 180–1; causes of terrorism in 176–7; civil war in 8; counter-terrorism of 186–7; economic targets of terrorism 183–4; ethnic Insurgency 179–80; impact of terrorism in 176, 184–5; massacres of civilians 181–2; suicide bombings in 182–3; Tamil militants in 15; Tamils of 8, 9; violence in 26
Srikrishna Commission 50–1
Srivastava, G.M. 107
Sunni Ahl-e-Hadith leaders, killing of 134
Swiss Federation of Tamil Associations 179
Swu, Isak Chishi 90

Taliban 141–2
Taliban took over Kabul and Jalalabad 144
Tamil Congress (TC) 177
Tamil Coordinating Committee in Norway 179

INDEX

Tamil Eelam Liberation Organisation (TELO) 178
Tamil United Liberation Front (TULF) 177
Tariq, Azam leader of Sipah-e-Sahaba 131
Tehrik-e-Islami Pakistan (formerly Tehrik-e-Jafria) 140
Tehriq-e-Nifaz-e-Fiqah Jafria (TNJF) as Tehrik-e-Jafria Pakistan(TJP) 132
terrorism 7–8, 13, definition 176
terrorist versus Freedom Fighter 13–15

ul-Haq, Zia 18; his Islamisation policies 123, 132
United Liberation Front of Asom (ULFA) 20, 106, 110–11 meet Gulbuddin Hekmatyar 110
United Naga Council, Manipur (UNC) 103–4
United National Liberation Front (UNLF) 111–13; killing Jat Regiment soldiers of Indian Army 111;
United People's Democratic Solidarity (UPDS) 108
United States, Army in Vietnam 84–5, 91; consulate killing 145; September 11 attack in 7, 27; war against terrorism 20, 143, 147

Unlawful Activities (Prevention) Act of 1967 100
US Agency for International Development (USAID) 33
Usmani, Maulana Shabbir Ahmad 121

Vajpayee, Atal Behari 103, 113

Wahhabi Jamaat Ulema-e-Ahl-e-Hadith (Society of the Ulema of 'the People of the Hadith') 133
Wickramasinghe, Ranil 187
Wijetunghe, D.B. 187
World Tamil Association (WTA) 179
World Tamil Movement (WTM) 179
World Trade Centre attacks *see under* United States, 11 September attack

Young Mizo Association 107

Zahab, Mariam Abou 135
Zaheer, Allama Ehsan Elahi 134
Zia, Khaleda (1991–96) 20, 157, 162, 172; 1 her success in Jatiya Sangsad elections 23

For Product Safety Concerns and Information please contact our EU
representative GPSR@taylorandfrancis.com
Taylor & Francis Verlag GmbH, Kaufingerstraße 24, 80331 München, Germany

www.ingramcontent.com/pod-product-compliance
Lightning Source LLC
Chambersburg PA
CBHW070613300426
44113CB00010B/1508